Incomes policy and inflation

This is the first volume in a projected series of studies in inflation. General editors Professors D. Laidler and M. Parkin. Future volumes will deal with inflation and the labour market, and inflation and expectations.

Incomes policy and inflation

Edited by Michael Parkin
and Michael T. Sumner

University of Toronto Press

First published 1973 in Canada
and the United States by
University of Toronto Press
Toronto and Buffalo

ISBN 0-8020-2111-5

Made and printed in Great Britain by
William Clowes and Sons Limited
London, Beccles and Colchester

Contents

Foreword

In July 1971 a group of some twenty economists, econometricans and accountants, financed by the Social Science Research Council began work at the University of Manchester on a three year research programme, on the problem of inflation. The research consists largely of a series of self-contained investigations of various aspects of the inflationary process. In order to ensure that our own work does not develop in isolation from that being carried out elsewhere, it is the policy of the Manchester-S.S.R.C. Inflation Programme regularly to invite scholars from other Universities in the United Kingdom and elsewhere to present papers at Manchester. Though our own work, and that of our colleagues at other institutions, consists of self-contained projects, certain common themes continue to emerge as research progresses.

The purpose of this series of volumes is to bring together in a convenient form papers on related aspects of inflation so that other research workers and students will have easy access to a relatively integrated body of material. Though each volume will contain a large proportion of previously unpublished work, previous publication in a learned journal will not disqualify an otherwise relevant paper from being included in this series.

In promoting a wider understanding of the inflationary process original research is vital, but the dissemination of the results of that research is just as vital. It is our hope that this series of volumes will enable the results of our own work at Manchester, and that of our colleagues elsewhere, to reach a wide audience.

Michael Parkin
David Laidler

Preface

Inflation and its consequences has possibly constituted the most serious economic problem which governments of all the advanced industrial countries have had to face in the past few years. In prolonged periods of rapid inflation, there is a strong temptation, fostered both by popular and serious press opinion, to find solutions summarized by the term, 'prices and income policies'. Such policies usually take the form of norms or guidelines for wage and price increases and are seen as a superior alternative to deflationary demand management policies. Clearly, if prices and incomes policies are capable of lowering the inflation rate independently of the pressure of demand they must be taken seriously. They undoubtedly will have side effects and those, of course, will have to be weighed against the potential reduction in the inflation rate. If, however, such policies do not materially affect the inflation rate then, because they have undesirable side effects, especially on the allocation of resources, they are positively damaging and should be avoided. The policy alternatives then reduce to demand deflation or learning to live with inflation and making whatever other adjustments are necessary to minimize its costs.

Against this background, the question as to the effects of prices and incomes policy on the rate of inflation assumes considerable importance.

Economic research over the past few years has not been insensitive to this question, and a large volume of published literature already existed by the time the last United Kingdom incomes policy experiment ended and the latest United States policy was introduced. Additionally though, we became aware that there was an almost equally large volume of new work bearing on the question which had not appeared in the literature.

It seemed appropriate, therefore, to arrange a conference of those researchers working on the effects of incomes policy, together with officials from Government Departments and the Bank of England, to consider all the work—published and unpublished—in this area.

With the financial help of the Social Science Research Council, a one-day conference was held at the University of Manchester on 24 March 1972, at which the previously unpublished papers were presented and discussed, and for which the previously published literature (and one early but unpublished paper by Professor Frank Brechling) served as background papers. It seemed to us that this entire collection of papers, together with our own survey of the literature, would prove useful to students and other research workers in this area.

There is one notable omission from the collection and one bonus. The omission is a sample of the important work of Professor A. G. Hines. We were fortunate in having Professor Hines at the conference but, unfortunately, one of his two papers on the effects of incomes policy on the inflation rate was committed to *Economica* and cannot be included here. His other was published only very recently in *The Current Inflation*, and is therefore highly accessible.[1] The bonus is a note by Professor Harry Johnson who, whilst not presenting a paper at the conference, made an important contribution to the discussion, the substance of which (together with additional material) is contained in Chapter 14.

The papers in this volume, with one exception, necessarily do not deal with very recent events and the reader might feel that the main conclusion which emerges is in need of substantial modification in the light of subsequent developments. We take this opportunity of commenting briefly on these developments and drawing what limited conclusions we can from them.

First, there has been a voluntary initiative taken by the C.B.I. (Confederation of British Industry) to limit price rises to not more than 5% p.a. The O.E.C.D. in their *Economic Outlook* for July 1972 have commented that: 'the voluntary price initiative of the C.B.I. in the U.K., although by no means a freeze, has undoubtedly contributed to a rapid deceleration in the rate of price increase' (p.77). There are two things to be said about this. First, it is a classic example of *post*

---

[1] The reader should refer to: Hines, A. G., 'Incomes Policy and Wage and Price Inflation', *Economica*, November 1972; and Hines A. G., 'The Determinants of the Rate of Change of Money Wage Rates and the Effectiveness of Incomes Policy' in H. G. Johnson and A. R. Nobay (eds) *The Current Inflation*, The Money Study Group, 1971; which should be regarded as complementary to the collection presented here.

hoc ergo propter hoc reasoning. Second, Bispham (Chapter 13) in analysing the development of prices over the period to the end of 1971 finds that: 'this deceleration can be almost wholly ascribed to falls in import prices of basic materials and particularly of fuels since July [1971], rather than to any paring of profit margins.'

The second additional evidence is more subtle and indirect. It is argued by some commentators (and economists) that the wage explosion from the last quarter of 1969 bears testimony to the effectiveness of incomes policy. The only interpretation of this episode which makes sense to us is that the recent inflation, like that in earlier periods, is generated by a mixture of excess demand and inflationary expectations. Specifically, in this period, the excess demand originated not in the United Kingdom economy, but in the United States. The massive reflation of the American economy in 1966, and the associated United States balance of payments deficit put inflationary pressure on the whole of Europe. As this pressure was building up, the devaluation of sterling gave a further upward twist to the British inflationary spiral. Inflationary expectations were building up throughout the last few years of the '60s. There is strong indirect evidence for this in the movements of bond and equity rates[2] over this period and in the work of Parkin (Chap. 5) and Nobay and Saunders (Chap. 12). More direct evidence is available from survey data on expectations which we are currently investigating; the results of our work on this will form the basis of a subsequent volume in this series.

The timing of the build-up in the world inflation rate and the take-off of United Kingdom inflation suggests that the latter phase of incomes policy did have the effect of postponing, though not of preventing, the wage explosion.[3] Of course, we cannot be sure about this interpretation at this stage, and must await the outcome of our present research on the role of expectations. If incomes policy can postpone the acceleration of inflation predicted by the expectations hypothesis, then the question posed above of the relative costs of inflation and resource misallocation becomes crucial.

It now only remains for us to acknowledge our considerable debt to the members of the S.S.R.C.—University of Manchester Inflation

[2] See Laidler, D. E. W., 'The Current Inflation—The Problem of Explanation and the Problem of Policy', the Lister Lecture to the British Association for the Advancement of Science, 1972.
[3] It should be noted that it probably also had the effect of delaying the balance of payments improvement following the 1967 devaluation, since it delayed the relative price changes which were necessary to effect the reallocation of resources.

Workshop for stimulation and practical help in organizing the Conference. We are especially grateful to Richard Harrington who did a superb job as Conference Secretary. Finally we would like to record our thanks to the Inflation Workshop Secretaries, Mrs. Vicki Whelan and Mrs. Betty Newman, who prepared the papers for the conference, handled the heavy correspondence and typed our own contribution to this volume.

Michael Parkin
Michael T. Sumner
Manchester
April 1972

Michael Parkin
Michael T. Sumner
and Robert A. Jones[1]

Chapter 1 A survey of the econometric evidence
of the effects of incomes policy on the
rate of inflation

1 Introduction

What are the effects of incomes policy on the rate of inflation? This
question has attracted a great deal of attention, especially in the
United Kingdom, but also in many other countries. It now appears
more important than ever as the United States moves into a new
attempt at incomes policy and the United Kingdom hovers around
the one million unemployed level with only a small abatement in the
rate of inflation. More and more people are arguing that the traditional cures for inflation are not working and therefore that some form
of incomes policy is needed. This raises a refinement on the question
posed above which is probably more important than the basic
question. That is, what are the effects of various well-defined alternative forms of incomes policy on the rate of inflation? Clearly incomes
policies vary in several important ways: statutory or voluntary; with
norms (guidelines) or without; with productivity agreements en-
couraged or not; threshold, indexation or no allowance for price
changes are a few examples of differences.

The purpose of this paper is to survey the existing econometric
literature on the effects of incomes policy. As such, we can only deal
with the first basic question. The answer to that is by no means
certain, although the evidence points in one main direction. The
second question has not been studied systematically at all.

To deal with our main question it is necessary to answer the prior
question, namely, what determines the rate of inflation? If this
question had been posed in the middle 1960's there would have been
little argument about the answer. However, since 1966, and more so

[1] University of Manchester. We are indebted to members of the Manchester
University Inflation Workshop, and to Ken Wallis of the London School of
Economics for discussion and comments on an earlier draft.

since the end of 1969, there is considerable confusion and disagreement on this question. It is therefore necessary to examine the alternative views about the causes of inflation, and to assess how each alternative view affects the conclusions which we can reach about the effects of incomes policy.

We do not, in this paper, present any new results. Rather, we survey the existing literature and draw from it what conclusions we can. We also attempt to highlight the important outstanding issues.

The starting point of all the studies surveyed in this paper is the notion that, in order to study the effects of incomes policy on the rate of inflation, we need first a model of the inflationary process and, second, some *a priori* ideas as to how incomes policy might affect that process so that we know where to look for its effects. The framework most commonly used to study the inflationary process and the effects of incomes policy is a two-equation system of wage and price inflation.[2] In the most general terms, such a system may be represented as

$$\dot{p} = f(\dot{w}, x) \tag{1}$$

$$\dot{w} = g(\dot{p}, y) \tag{2}$$

where $\dot{p} =$ proportionate rate of change of prices
$\dot{w} =$ proportionate rate of change of wages
x, y, vectors of additional variables.

In such a system, the rate of inflation can be influenced by incomes policy either by changing the functions $f(\ )$ and $g(\ )$, or by changing the values of the x and y variables. Two qualifications must however be noted. First, a change in $f(\ )$ or $g(\ )$ does not necessarily imply that the rate of inflation will be affected by incomes policy. There are two potential reasons for this. A change in $f(\ )$ could be offset by a change in $g(\ )$, or the functions could change in such a way that for certain values of x and y the inflation rate falls and for other values it rises. The second qualification concerns the distinction between 'demand management' and incomes policy. One of the components of the y vector in all empirical studies is the unemployment rate (or a closely related variable). This is the variable which captures the

---

[2] There are two exceptions to this. Klein and Ball [17] have a four equation system involving wage rates, earnings, hours and prices. Hines [12] uses a three equation model involving, in addition to wages and prices, a unionization variable. However, both of these models can be reorganized to reduce them to two equation systems in only wages and prices.

effects of 'demand management' policies on the inflation rate. The term 'incomes policy' as conventionally used excludes demand management and stands in contrast to it. Hence, variations in the inflation rate attributable to variations in the unemployment rate are not to be regarded as the effects for which the literature reviewed here is testing.

In what follows we examine the effects of incomes policy on the wage equation (part 2) and the price equation (part 3). In part 4 we summarize the principal outstanding issues and consider what conclusions can be drawn in the present state of knowledge.

2 The determinants of the rate of wage change and assessments of incomes policy

This review of the determinants of, and effects of incomes policy on, the rate of wage changes will be limited to empirical work. There is no well-defined, unified theory of inflation and incomes policy, and to undertake a discussion of inflation theory would divert attention too far from the main problems with which this paper seeks to deal.

The most comprehensive empirical proposition about wage inflation is that the rate of change of money wages depends positively on

    (i) excess demand for labour,
    (ii) the dispersion of that excess demand across individual labour markets,
    (iii) the expected (or actual) rate of change of prices, and
    (iv) the strength of Trade Unions.

The pioneering study of the determination of the rate of change of money wages by Phillips [29] concentrated exclusively on the role of the excess demand for labour as proxied by the unemployment rate. He used informal empirical methods which make it impossible to assess the statistical significance of his results. Lipsey [20], working with Phillips' data, used conventional econometric methods to test the Phillips hypothesis and estimate the relationship between the rate of change of money wages and the unemployment rate.

It is clear from Lipsey's paper that a monocausal explanation of changes in money wages as a function of the unemployment rate provides a poor fit to the data. The model which Lipsey suggests is one in which the rate of change of money wages depends on the unemployment rate (excess demand proxy), the rate of change of unemployment (structure of excess demand proxy) and the rate of change of prices. This model, when fitted to data for 1923–39/1948–57, has a coefficient of determination of 0·89,[3] with all three variables contributing significantly to this.

A much neglected paper, which must rank with that of Phillips as being one of the seminal empirical studies of inflation is that by Klein and Ball [14]. This study is also the first to look for the effects of incomes policy, although under the name of the 'political factor'. This 'political factor' is associated more with the political party in power than with incomes policy in the Klein-Ball paper although, in the later writings which we shall consider shortly, the same phenomenon is regarded as representing the first post-war incomes policy period. The broad findings of Klein and Ball agree with those of Phillips and Lipsey. Unemployment and the rate of change of prices are important variables in their sample (1948–58 quarterly). Additionally, the 'political factor' is very important and shows that inflation of wage rates was some $2\frac{1}{2}\%$ higher from 1952 onwards than in the earlier post-war years.

All three of the studies so far discussed ignore two problems. One is the appropriate measurement of the excess demand for labour and the other is the effect on the inflation rate of 'cost push' in the form of changes in the strength of trade unions and the ability of firms to meet claims as measured by profitability. The first of these problems had already received attention by Dow and Dicks-Mireaux [10] at the time when Phillips was writing. They produced for the post-war period only [4] an index of the excess demand for labour based on both unemployment and vacancies. This index was used in subsequent studies of the wage inflation process by Dicks-Mireaux and Dow [8] and by Dicks-Mireaux [7]. The results of these studies confirm the importance of price changes and the excess demand for labour (measured as the Dow–Dicks-Mireaux index) in explaining wage changes.

The first study of the role of variables other than excess demand and price changes was that by Lipsey and Steuer [22]. They examined the effects of profits to test the hypothesis that Phillips' results were a statistical artifact, which stemmed from a correlation between profits and unemployment and which diverted attention from the

[3] Lipsey [20], footnote 52.
[4] Vacancies data became available only after the second world war.

'true' relationship between wage-changes and profits, the latter indicating vulnerability to cost-push pressures. While tests at the aggregate level failed to discriminate sharply between the hypotheses considered, tests on industry data revealed that profits added nothing to the explanatory power of a relation which included unemployment.

The most influential attempt to establish a 'cost-push' explanation of wage change is that of Hines [12]. He postulated that union strength is a source of wage inflation and that it can be appropriately proxied by the change in the percentage of the labour force unionized. Using a sample period from 1893 to 1961, he found that his hypothesis was superior to that of Phillips and Lipsey, and in equations with the level of and change in unionization, and with current and lagged changes in prices, the level of unemployment ceased to be a significant variable in the determination of the rate of change of wages.[5]

The literature was in the state which we have just reviewed when the first systematic attempts to assess the effects of incomes policy were made. The first of these attempts, by Bodkin et al. [2], Brechling [3], the Prices and Incomes Board [26] and Smith [34], used the approach adopted earlier by Klein and Ball and looked for intercept shifts between incomes policy 'on' and 'off' periods. The possibility of heterogeneity among periods in which incomes policy was in use was admitted (except by Bodkin et al.) in varying degrees by using multiple shift dummies. An attempt was made by the P.I.B. to distinguish between voluntary policies (1948–50 and 1965) and 'years of tight control' (1961–2 and 1966);[6] Brechling and Smith used the same device more liberally to allow for differences in the impact of successive policy interludes. One problem which emerged quite clearly at this stage but which has received little attention is the difficulty of deciding whether or not incomes policy was in force in particular periods; Smith, for example, was alone in characterizing 1956 as a period in which incomes policy was operative. We return to this point at a later stage.

Although the results of the 'shift dummy' studies of incomes policy varied according to the wage series employed (see especially Smith), and indicated little consistency in the effects of policy in successive periods, their central conclusion was that incomes policy

[5] See Hines [12] equations (1.a)', (1.b)', p. 239 and 1, p. 240. In passing, it should be noted that Hines's model has been critically examined in a recent paper by Purdy and Zis [30]. See also Thomas and Stoney [38].
[6] The coefficients on the two shift dummies were virtually identical.

had succeeded in shifting the wage equation in a favourable manner.[7] This beneficial effect was, however, questioned by Jefferson, Sams and Swann [14] and by Lipsey and Parkin [21]. In the first of these investigations Lipsey's model [20] was fitted to annual data for 1950–60 and 1962–4, and predictions were thence derived for incomes policy periods (identified as 1948–9, 1961 and 1965–7). Except for 1965–6 the policy was found to have reduced the rate of increase of hourly wages, though the magnitude and statistical significance of the reductions varied widely. The authors, however, cast grave doubt on the economic significance of incomes policy, and particularly its ability to rectify a large payments imbalance within an acceptable period. Lipsey and Parkin attempted to establish the precise form of the policy-induced shift of the wage equation, an attempt which has in turn generated a series of studies of this problem, notably those by Burrows and Hitiris [5], Godfrey [11], Hines [13], Sargan [33], Taylor [37], Thomas and Stoney [39], and Wallis [41].

The method adopted in all these studies has been to estimate wage equations for 'policy on', 'policy off', and the entire sample periods, and to test the hypothesis that the wage determination equation has been stable through the entire sample regardless of whether policy is operating or not. The outcome of this test answers the question as to whether the wage determining equation shifts with policy, but it does not deal with the question of the effects of policy on the average wage inflation rate. This is examined, for cases where a structural shift is found, by using the 'policy off' equation to predict the rate

---

[7] An unnoticed by-product of Brechling's study concerns the role of price expectations in the wage equation, and stems from his use of the current and two lagged values of the rate of change of (consumer) prices in place of the usual single price term. Two points are of interest: the coefficients on the price variables do not decline monotonically, as is implied in the adaptive expectations formulation which has been extensively used in the recent past; and the sum of the price coefficients is 0·9, much higher than other estimates and probably insignificantly different from unity (though insufficient information is given for a test to be made). This last aspect of Brechling's results is particularly interesting in view of the contention that in the long run the Phillips curve becomes vertical.

A later re-estimation of Brechling's model over a slightly longer period by Mitchell [24] produced a lower (point) estimate of the price effect (0·81); again, he did not show awareness of the relevance of his results to the strict expectations hypothesis, and hence did not provide enough information for a significance test to be made. It is notable, however, that the later data tended to produce results less close to the extreme neoclassical prediction.

Mitchell's formulation differed from Brechling's in two respects: he included only one lagged value of the price term; and he employed a transformation to eliminate first-order autocorrelation, whereas Brechling's Durbin-Watson statistics are suspect. Either factor might account for the numerically small but economically interesting difference in the results.

of wage change in 'policy on' periods and the average prediction errors are then calculated.

We examine first the findings about structural stability of the wage determination equation. Lipsey and Parkin found the following relationship for 'policy off' and 'policy on':[8]

'Off' $\dot{w}_{W1} = 6 \cdot 672 - 2 \cdot 372 + 0 \cdot 457\dot{p} + 0 \cdot 136T$
$\quad\quad\quad$ [5·79] $\quad$ [3·64] $\quad$ [6·25] $\quad$ [0·07]
$\quad\quad\quad R^2 = 0 \cdot 856 \quad\quad d = 1 \cdot 231$

'On' $\dot{w}_{W1} = 3 \cdot 919 - 0 \cdot 404U + 0 \cdot 227\dot{p} + 3 \cdot 764\dot{T}$
$\quad\quad\quad$ [2·27] $\quad$ [0·56] $\quad$ [0·93] $\quad$ [1·161]
$\quad\quad\quad R^2 = 0 \cdot 138 \quad\quad d = 0 \cdot 724$

'Entire' $\dot{w}_{W1} = 4 \cdot 147 - 0 \cdot 891U + 0 \cdot 482\dot{p} + 3 \cdot 315\dot{T}$
$\quad\quad\quad$ [4·26] $\quad$ [1·77] $\quad$ [5·76] $\quad$ [2·09]
$\quad\quad\quad R^2 = 0 \cdot 616 \quad\quad d = 0 \cdot 742$

An F-test was performed on the structural stability of the 'on' and 'off' equations, and the hypothesis that the two coefficient vectors are the same was rejected.[9] The most significant finding was the flattening of the $\dot{w}$, U relationship and the drop in the intercept, indicating a pivoting of the Phillips curve at about 1·8% unemployment and a wage inflation rate of 4%. The subsequent work by Parkin [28]

[8] Summary statistics quoted for all regression results are the adjusted ($\bar{R}^2$) or unadjusted (R^2) coefficient of determination, and the Durbin-Watson statistic (d); a t-statistic [ ] or standard error ( ) is given below each regression coefficient. The variables used by Lipsey and Parkin are defined as follows:

W_{W1} is weekly wage rates for all industries, all workers,

$$\dot{w}_{W1} = \frac{W_{t+2} - W_{t-2}}{\frac{1}{2}(W_{t+2} + W_{t-2})} \cdot 100$$

U is the moving average of the percentage of labour force registered as wholly unemployed,

$$U = \frac{U_t + U_{t-1} + U_{t-2}}{3}$$

T is the percentage of labour force unionized, $\dot{T} = T - T_{-1}$.
Quarterly data, 1947(3)–1967(2) obtained by interpolating annual data.
P is the index of retail prices, all items,

$$\dot{p} = \frac{P_{t+2} - P_{t-2}}{\frac{1}{2}(P_{t+2} + P_{t-2})} \cdot 100$$

The same data (for policy-off) was used by Sumner.
[9] Strictly, the F test is inappropriate because of the presence of serial correlation, and it can only be interpreted as a rough indication of a shift.

apparently strengthened this conclusion. However, the work of Godfrey and Wallis suggests that when appropriate allowance is made for both simultaneous-equation and higher-order autocorrelation problems, this inference is invalid. Godfrey tested for the slope and intercept changes using shift and slope dummies and found that the only significant change, using Sargan's autoregressive instrumental variable estimator [32], was on the union pushfulness proxy.[10]

Wallis reports that 'a number of people [including Godfrey, Trivedi and Wallis]...[have]...put the Lipsey-Parkin model through computer programmes for various estimation methods, such as 2SLS, autoregressive 2SLS, instrumental variables and various maximum likelihood methods. Generally speaking, what happens is that the variables of the L-P model very quickly lose their apparent significance and thus the model ceases to be identified.'

The Lipsey-Parkin conclusions have also been questioned within the confines of OLS estimation. Sumner [36] argued that before we can have sufficient faith in the Lipsey-Parkin equation to use it as a basis for assessing the effects of incomes policy, we need to be satisfied that the 'policy off' equation is structurally stable. He divided the policy off sample into two sub-samples, (A) 1950(4)–1955(4) and (B) 1957(1)–1961(2), and estimated the equations for the two sub-periods separately. The result was:

$$\text{(A)} \quad \dot{w}_{w1} = 7 \cdot 80 - 2 \cdot 85 U + 0 \cdot 44 \dot{p}$$
$$[4 \cdot 72] \qquad [10 \cdot 40]$$
$$\bar{R}^2 = 0 \cdot 93 \qquad d = 2 \cdot 20$$

$$\text{(B)} \quad \dot{w}_{w1} = 8 \cdot 12 - 2 \cdot 85 U + 0 \cdot 004 \dot{p}$$
$$[2 \cdot 47] \qquad [0 \cdot 02]$$
$$\bar{R}^2 = 0 \cdot 51 \qquad d = 1 \cdot 27$$

It is immediately apparent that, according to these findings, the relationship between wage changes and price changes collapses completely after the middle 1950's, but the relationship between wage changes and unemployment remains remarkably stable.

Hines reports a large number of equations. We think that we fairly represent his findings by quoting here his best quarterly model for

---

[10] Union militancy is proxied by the number of stoppages, excluding coal-mining.

'policy off'. Since he gives both OLS and 2SLS we report both. His findings are: [11]

'Off' $\dot{w}_{H1} = 7\cdot145 - 1\cdot384U + 0\cdot211\dot{p} + 7\cdot844\dot{T}/T$
$\quad\quad\quad\quad\quad [2\cdot50] \quad\quad [2\cdot383] \quad\quad [3\cdot78]$
$\quad\quad\quad\quad \bar{R}^2 = 0\cdot840 \quad\quad d = 1\cdot57$

'On' $\dot{w}_{H1} = 5\cdot165 - 0\cdot589U + 0\cdot285\dot{p} + 9\cdot793\dot{T}/T$
$\quad\quad\quad\quad\quad [0\cdot81] \quad\quad [0\cdot92] \quad\quad [3\cdot01]$
$\quad\quad\quad\quad \bar{R}^2 = 0\cdot382 \quad\quad d = 0\cdot82$

'Entire' $\dot{w}_{H1} = 6\cdot076 - 0\cdot918U + 0\cdot229\dot{p} + 8\cdot900\dot{T}/T$
$\quad\quad\quad\quad\quad [2\cdot08] \quad\quad [2\cdot43] \quad\quad [4\cdot62]$
$\quad\quad\quad\quad \bar{R}^2 = 0\cdot656 \quad\quad d = 0\cdot98$

OLS

and

'Off' $\dot{w}_{H1} = 6\cdot394 - 1\cdot048U + 0\cdot264\dot{p} + 7\cdot850\dot{T}/T$
$\quad\quad\quad\quad\quad [10\cdot44] \quad\quad [13\cdot81] \quad\quad [15\cdot87]$
$\quad\quad\quad\quad \bar{R}^2 = 0\cdot994$

'On' $\dot{w}_{H1} = 12\cdot983 - 2\cdot550U - 0\cdot979\dot{p} + 17\cdot750\dot{T}/T$
$\quad\quad\quad\quad\quad\quad [3\cdot62] \quad\quad [2\cdot40] \quad\quad [5\cdot59]$
$\quad\quad\quad\quad\quad \bar{R}^2 = 0\cdot672$

'Entire' $\dot{w}_{H1} = 6\cdot234 - 0\cdot982U + 0\cdot214\dot{p} + 8\cdot800\dot{T}/T$
$\quad\quad\quad\quad\quad [7\cdot05] \quad\quad [5\cdot19] \quad\quad [10\cdot68]$
$\quad\quad\quad\quad \bar{R}^2 = 0\cdot953$

2SLS

Hines's results, in qualitative terms, are straightforward. They differ from Lipsey and Parkin in finding a significant role for unionization in both 'policy on' and 'policy off' periods; failing to find a non-significant unemployment effect in 'policy on', and in the effects of price changes. We take up subsequently the question as to whether these differences affect our view as to the overall effect of incomes policy on the rate of wage change.

So far, we have looked at models based directly on the earlier

[11] Hines's variables, where they differ from those used by Lipsey and Parkin, are defined as follows:

W_{H1} is hourly wage rates,

$$\dot{w}_{H1} = \frac{W_t - W_{t-1}}{W_{t-1}} \cdot 100$$

$\dot{p}$ is differenced as $[(P_t - P_{t-1})/P_{t-1}] \cdot 100$.
Quarterly data, 1949(1)–1969(4).

literature on the wage inflation process. Two recent studies by
Taylor [37], and Thomas and Stoney [39], have both advanced our
understanding of the wage inflation process and at the same time,
tested for the effects of incomes policy.

Taylor argues that the excess demand for labour is better proxied
by allowing for labour hoarding as well as unemployment. Using a
model in which unemployment and hoarding are added together he
finds the following:[12]

'Off' $\dot{e} = 3\cdot48 - 0\cdot68(U + D) + 0\cdot36\dot{p} + 5\cdot00S$
        $[1\cdot43]$ $[4\cdot17]$ $[1\cdot85]$ $[2\cdot16]$
        $\bar{R}^2 = 0\cdot70$ $d = 2\cdot61$

'On' $\dot{e} = 9\cdot13 - 0\cdot69(U + D) + 0\cdot03\dot{p} + 1\cdot20S$
        $[2\cdot57]$ $[2\cdot59]$ $[0\cdot06]$ $[0\cdot52]$
        $\bar{R}^2 = 0\cdot48$ $d = 1\cdot57$

'Entire' $\dot{e} = 3\cdot78 - 0\cdot57(U + D) + 0\cdot37\dot{p} + 4\cdot22S$
        $[2\cdot48]$ $[4\cdot04]$ $[1\cdot74]$ $[4\cdot21]$
        $\bar{R}^2 = 0\cdot73$ $d = 1\cdot97$

These equations have high coefficients of determination and satisfactory Durbin-Watson statistics, and the 'off' and 'on' equations
are not significantly different from the 'entire' equation. However,
the theoretical underpinnings of the model have not yet been fully
developed.

Thomas and Stoney approach the problem of deriving an explanation for the average rate of wage change from rather more rigorous
micro-behaviour propositions and aggregation than has been common in this field. The notable exception is the work of Archibald [1].
Their work was developed entirely independently of Archibald's but
is in many ways very close to it. They propose that for each individual

[12] Taylor's variables are defined as follows:

E is hourly earnings adjusted for overtime,

$$\dot{e} = \frac{E_{t+1} - E_{t-1}}{E_t} \cdot 100$$

$(U + D)$ is the sum of the percentage of labour force registered as unemployed
and rate of labour hoarding.

$$\dot{p} = \frac{P_{t+1} - P_{t-1}}{\frac{1}{2}(P_{t+1} + P_{t-1})} \cdot 100$$

S is the total number of stoppages (thousand) semi-annual data, 1953(2)–
1970(1); the data used in the sub-period regressions ends in 1969(1).

labour market, the rate of wage change depends on the unemployment rate in that market and on the rate of wage change in the 'leading' market. Explicit statistical aggregation (with the help of some strong assumptions) yields an equation to explain aggregate wage change which is a function of the average unemployment rate, its dispersion, the unemployment rate in the 'leading' sector and, where that sector has more than one individual market, the dispersion of unemployment in that sector. Their estimating equations take advantage of explicit assumptions about the functional form of the micro-relations.

The Thomas-Stoney results are, from the point of view of incomes policy, like Taylor's, although they, unlike him, do not go beyond 1966 with their data. They obtain the following results:[13]

'Off' $\dot{w}_{H2} = 3·05 + 0·416\dot{p} - 3·08S_1^* + 7·10A_1$
       $(0·62)$ $(0·067)$ $(0·62)$ $(2·56)$
       $\bar{R}^2 = 0·942$ $d = 2·21$

'On' $\dot{w}_{H2} = 2·59 + 0·343\dot{p} - 2·32S_1^* + 10·08A_1$
      $(0·77)$ $(0·094)$ $(0·49)$ $(4·42)$
      $\bar{R}^2 = 0·963$ $d = 2·50$

'Entire' $\dot{w}_{H2} = 3·04 + 0·431\dot{p} - 2·57S_1^* + 6·56A_1$
         $(0·44)$ $(0·048)$ $(0·41)$ $(1·95)$
         $\bar{R}^2 = 0·946$ $d = 1·97$

and, in an F-test, show that the 'on' and 'off' equations can be regarded as the same as that for their 'entire' sample.

From this brief survey of tests for the structural stability of the

---

[13] Thomas and Stoney's variables are defined as follows:
W_{H2} is hourly wage rates,

$$\dot{w}_{H2} = \frac{W_{t+1} - W_{t-1}}{2W_t} \cdot 100$$

$$\dot{p} = \frac{P_{t+1} - P_{t-1}}{2P_t} \cdot 100$$

$$S_1^* = \log U - \frac{S^2}{2U^2}$$

$$A_1 = \log U - \log \hat{U} + \frac{\hat{S}^2}{2\hat{U}^2} - \frac{S^2}{2U^2}$$

$U =$ unemployment rate
$S^2 =$ variance of regional unemployment rates
$\wedge$ denotes leading sectors
annual data, 1950–66.

wage equation, it seems that we may conclude, tentatively, that there is little evidence for significant movements of that relationship. Lipsey and Parkin's findings of a structural shift need modification in the light of the work by Wallis and Godfrey. Taylor and Thomas and Stoney find no significant changes in their respective formulations of the function, and similar conclusions are reached by Burrows and Hitiris [5] and Sargan [33], who adopt more conventional estimating equations; a common, and possibly significant, characteristic of these four studies is that the data period excludes all or (in Sargan's case) most of the Cripps wage freeze. Only Hines's results appear to indicate shifts, and it would be premature to attribute much

Table 1   Estimated effects of incomes policy on the rate of wage inflation

+ = number of quarters in which inflation was higher than predicted

− = number of quarters in which inflation was lower than predicted

$\hat{\varepsilon}$ = estimated effect of incomes policy (% p.a.) mean

σ_ε = standard deviation of residuals for 'policy off' equation

Incomes Policy Yrs.	Lipsey-Parkin			Hines		
	+	−	$\hat{\varepsilon}$	+	−	$\hat{\varepsilon}$
1. 1948(3)–1950(3) 1949(1)H	0	9	−2.369	0	7	−1.440
2. 1956(1)–1956(4)	2	2	−1.050	2	2	−0.073
3. 1961(3)–1967(2) 1968(2)H	11	13	−0.127	14	14	−0.050
4. 1968(3)–1969(4) Hines only	—	—	—	2	4	−0.056
All periods	13	24	−0.772	18	27	−0.267
	$\sigma_\varepsilon = 1.058$			$\sigma_\varepsilon = 0.851$		

1. The Lipsey-Parkin results are those derived by Wallis from the reduced-form equation ([36], Table 1).

2. Hines' results are obtained from Table XI of 'What Does the Phillips Curve Show?', a revised extended version of [13], mimeo, May 1971.

3. Hines' results have been re-grouped to facilitate comparison with those of Wallis.

significance to his findings until their ability to withstand closer scrutiny has been investigated.

The findings of Lipsey and Parkin and Hines of structural shifts in the wage determination equation, even if correct, do not imply that incomes policies necessarily moderate the rate of wage inflation. Using their equations for policy-off to predict the policy-on inflation rate still might show no significant impact of policy even though their equations for 'on' and 'off' look different. Table 1 summarizes the results of such an exercise and shows very clearly that, even in studies where the wage equation seems to shift between policy on and off, the impact on the rate of wage inflation is so small on average as to be economically insignificant. It is important, however, to notice that the sub-periods of incomes policy are very different from each other, with all studies agreeing that the Cripps' policy achieved a significant reduction in the wage inflation rate.

The conclusion of this section is therefore that, on the basis of our present knowledge, it is possible to say that, with the exception of the immediate post war experiment, incomes policy apparently has little effect either on the wage determination process or on the average rate of wage inflation, given the values of the explanatory variables.[14] Possible effects on the determinants of wage changes are considered in the next section.

3   The price equation

Compared with the detailed attention devoted to the behaviour of wages, this branch of the empirical literature on inflation has suffered some neglect, both in general and in relation to the impact of incomes policy. This neglect becomes even more apparent when the underlying theory is considered.

The next sub-section reviews those studies of incomes policy which include a price equation. As above, the discussion will be confined to the estimated effects on the parameters of the price equation itself, and will not attempt to gauge that part of the total effect on the inflation rate which results from effects on the arguments of the price equation. After some digression, an alternative to the typical form of the price equation is evaluated.

More than half of the discussion which follows is devoted to the

[14] A recent study by the Department of Employment [6] reaches the same conclusion for earnings averaged over the period 1965-9. However, they ignore earlier experiments with incomes policy in fitting their equations.

relationship between excess demand and the rate of change of prices; references to incomes policy seldom intrude. Some justification for the apparent lack of correspondence between title and contents should be offered at the outset. Briefly, almost all empirical studies of the price equation, whether or not they have been specifically concerned with incomes policy, have adopted the cost-plus hypothesis; and the theoretical underpinnings of such attempts as have been made to test for a demand influence have rarely been made explicit. It is argued below that cost-plus pricing leaves little or no room for the operation of incomes policy; on the other hand, if excess demand enters the price equation directly then the search for policy effects can no longer be dismissed *a priori* as a lost cause. Hence, thorough testing of an excess demand hypothesis, including comparison with the cost-plus alternative, emerges as a pre-condition of tests for effects of incomes policy.

3.1 *The price equation and incomes policy*

Most studies of the price equation have wasted little time on theoretical niceties before getting down to the serious business of estimation. Solow's [35] statement of the underlying theory is a fair example: 'In general, one expects the rate of change of the price level to depend on current and recent changes in unit costs, and on the supply-demand balance in the current period and the recent past.' Similar statements, more or less terse, can be found in the investigations cited below. Moreover, at least for the U.K., the set of independent variables usually reduces to the components of changes in unit costs, for most subsequent students of the price equation have accepted Neild's conclusion [27, p. 51]: '...that manufacturers' prices are set by reference to costs when operating at some normal level of capacity and that they are not sensitive to moderate fluctuations in demand.' Admittedly, few have taken note of his caveat (p. 20) that: 'This rejection of demand influence seems fairly decisive, but it remains possible that a more complex formulation or a different indicator might lead to a different conclusion.' In the spirit of the work to be surveyed, demand will be ignored in the remainder of this section.

Attempts to isolate direct effects of incomes policy on prices have followed the same two routes as were used in the study of wages, *viz.* insertion of several intercept dummies for the various policy-on interludes or estimation of separate functions for 'on' and 'off' periods. Examples of the first approach are provided by the work of

Bodkin *et al.* [2], Smith [34], the Prices and Incomes Board [22] and Solow. Smith and the P.I.B. adopt Dicks-Mireaux's specification [7]:

$$\dot{P} = a + b\dot{W}_{-i} + c\dot{M}_{-j} + d\dot{Q}_{-k} + \varepsilon$$

where a dot above a variable indicates its proportional rate of change and the symbols have the following definitions:

$P = $ price level: wholesale or retail, (Smith) or implicit deflator of total final expenditure at factor cost (P.I.B., and also Solow)

$W = $ labour income, variously measured as wage rates or earnings, hourly or weekly (all of which are tried by Smith), or wages and salaries per head (P.I.B.)

$M = $ import prices

$Q = $ output per head

$i, j, k = $ empirically determined lags.

Bodkin *et al.* use a similar form but without allowance for $\dot{Q}$. Neither Smith nor the P.I.B. points out that in the absence of systematic changes in gross profit margins the intercept should be insignificantly different from zero; Smith's estimates of the intercept are small in absolute value,[15] but the restriction is not satisfied by the P.I.B.'s estimates: as always, an unexplained trend is an admission of ignorance. A further requirement is that $b = -d$; however, in these, as in other examples of the Dicks-Mireaux specification, the coefficient on changes in labour costs persistently exceeds the coefficient on changes in labour requirements per unit of output.

Too much need not be made of this discrepancy between expectations and results. As is well known, the rate of change of labour productivity includes a large transitory component, arising from lags in the adjustment of employment to changes in output. The normal cost variant of the cost-plus hypothesis under discussion suggests that the appropriate variable for the price equation is a smoothed measure of $\dot{Q}$. This point was discussed by Neild, but in his experiments he used unit labour cost as a composite variable, so that in the present context the success of the experiment cannot be judged. In passing, it may be noted that the unspecified but 'senseless' outcome of an attempt to include $\dot{W}$ and $\dot{Q}$ as separate determinants of $\dot{P}$ led Solow to adopt the composite variable, unit labour costs.

---

[15] Standard errors are not reported for the intercepts.

The bearing of these three sets of results on the success of incomes policy is not easy to determine. The results themselves are contradictory. The P.I.B. reports positive but insignificant coefficients on the two shift dummies for the period studied (1946–66). Bodkin *et al.* also discover a positive coefficient, which in their case is significant. Smith presents several alternative tables, in which the direction of effect and statistical significance of incomes policy turns out to be very sensitive to the estimation method and the labour cost and price variables adopted. OLS estimates of retail price index regressions produce no significant results using earnings variables, a significant reduction in the inflation rate in 1956 using hourly wage rates, and an increase (1948–50), a decrease (1956) and an increase (1961–2) using weekly wage rates. Wholesale price index OLS regressions produce significant increases in the inflation rate in 1948–50 and 1956, using earnings. The two-stage least squares estimates are similar in pattern. Since Smith does not report the results of standard tests for autocorrelation of residuals, this summary of his results may well overstate their significance. Solow's regressions for 1948–66 include intercept dummies for 1948–9 and 1961; he was 'unable to make a Wilson dummy work'. Both coefficients are negative and appear to be highly significant, though again autocorrelation tests are not fully reported. However, he is 'reluctant to place a lot of weight on this indication of the effectiveness of incomes policies', a surprising comment in view of the magnitude of the coefficients, approximately 0·05 in 1948–9 and 0·02 in 1961, for a definition of the dependent variable apparently in terms of proportional, not percentage, changes. The practice of drawing the reader's attention to the statistical significance of results, which he could judge for himself, while ignoring some of their economic implications and providing insufficient information for the reader to be sure of making correct inferences, is a lamentable feature of much applied work.

That the results of these exercises should fail to indicate a stable negative coefficient on the various shift dummies is scarcely surprising. As Lipsey and Parkin [21] point out, to test for policy effects on the price equation by the simple expedient of incorporating a single intercept dummy amounts to assuming that the gross profit margin is steadily reduced (or increased) during the operation of incomes policy. Any such effect on profit margins, however, could hardly be consistent and prolonged. Conversely, an insignificant coefficient on a shift dummy does not rule out the possibility that incomes policy produced some effect on margins during part of the period of operation.

The alternative approach of estimating and comparing separate price equations for 'on' and 'off' periods has been used by Lipsey and Parkin, Hines [13] and Burrows and Hitiris [5]. The latter report that none of the slope or intercept dummies which they used in preference to the computation of separate 'on' and 'off' regressions is significant, either alone or in any combination, with the single exception of the shift dummy when the regressors include the lagged dependent variable as a proxy for the expected rate of change of prices. However, the magnitude of the coefficient is small -0.194 even in the steady state, with the dependent variable apparently (again!) expressed in percentage terms: and its statistical significance is dubious, for the authors quote only the conventional form of the Durbin-Watson statistic: at 1.7, this is only fractionally above the upper bound, and the statistic for the corresponding equation with the lagged dependent variable excluded is less than unity. Serial correlation appears to be a feature of all the equations estimated by Burrows and Hitiris, and indeed of all the price equations surveyed for which test statistics are reported.[16] Two other characteristics of the results are of interest, but received no comment: one is the low coefficient (typically 0.22) on the rate of change of labour cost per unit of output, the other is the consistency of the intercept (in the range of 1.0–1.6) for which a standard error is not provided.

Burrows and Hitiris conclude that their 'tests do not support Lipsey and Parkin's contention that the price equations collapse when incomes policy is operating'. This is a fair indication of the L-P regression results: in the policy-on equation $\dot{W}$ and $\dot{M}$ lose all significance, the intercept rises from -0.140 to 3.874 and becomes significant,[17] and the (unadjusted) coefficient of determination falls from 0.843 to 0.241. The changes between Hines's policy-on and off regressions are similar in direction, though much less dramatic. However, Lipsey and Parkin seem to regard the apparent instability of the price equation as a statistical illusion which stems from the replacement in incomes policy periods of the Phillips relation by a wages norm. While they are sceptical about the existence of consistent differences between the 'on' and 'off' price equations, the

[16] Lipsey and Parkin are the only other authors to do so.
[17] The D.W. statistic is, however, unacceptably low.

prediction errors generated by their 'off' equation suggest departures from what would have been expected in two particular policy interludes, *viz.* an increase in the inflation rate of 0·75% during the Cripps period, and a decrease of 2% during 1956. Not surprisingly, these results correspond qualitatively to those of Smith, though in both cases their significance remains uncertain.

To conclude, there is no evidence that incomes policy has produced a consistent change in the price equation. It would indeed have been surprising if a policy-induced change in profit margins or in the rules of cost-plus pricing had been found to persist indefinitely. The use in the price equation of shift dummies alone does not appear to be an inappropriate technique, provided the policy-on period is not treated as homogeneous.[18] Such changes in gross margins as are suggested by the results are of doubtful significance, and there is a disturbing lack of correspondence among the various investigations as to the particular periods in which changes occurred. All the studies cited exhibit defects at the statistical level, and none of them deals convincingly with the problem of simultaneous equation bias.[19]

With the exception of Solow, who reported a puzzling difference between quarterly and annual results, none of the investigators attempted to test for a relationship between demand and price changes. This is surprising, for any such relationship would make a consistent effect of incomes policy on the price equation much more plausible than it is within the cost-plus framework considered so far. Moreover, evidence has been slowly accumulating to suggest the existence of a direct effect of demand on prices. This evidence is reviewed in the next section.

3.2   Demand and prices

A casual glance at the post-war time-series confirms Dow's statement [9, p. 348] that 'profits [as a proportion of output] have often been a little higher in the years of high demand'. Less casually, Brownlie [4] demonstrated the existence, in New Zealand, of a sig-

---

[18] The P.I.B. study, which employs only two shift dummies, comes perilously close to doing so. Two shift dummies are inserted in the price (and wage) equation, in an attempt to distinguish between voluntary policies (1948–50 and 1965) and 'years of tight control' (1961–2 and 1966).

[19] Hines's and Smith's two-stage least squares estimates are obtained within the confines of a model in which $\dot{p}$ and $\dot{w}$ cannot be regarded as the sole endogenous variables; they introduce no extraneous regressors at the first stage. This point is considered further in section 4.

nificant relationship between the aggregate profit margin, defined as the ratio of pre-tax profit to the value of output, and demand pressure, proxied by the ratio of production to horsepower installed. However, Dow chooses to attribute pro-cyclical variations in the share of profits not to a direct influence of demand on pricing decisions, but to inertia in the form of a 'tendency...not fully to adjust prices to short-term fluctuations in output per head'. This interpretation appears to be based on Neild's analysis, cited above.

Neild reached the conclusion that demand has no direct effect on prices after noting that the addition of a demand variable to the model discussed in the preceding section added nothing to the results; on the contrary, the coefficient was persistently negative, significantly so in the period 1950–60. The demand variable used in these experiments was 'the index of demand [for labour] in cumulative form', on the grounds that it 'seemed most reasonable to assume that a given level of excess demand would be associated with a change in price'. These experiments appear to be the only statistical foundations for the decision of many subsequent investigators to exclude demand from the price equation *ab initio*.

The validity of Neild's conclusions has been challenged by Rushdy and Lund [31]. To appreciate their reasoning, and the recent criticisms by McCallum [23], it is necessary to spell out Neild's basic model in more detail. Price is set by marking up prime costs per unit of output (K), plus any fixed absolute charge, hence:

$$P_t = \alpha_0 + \alpha_1 K_t \tag{a}$$

Prime costs consist of unit labour (L) and material (J) costs, but the appropriate values of L and J are not their current levels, but distributed lag functions, here denoted by tildes,

$$K_t = \beta_1 \tilde{L}_t + \beta_2 \tilde{J}_t \tag{b}$$

The forms of lag function adopted are for labour costs

$$\tilde{L}_t = (1 - \lambda)L_t + (1 - \lambda)\lambda L_{t-1} + (1 - \lambda)\lambda^2 L_{t-2} + \cdots \tag{c}$$

and for material costs

$$\tilde{J}_t = \mu_0 J_t + \mu_1 J_{t-1} + \mu_2(1 - \lambda)J_{t-2} + \mu_2(1 - \lambda)\lambda J_{t-1} + \cdots \tag{d}$$

The estimating equation is therefore:

$$P_t = \alpha_0(1 - \lambda) + \alpha_1\beta_1(1 - \lambda)L_t + \alpha_1\beta_2\mu_0 J_t + \alpha_1\beta_2(\mu_1 - \mu\lambda_0)J_{t-1}$$
$$+ \alpha_1\beta_2[\mu_2(1 - \lambda) - \lambda\mu_1]J_{t-2} + \lambda P_{t-1}. \tag{e}$$

To return to the criticisms of Rushdy and Lund, two specific points are raised: Neild's preferred form, involving labour costs deflated by trend productivity, implicitly includes demand because of the pro-cyclical behaviour of measured output per head; and the cumulated demand variable (C) is appended not to the structural equation,

$$P_t = \alpha_0 + \alpha_1\beta_1\tilde{L}_t + \alpha_1\beta_2\tilde{J}_t + \alpha_2 C_t \tag{a'}$$

but to the estimating equation (e). The estimating equation derived from (a') is given by (e) above plus:

$$\alpha_2[D_t + (1 - \lambda)C_{t-1}]$$

where D_t denotes the current excess demand. Conversely, as Rushdy and Lund state, the structural equation implied by Neild's aug-mented estimating equation, (e) $+ \alpha_2 C_t$, includes 'a distributed lag of demand experience with increasing weights'. However, they con-tinue: 'Neild thus reversed the acceptable distributed lag form and it is, therefore, not surprising that he failed to obtain significant results for his demand variable.' Their next step is to add D_t (not C_t) to Neild's estimating equation, presumably to test their assertion that his use of trend productivity implicitly includes the current level of excess demand.

The results will be discussed presently. Meanwhile, it may be help-ful to dispose of a potential source of confusion provided for assidu-ous readers of the *R.E.S.* by McCallum. He appears to have been misled by the irrelevant sentence quoted above and by the subsequent search for a partial relation between the price level and current excess demand into thinking that Rushdy and Lund reject Neild's 'reason-able assumption' that cumulated excess demand belongs in the price-level equation. On the contrary, they explicitly accept it. He proceeds by postulating an 'equilibrium' price equation of the form

$$P_t^* = a + bLt + cJt + dCt$$

and invoking the partial adjustment hypothesis to derive an esti-mating equation that includes among the regressors C_t, 'which was used by Neild'. He admits in a footnote that 'this way of viewing Neild's model is strictly appropriate only when the terms J_{t-1} and J_{t-2} are not used...'. The point is simply that these terms are used. Thus are Notes and Comments generated.

Reverting to matters of substance, Rushdy and Lund's results con-firm their expectation that any influence of current (or, more accurately, last quarter's) excess demand on the price level is hidden when trend productivity is used in the measurement of unit labour costs. Demand enters significantly with the appropriate sign when included with measured unit labour costs, though, as in Neild's own analysis, the latter is insignificant. There is nothing to choose between these competing formulations on statistical grounds. Rushdy and Lund object to the productivity trend version on the grounds that: 'strictly interpreted, this costing hypothesis assumes that manufacturers at any point in time during 1950–60 were aware of the productivity trend for these 11 years, and adjusted their prices according to a distributed lag of the unit wage costs implied by it.' Further testing is required to determine the relative merits of these alternative hypotheses.

Rushdy and Lund finally list (some of) the results of price-change[20] regressions including and excluding last quarter's level of excess demand. These are too diverse to permit a useful summary to be given here, as the coefficient estimates but not $\bar{R}^2$'s are very sensitive to the precise specification adopted. The results may, however, be characterized as providing evidence not only of a direct influence of demand on prices but also of mis-specification: in particular, of the 24 equations published all but three (in which demand is either excluded or enters insignificantly) contain significantly positive intercepts.

An issue more important than the empirical results is their theoretical foundation. Neild, his critics, and their critic, all accept the proposition that the appropriate demand variable in a price-level equation is cumulated excess demand. Conversely, the current level of excess demand should feature in a price-change equation. This apparently innocuous statement has been challenged by Johnson [15] on the following grounds: 'It might be plausible to use a cumulative demand variable if this were the *only* explanatory variable being used, but Neild, [*et al.*] is relating current price to current and recent prime costs, and if a demand influence is at work as well, it seems plausible to expect that the current margin between price and prime costs will be affected by the current, or very recent, level of demand pressure.'[21] Conventional theory argues that price changes in response to excess demand alone; costs elements have no place in the price equation

---

[20] In absolute rather than relative form.
[21] Italics in original. Apparently ([16] p. 4) Neild experimented unsuccessfully with current excess demand as an argument of his price-level equation.

3

since the influence of supply shifts will be reflected in the single explanatory variable.[22] There is no warrant for Solow's statement with which this survey began,[23] or for McCallum's objection to Rushdy and Lund's addition of current excess demand to Neild's model of the price level: '...that would make the price level a function of excess demand. This in turn would imply that a non-zero level of excess demand which remained constant period after period would not induce, *ceteris paribus*, a change in the price level. The "Law of Supply and Demand" would not be in force.' The Law of Supply and Demand is quite irrelevant to cost-plus pricing, the theoretical basis for which has yet to be provided.

The conclusion, mildly surprising, is that the excess demand hypothesis has received little or no testing. The only exceptions of which we are aware are a paper by Johnston, Bugg and Lund [16], and the positive section of McCallum's previously cited paper. These are discussed in the final sub-section. First, the relevance of Rushdy and Lund's results to a topic outside the scope of this survey but of considerable interest to the policy-maker, is examined briefly.

3.3   *A digression*

Whatever the status of Rushdy and Lund's work as a test of the effect of demand on prices, their first set of results, on the partial relation between the price level and current or recent excess demand, serves the valuable function of disposing, at least at the aggregate level, of a pricing hypothesis unrecognized in economic theory but dear to the heart of the Society of Motor Manufacturers and Traders. In the words of the P.I.B. [25] a problem arises in

...capital-intensive industries...whose overhead or indirect costs cannot be adjusted downwards as demand falls, with the result that in periods of recession their unit costs rise... The normal reaction of firms to a rise in unit costs is to raise their prices... If it be assumed—and the assumption is surely fair—that the proportion of industries in the

---

[22] This simple point, and its neglect by economists in their applied work, will be familiar to historians of economic thoughts on the Phillips curve.

[23] At least in orthodox theory. Williamson [42] has proposed a model in which the height of an individual imperfectly competitive firm's demand curve is positively related to the prices charged by its competitors; adopting Neild's assumption about cost structure, he obtains an estimating equation which differs from Neild's by including P_{t-2} and excluding the intercept. The model is fitted to data for British manufacturing, and the results are shown to be consistent with Williamson's predictions: it is impossible, however, to distinguish between Williamson's model and a version of Neild's which incorporates an alternative lag structure.

economy which are unable quickly to decrease their overhead costs is rising, the inference must mean that a period of recession can well be accompanied by rising costs and prices...

The co-existence of inflation and recession is hardly a discriminating test of the hypothesis under discussion, but such a test is provided, perhaps inadvertently, by Rushdy and Lund.

Clearly, this extreme version of full-cost pricing implies a negative relationship between demand and price in a regression which includes prime costs. This implication is strongly rejected by the empirical results. Demand enters positively and significantly when measured unit labour costs are included, negatively but highly insignificantly in association with unit labour costs based on trend productivity; the alleged distinction between 'full cost' and 'normal cost' pricing in the work of (e.g.) Andrews suggests that the former results relate directly to the question at issue.

3.4   Testing the excess demand hypothesis

The first attempt at a direct test of the excess demand hypothesis by Johnston, Bugg and Lund, develops a succession of increasing complex macro models in order to approximate the discrepancy between aggregate demand and supply. Initially, the full burden of adjustment to excess demand, in the form of unfulfilled plans, is borne by consumers. Subsequently, data on machine tool orders and approvals of industrial building applications are considered in an endeavour to measure excess demand for capital goods. However, the apparent lack of response to, or development of, the ideas presented suggests that a simpler approach might be more fruitful. Moreover, one of the central concepts discussed, the principle that some increase in supply is always forthcoming in response to an increase in demand (the output-response function), provides some justification for adoption of a simpler model.

McCallum's contribution falls into this latter category. A linear homogeneous relation between (absolute) price changes and excess demand for products is postulated, but the relationship is not instantaneous: 'It seems reasonable to believe that response lags exist in this relationship as they do in most others. Let us, therefore, posit a geometric distributed lag model.' Excess demand is measurable in the labour market but not directly in the product market. Excess demand for labour is assumed to be a distributed lag function of excess demand for commodities.

McCallum's own view of the outcome is admirably succinct: 'Results of estimating these pure excess demand models are very favourable. The R^2 figures are respectably high though lower than for the models in which price changes are related to costs. A comparative strong point of the excess demand results is the apparent absence of autocorrelation.' The obligatory plea for more empirical work evokes three immediate simple suggestions for improving his model while remaining within the single-equation framework.

The first is to use a direct proxy for excess demand in the product market in place of the measure based on vacancies and unemployment. The notion of the output-response function suggests that a variable as crude as deviations of (manufacturing) production from trend would be worthy of experimentation, and it would certainly eliminate one timing problem.

The second is to substitute for the *ad hoc* appeal to inertia as justification for a distributed-lag formulation the marginally less *ad hoc*, or at least more respectable, 'new microeconomic' stress on the role of price anticipations, formed adaptively. Solow claimed to have tested the 'expectations hypothesis' associated with Friedman by including a Cagan-type weighted average of past price changes in the mark-up equation discussed in the first sub-section, but, as noted by Laidler [18] and Vanderkamp [40], Solow's discovery that the coefficient on past price changes is always significantly below unity is irrelevant in terms of the Friedman view, since inflationary anticipations may be presumed to operate through the separately-entered labour cost variable as well as directly. An upper limit on the point estimate of the total effect of expectations is provided by the sum of Solow's labour-cost and price-expectations coefficients, always less than one for both the United States and the United Kingdom; but a more direct test and confidence interval might be of interest.

Thirdly, direct measures of expected price changes would be worth consideration. These would permit a very strong test of the excess demand hypothesis, since a distributed-lag formulation would then lack all theoretical justification.

Within this framework, incomes policy may affect the formation of price expectations or the response of prices to either excess demand or expectations. The last possibility appears implausible, and the first has been extensively discussed by Laidler [19] in the context of the wage equation. The possible effects of incomes policy on the wage-change/unemployment relation enumerated by Lipsey and Parkin

[21] apply almost equally to the response of goods prices to excess demand; the only obvious difference is the absence of a non-zero norm for price increases.

The argument of this section of the survey can be summarized very briefly. The existing evidence indicates that incomes policies have had no identifiable effect on the price equation. Unless further tests demonstrate that the excess demand model can compete successfully with the cost-plus hypothesis, it is difficult to see why the consensus should be questioned.

4   Outstanding issues

In this concluding section, we focus attention on those problems which appear most urgent. At this stage we can offer no solutions.

References have already been made to the bias introduced into many studies by neglect of the interdependence between wage-and-price changes. Three attitudes to the simultaneity problem are found in the literature. Most students of the inflationary process have 'solved' the problem by ignoring it, and have persisted in the application of ordinary least squares techniques. Justifications invoked for this procedure include appeal to the fact that the direction of bias is known, (e.g., Lipsey [20], note 47). On occasion, an endogenous variable which appears among the regressors of another equation has been subjected to the imposition of an arbitrary lag as a way of circumventing the problem regardless of the cost of mis-specification.

An ostensibly more substantial justification derives from the results of many of the studies which adopt the second approach to simultaneity, *viz.* estimation of a (usually) two-equation model by two-stage-least-squares. Typically the results of such an exercise differ only slightly from those of OLS estimation.[24] It is not clear, however, whether the similarity between the two sets of results should be regarded as a source of joy or dismay. The first reaction has been prevalent, but the second might be more appropriate in view of the limitations of the 2SLS method as generally applied. The dubious validity of this second approach stems from the treatment of $\dot{p}$ and $\dot{w}$ as the only endogenous variables of the model. This basic assumption has received surprisingly little probing until recently.

---

[24] Hines's policy-off results reproduced in section 2 give a fair indication of the magnitudes typically involved. Similar results are to be found in the work of Dicks-Mireaux [7], the P.I.B. [26] and Smith [34].

This probing, which represents the third approach to the simultaneity question, employs maximum likelihood methods, which additionally take account of autocorrelation in the residuals, and typically, (for example, in the work of Godfrey [11]), recognizes that all the variables in the conventional two-equation model, with the single exception of the rate of change of import prices, are endogenous. The results of applying these more sophisticated techniques have already been summarized in the extract from Wallis's paper [41] quoted in section 2; the obvious inference is that the scepticism expressed above about the effects of incomes policy applies equally to what economists thought they knew about the inflationary process itself.

A retreat into economic nihilism will contribute little to the solution of economic problems. The results of Wallis *et al.* make rigorous re-estimation of the alternative models discussed above all the more urgent. A particularly promising line of approach is presented by the models, typified by the work of Thomas and Stoney [39], which take account of the dispersion of excess demands as a determinant of the rate of wage inflation. Apart from its potential contribution to our understanding of inflation *per se*, a disaggregated study of the wage equation will be necessary to test hypotheses as to the effects of incomes policy which have been formulated in the light of existing, and admittedly deficient, investigations. As an illustration, systematic differences between behaviour in the public and private, or competitive and non-competitive sectors, have been suggested[25] but no tests have yet been made. Another potentially important, but so far underdeveloped approach, is Taylor's experimentation with more accurate proxies for excess demand [37].

A more mundane, but none the less important, problem arises in assigning particular historical episodes to the 'policy-on' or 'off' categories. This has already been mentioned in the discussion of those studies of the wage equation which used only shift dummies. The problem arises in a more acute form in relation to the very recent past. The formal demise of incomes policy coincided with that of the Labour Government, but it seemed reasonable to one of the present authors 'to regard the publication of the final White Paper in December 1969 as no more than a belated epitaph' [36]. On the other hand, despite its formal demise, incomes policy has arguably been operative since June 1970, as evidenced by ministerial attempts

[25] See, for example, Laidler [19].

to moderate wage increases in the public sector and by official interest in the C.B.I.'s endeavours to limit price increases. Given the inflation rate since 1969, the classification of this period as 'on' or 'off' makes a major difference to the evaluation of incomes policy during the entire post-war period.

A related issue, also touched on earlier, concerns the form of policy in 'on' periods. Treatment of a wage freeze and mild moral suasion on the same footing is clearly inadequate, but that is the procedure followed in most of the existing literature. It may be fruitful to examine foreign experience of different types of policy in order to gain degrees of freedom in future investigations. The treatment of incomes policy as an at least approximately continuous variable would, moreover, facilitate examination of a problem noted by Wallis [41], *viz.* '...the decision to impose an incomes policy is not independent of the values of the variables in the model, and...the policy itself must surely also become a jointly dependent endogenous variable'. As far as we are aware, no attention has yet been devoted to this issue.

The final area in which additional effort appears needed is the proxying of price expectations. The inadequacy of using current or a distributed lag function of past actual price changes requires little comment, for it has been much discussed in the literature. Particular illustrations of the magnitude of this problem are provided by Hines's finding of a significantly *negative* coefficient on $\dot{p}$ in the 'policy-on' wage equation [13], Taylor's insignificant coefficient on $\dot{p}$ in his corresponding equation [37], and Sumner's results on the inexplicable influence of $\dot{p}$ on $\dot{w}$ in the latter part of the 1950's [36]. To date, little progress has been made in experiments with more sophisticated alternatives. One such alternative which is certainly worth exploring is the neglected questionnaire evidence which seeks answers to direct questions on the price expectations of consumers or businessmen.

To end a paper with the assertion that further research is urgently needed is universally recognized as the acme of professional performance. In the light of the foregoing, however, such an assertion does not seem difficult to justify.

References

[1] G. C. Archibald, 'The Phillips Curve and the Distribution of Unemployment', *American Economic Review*, May 1969.

[2] R. G. Bodkin, E. P. Bond, G. L. Reuber and T. R. Robinson, *Price Stability and High Employment: The Options for Canadian Economic Policy*, Special Study No. 5 for the Economic Council of Canada, Queen's Printer, Ottowa, 1967.

[3] F. P. R. Brechling, 'Some Empirical Evidence on the Effectiveness of Prices and Incomes Policies', Chapter 2 below.

[4] A. D. Brownlie, 'Some Econometrics of Price Determination', *Journal of Industrial Economics*, March 1965.

[5] P. Burrows and T. Hitiris, 'Estimating the Impact of Incomes Policy', *Bulletin of Economic Research*, May 1972, and Chapter 8 below.

[6] Department of Employment, *Prices and Earnings in 1951–69*, H.M.S.O. 1971.

[7] L. A. Dicks-Mireaux, 'The Inter-relationship between Cost and Price Changes, 1945–1959: A Study of Inflation in Postwar Britain', *Oxford Economic Papers*, 1961.

[8] L. A. Dicks-Mireaux and J. C. R. Dow, 'The Determinants of Wage Inflation in the United Kingdom, 1946–1956', *Journal of the Royal Statistical Society*, Series A (General) 1959.

[9] J. C. R. Dow, *The Management of the British Economy 1945–60*, C.U.P. 1965.

[10] J. C. R. Dow and L. A. Dicks-Mireaux, 'The Excess Demand for Labour', *Oxford Economic Papers*, 1958.

[11] L. G. Godfrey, 'The Phillips Curve: Incomes Policy and Trade Union Effects', Chapter 6 in H. G. Johnson and A. R. Nobay (eds.) *The Current Inflation*, Macmillan 1971. Abridged and amended as Chapter 7 below.

[12] A. G. Hines, 'Trade Unions and Wage Inflation in the United Kingdom 1893–1961', *Review of Economic Studies*, 1964.

[13] A. G. Hines, 'The Determinants of the Rate of Change of Money Wage Rates and the Effectiveness of Incomes Policy', Chapter 8 in *The Current Inflation* (see 11).

[14] C. W. Jefferson, K. I. Sams and D. Swann, 'The Control of Incomes and Prices in the U.K., 1964–7: Policy and Experience', *Canadian Journal of Economics*, 1969.

[15] J. Johnston, 'The Price Level under Full Employment in the U.K.' In D. C. Hague (ed.) *Price Formation in Various Economies*, International Economic Association, Macmillan, 1967.

[16] J. Johnston, D. D. Bugg and P. J. Lund, 'Some Econometrics of Inflation in the U.K.', in P. E. Hart, G. Mills and J. K. Whittaker (eds.) *Econometric Analysis for National Economic Planning*, Colston Papers Vol. XVI, Butterworth, 1964.

[17] L. R. Klein and J. R. Ball, 'Some Econometrics of the Determination of the Absolute Level of Wages and Prices', *Economic Journal*, 1959.

[18] D. Laidler, 'Discussion', in D. R. Croome and H. G. Johnson (eds.) *Money in Britain 1959–69*, O.U.P. 1970.

[19] D. Laidler, 'The Phillips Curve, Expectations and Incomes Policy', Chapter 5 in *The Current Inflation* (see 11).

[20] R. G. Lipsey, 'The Relation between Unemployment and the Rate of Change of Money Wage Rates in the U.K., 1862–1957: Further Analysis', *Economica*, 1960.

[21] R. G. Lipsey and J. M. Parkin, 'Incomes Policy: A Reappraisal', *Economica*, May 1970, and Chapter 4 below.

[22] R. G. Lipsey and M. D. Steuer, 'The Relation between Profits and Wage Rates', *Economica*, 1961.

[23] B. T. McCallum, 'The Effect of Demand on Prices in British Manufacturing: Another View', *Review of Economic Studies*, January, 1970.

[24] D. J. B. Mitchell, 'British Incomes Policy, the Competitive Effect and the 1967 Devaluation', *Southern Economic Journal*, July 1970.

[25] National Board for Prices and Incomes, Second General Report, Cmnd. 3394, August 1967.
[26] National Board for Prices and Incomes, Third General Report, Cmnd. 3715, July 1968.
[27] R. R. Neild, *Pricing and Employment in the Trade Cycle*, C.U.P. 1963.
[28] J. M. Parkin, 'Incomes Policy: Some Further Results on the Determination of the Rate of Change of Money Wages', *Economica*, November 1970, and Chapter 5 below.
[29] A. W. Phillips, 'The Relationship between Unemployment and the Rate of Change of Money Wage Rates in the United Kingdom, 1861–1957', *Economica*, 1958.
[30] D. Purdy and G. Zis, 'Trade Unions and Wage Inflation in the U.K.: A Reappraisal', Manchester University mimeo, 1972.
[31] F. Rushdy and P. J. Lund, 'The Effect of Demand on Prices in British Manufacturing Industry', *Review of Economic Studies*, Oct. 1967.
[32] J. D. Sargan, 'Wages and Prices in the United Kingdom', in Colston Papers (see 16).
[33] J. D. Sargan, 'A Study of Wages and Prices in the U.K., 1949–1968', in *The Current Inflation* (see 11).
[34] D. C. Smith, 'Incomes Policy', in R. E. Caves (ed.) *Britain's Economic Prospects*, The Brookings Institution, 1968, and Chapter 3 below.
[35] R. M. Solow, *Price Expectations and the Behaviour of the Price Level*, M.U.P. 1969.
[36] M. T. Sumner, "Aggregate Demand, Price Expectations and the Phillips Curve: A Comment on Lipsey and Parkin', Chapter 9 below.
[37] J. Taylor, 'Incomes Policy: A Further Reappraisal', Chapter 10 below.
[38] R. L. Thomas and P. J. M. Stoney, 'A Note on the Dynamic Properties of the Hines Inflation Model', *Review of Economic Studies*, April 1970.
[39] R. L. Thomas and P. J. M. Stoney, 'Unemployment Dispersion as A Determinant of Wage Inflation in the U.K. 1925–66', *The Manchester School*, June 1971, and Chapter 11 below.
[40] J. Vanderkamp, 'Wage Adjustment, Productivity and Price-Change Expectations', *Review of Economic Studies*, Jan. 1972.
[41] K. F. Wallis, 'Wages, Prices and Incomes Policies: Some Comments', *Economica*, August 1971, and Chapter 5 below.
[42] J. H. Williamson, 'The Price-Price Spiral', *Yorkshire Bulletin*, May 1967.

Frank P. R. Brechling

Chapter 2 Some empirical evidence on the effectiveness of prices and incomes policies[1]

1 Introduction

In post-war years the governments of several Western countries have attempted to reduce the rate of inflation by regulating in some manner the process by which wages and prices are usually formed. It is comparatively easy to point to specific instances in which government pressure has resulted in reducing increases in particular wages or prices. It would appear, however, that the success or failure of a price and incomes policy should be judged by its impact on the *general* level of wages and prices. In this paper an attempt will, therefore, be made to analyze and assess the effects of price and incomes policies in the United Kingdom and the United States upon the general indices of inflation: the level of wages, the GNP deflator and wholesale prices in manufacturing.

One reason why empirical investigations of the effectiveness of price and incomes policies are particularly difficult, is that there are only a small number of periods during which such policies were implemented. Thus in the United States the guideposts and the occasional interferences with price formation have been in effect only in one period, namely since 1961–2. In the United Kingdom there is slightly more information. Income policies were implemented in three post-war periods: the first was in 1948–50 under Sir Stafford

[1] This paper was written early in 1966 and read to the Canadian Political Science Association, 8 June 1966. Since I intended originally to extend the empirical analysis, I did not submit it for publication. To the best of my knowledge, this paper contains one of the first, moderately successful, attempts to obtain empirical estimates of the effectiveness of price and incomes policies. The results are now, however, superceded by those of more recent researches, particularly by Perry, Lipsey and Parkin. On re-reading the manuscript I was pleased by my conjecture in section 5(i) that 'we must expect a rather vigorous inflation in the not too distant future when the money illusion will have disappeared'. Apart from some minor corrections the manuscript has not been changed.

Cripps, the second was the period of the Pay-Pause under Selwyn Lloyd in 1961–2 and the third started with the new Labour government in the autumn of 1964. The evidence which will be presented later in this paper suggests that wages and prices tended to rise more slowly in these than in other comparable periods. Since, however, the number of price and incomes policies is so small, we cannot be too confident about their apparent deflationary impact.

In the next section a sketch of the theoretical model, which underlies the later statistical investigations, will be given. In section 3 the United Kingdom evidence will be examined; we shall look at, in turn, wages, the GNP deflator and manufacturing wholesale prices. In section 4, the same order will be adopted for the examination of the United States evidence. In section 5, some alternative explanations of the empirical results will be presented and, finally, section 6 will contain the main conclusions of the study.

2   The theoretical framework

In order to be able to assess the impact of price and incomes policies upon the rate of inflation, we must have a model of the determination of wages and prices in periods when there are no price and incomes policies. Such models may have varying degrees of complexity. The one used in the present study is comparatively simple. It contains both demand-pull and cost-push elements.

The demand-pull elements of our theoretical model are well-known from the empirical investigations of Phillips [8], Lipsey [5] and, more recently in Canada, Kaliski [3]. According to these elements, the change in the level of prices or wages is a function of the level of excess demand. Figure 1 illustrates such a functional relationship. Excess demand is measured along the horizontal axis and the change in prices (or wages) along the vertical axis. It is plausible that the A-curves are non-linear, becoming steeper as the level of excess demand rises. The procedures adopted for the present purposes, however, depend only on the positive slope (and not on the degree of curvature) of the A-curves.

The cost-push elements of our model shift the A-curves and, thereby, create a higher or lower increase in prices at the same level of excess demand. There are no hard and fast rules for the inclusion of cost-push variables and, indeed, the factors which exert cost-push pressure vary between markets and between countries. In the

Figure 1

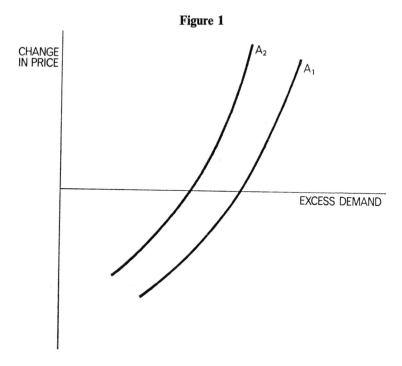

empirical investigations the following cost-push variables have been included in the analysis:

(i) A cost-push variable which has performed well in models of the labour market for both the United Kingdom and the United States is the price of consumer goods.[2] In other words, the A-curve in Figure 1 must be expected to shift to the left with a rise in the rate of increase of consumer goods prices. Plausible theoretical reasons for this relationship are that some wage contracts have a cost-of-living clause and that wage-earners strongly resist reductions in their real wages.

(ii) A cost-push variable which is known to have an important influence upon the average price level in the United Kingdom is the level of import prices.[3] Hence, a rise in the rate of increase in import prices will shift the A-curves in Figure 1 to the left. The importance of import prices arises from the comparatively high British average propensity to import.

[2] See, for instance, Perry [7].
[3] See, for instance, Dicks-Mireaux [2].

(iii) A variable which is or acts like a cost-push variable in the United States is the level of farm prices. Hence, a rise in the rate of increase in farm prices will shift the A-curve in Figure 1 to the left. There are two reasons for the strong influence of farm prices upon the average price level: First, farm prices may be fixed predominantly by non-competitive arrangements and second, farm prices may respond to their *own* excess demand. In either case, farm price changes are unlikely to be related closely to the overall level of excess demand in the economy. Consequently, the rate of change in farm prices was allowed to have an independent influence upon changes in the GNP deflator. Changes in manufacturing wholesale prices, on the other hand, should not be influenced much by changes in farm prices and, hence, the latter were not included in the analysis of manufacturing wholesale prices.

This model, which consists of both a general demand-pull and various cost-push elements, is assumed to give an adequate explanation of all but the random changes in wages and prices in those periods when no price and incomes policies are operative. A successful price and incomes policy is then defined as one which autonomously reduces the increases in wages and prices. In terms of Figure 1 a successful price and incomes policy shifts the A-curve to the right, so that with a given level of excess demand and given cost-push elements there is a lower rate of change in prices or wages. The statistical task thus consists, first, of establishing whether the A-curve does move significantly to the right and, second, of measuring the amount by which the A-curve moves to the right in times of price and incomes policies.[4]

One important implication of the above argument is that a government policy which succeeds in reducing the rate of inflation either through a reduction in excess demand or a change in the cost-push variables is *not* a price or incomes policy. In other words, a price and incomes policy is here treated as an alternative means of reducing the rate of price and wage inflation, the customary means being a reduction in excess demand. These definitions reflect the aims and methods of price and incomes policies. Governments typically implement them because they wish to maintain a high level of

---

[4] It might also be interesting to discover whether the price and incomes policy affects the slopes of the relationship between the change in prices (or wages) and the level of excess demand and the cost-push variables. This possibility was not investigated in the present study.

activity (i.e., high excess demand) without having to accept the ensuing inflation.

The main points of this section of the paper can now be summarized as follows: The effectiveness of a price and incomes policy in reducing the increase in wages and prices can be assessed only against the background of a model which predicts how wages and prices would move in the absence of a price and incomes policy. According to the model used in the present study changes in wages and prices are determined normally by the level of excess demand and by a variety of cost-push factors, namely consumer prices in the case of wages and import or farm prices in the case of the GNP deflator and manufacturing wholesale prices.

3   The British evidence

Let us now proceed to examine the empirical evidence. As was pointed out in the previous section, the analysis is designed to discover whether price and incomes policies exert an autonomous downward pressure on increases in wages and prices. We shall look, in turn, at wages, the GNP deflator and manufacturing wholesale prices.

(i) One of the earliest attempts to take into account the effects of an incomes policy in the United Kingdom was undertaken by Klein, Ball, Hazlewood and Vandome in their well-known 'Econometric Model of the United Kingdom' [4]. They related overlapping quarterly changes in the index of weekly wage rates to four-quarter moving average of the level (and *not* ratio) of unemployment (U), a four-quarter moving average of overlapping changes in the price index of total consumption ($\bar{p}$), seasonal dummies (Q) and a shift dummy (F) which took on the value of zero before 1 January 1952 and of one after 1 January 1952.[5] The equation, fitted by the limited information maximum likelihood method, turned out as follows:

$$w_t - w_{t-4} = 10 \cdot 26 - 0 \cdot 091\bar{U} + 0 \cdot 85\bar{p} + 2 \cdot 90F$$
$$\phantom{w_t - w_{t-4} =} (1 \cdot 41) \quad (0 \cdot 013) \quad (0 \cdot 09) \quad (0 \cdot 40)$$
$$+ 0 \cdot 10Q_1 + 0 \cdot 30Q_2 + 0 \cdot 19Q_3 \quad (1)$$
$$(0 \cdot 57) \qquad (0 \cdot 57) \qquad (0 \cdot 57)$$
$$(\bar{R} = 0 \cdot 93) \qquad (d = 1 \cdot 02)$$

[5] In this and the following sections, I shall refer to differences or ratios over *four* quarters as *overlapping* first differences or ratios. Thus an overlapping first difference in wages is $w_t - w_{t-4}$ where the t's are quarters. It is clear that overlapping differences introduce a moving average into a time series. For the sake of brevity, I have changed slightly the notation of Klein, Ball, Hazlewood and Vandome. Their sample period was 1948,I to 1956,IV (36 quarters).

Thus the shift dummy for the incomes policy before 1952 is highly significant and quite large. The coefficient of 2·90 indicates that the annual change in weekly wage rates was 2·9 index number point lower before 1952 than after 1952.

In order to test whether the two later periods of price and incomes policy have also had depressing effects upon changes in wages, basically similar regression equations were fitted for the entire period 1948,I to 1965,IV (76 observations). These equations differed from equation (1) in the following respects:

First, ordinary least squares have been used instead of the limited information maximum likelihood method used by the previous authors. Since presumably changes in wages are likely to have some influence upon changes in consumer goods prices, the ordinary least squares approach is likely to yield biased estimates. It would appear, however, that these biases may be negligibly small. Thus Klein, Ball, Hazlewood and Vandome fitted equation (1) also by ordinary least squares and a comparison of the parameters suggests that the simpler fitting procedure would not have produced markedly different results. For example, the coefficient of F turned out to be 2·98 (compared with the 2·90 reported above) when the equation was fitted by ordinary least squares. Another reason for preferring at this stage a simpler fitting procedure is that the complex fitting procedures require a fully fledged model of the interaction of prices and wages, which has not been developed in this paper.

Second, Klein, Ball, Hazlewood and Vandome used absolute differences in wages rates and prices. In the present investigation proportionate changes are used instead.

Third, Klein, Ball, Hazlewood and Vandome used an index number of the absolute level of unemployment as an independent variable. Following the popular specification of the Phillips curve, we have used instead the reciprocal of the unemployment *ratio*.

Fourth, in the present study, the observations for unemployment and price changes are not averaged prior to their introduction in the regressions as independent variables. It was thought that averaging might blur some important and relevant relationships. Instead the observations of the current and the previous four quarters were used as independent variables in a first run and the least significant variables were then omitted from later regressions. The same basic procedure has been adopted for the other regressions to be reported later in this paper.

Fifth, in the present investigation we have four incomes policy dummy variables. The first (F_1) assumes the value of unity from 1948,I to 1950,IV, from 1961,III to 1962,II and from 1964,IV to 1965,IV and of zero in all the other periods. The second (F_2) assumes the value of unity only from 1948,I to 1950,IV, the third (F_3) only from 1961,III to 1962,II and the fourth (F_4) only from 1964,III to 1965,IV and of zero at all other times. The first period of incomes policy differs somewhat from that used by Klein, Ball, Hazlewood and Vandome because there is some evidence that—owing to re-armament—the incomes policy of the Labour government had already broken down in 1951. The other two periods of incomes policy were determined by a study of public announcements at that time.

Sixth, in addition to experimenting with overlapping quarterly changes in wages and prices, we also present the results of quarter-to-quarter changes. As was to be expected the latter contain a fair amount of noise and, hence, the overall fits are not very close.

In the following regression equations, w stands for the weekly money wage rate in all industries, U for the total unemployment ratio in Britain, p^c for the price of consumer goods, which is the implicit deflator of the published series of consumption expenditure. The equations involving quarter-to-quarter changes have also been fitted with quarterly dummies, but since they turned out to be insignificant, they were omitted in subsequent runs. The four relevant equations turned out as follows:

The British evidence

$$
\begin{aligned}
\frac{w_t - w_{t-1}}{w_{t-1}} = \ &-0.00288 + 0.0324 U_t^{-1} - 0.0175 U_{t-3}^{-1} \\
&(0.00414)\ \ \ (0.0072) \qquad\quad (0.0084)
\end{aligned}
$$

$$
\begin{aligned}
&+\ 0.1971\,\frac{p_{t-2}^c - p_{t-3}^c}{p_{t-3}^c} + 0.3380\,\frac{p_{t-3}^c - p_{t-4}^c}{p_{t-4}^c} \qquad (2)\\
&\quad (0.0829) \qquad\qquad\qquad (0.0846)
\end{aligned}
$$

$$
\begin{aligned}
&+\ 0.2113 + \frac{p_{t-4}^c - p_{t-5}^c}{p_{t-5}^c} - 0.00451 F_1 \\
&\quad (0.0875 \qquad\qquad\qquad (0.00177)
\end{aligned}
$$

$$
(R^2 = 0.43) \qquad (d = 1.94)
$$

$$\frac{w_t - w_{t-1}}{w_{t-1}} = -0.00324 + 0.0331 U_t^{-1} - 0.0179 U_{t-3}^{-1}$$
$$(0.00424) \quad (0.0076) \qquad (0.0087)$$

$$+ 0.1947 \frac{p_{t-2}^c - p_{t-3}^c}{p_{t-3}^c} + 0.3418 \frac{p_{t-3}^c - p_{t-4}^c}{p_{t-4}^c} \tag{3}$$
$$(0.0847) \qquad\qquad (0.0864)$$

$$+ 0.2174 \frac{p_{t-4}^c - p_{t-5}^c}{p_{t-5}^c} - 0.00504 F_2$$
$$(0.0902) \qquad\qquad (0.00226)$$

$$- 0.00153 F_3 - 0.00451 F_4$$
$$(0.00357) \qquad (0.00356)$$

$$(R^2 = 0.43) \qquad (d = 1.95)$$

$$\frac{w_t - w_{t-4}}{w_{t-4}} = -0.00679 + 0.0626 U_t^{-1} - 0.0167 U_{t-4}^{-1}$$
$$(0.00528) \quad (0.0087) \qquad (0.0095)$$

$$+ 0.3336 \frac{p_t^c - p_{t-4}^c}{p_{t-4}^c} + 0.3587 \frac{p_{t-2}^c - p_{t-6}^c}{p_{t-6}^c} \tag{4}$$
$$(0.0660) \qquad\qquad (0.1030)$$

$$+ 0.2108 \frac{p_{t-3}^c - p_{t-7}^c}{p_{t-7}^c} - 0.0186 F_1$$
$$(0.0863) \qquad\qquad (0.0021)$$

$$(R^2 = 0.89) \qquad (d = 1.45)$$

$$\frac{w_t - w_{t-4}}{w_{t-4}} = -0.01026 + 0.0687 U_t^{-1} - 0.0177 U_{t-4}^{-1}$$
$$(0.00508) \quad (0.0088) \qquad (0.0095)$$

$$+ 0.2852 \frac{p_t^c - p_{t-4}^c}{p_{t-4}^c} + 0.3618 \frac{p_{t-2}^c - p_{t-6}^c}{p_{t-6}^c} \tag{5}$$
$$(0.0649) \qquad\qquad (0.0985)$$

$$+ 0.2536 \frac{p_{t-3}^c - p_{t-7}^c}{p_{t-7}^c} - 0.0226 F_2 - 0.0101 F_3$$
$$(0.0824) \qquad\qquad (0.0028) \qquad (0.0039)$$

$$- 0.0209 F_4$$
$$(0.0038)$$
$$(R^2 = 0.90) \qquad (d = 1.56)$$

For the present purposes the following results should be emphasized: First, all the coefficients of the F-dummies have a negative sign, which means that in periods of incomes policies the proportionate increases in wages tended to be smaller than in other periods. Moreover, in the case of equations (2), (4) and (5) all the regression coefficients of the dummies are statistically significantly different from zero by conventional standards. The weakest results are obtained

4

in equation (3) in which only the coefficient of F_2 is more than twice its standard error. Second, the three incomes policies appear to have reduced wage increases by an average of 1·8 percentage points per annum. In the first period (1948–50) the reduction seems to have been highest at over 2 percentage points per annum; in the second period (1961–2) it seems to have been lowest at about 1 percentage point per annum; and in the third period (1964–5) it seems to have been about 2 percentage points. We must conclude, therefore, that this evidence suggests fairly convincingly that the three incomes policies which were implemented in the United Kingdom in post-war years, have had a substantial depressing influence upon the rate of increase of money wages.

(ii) To be successful, a price and incomes policy should ultimately result in a reduction of the rate of increase not only of wage rates but also of the average price level. Let us, therefore, now turn to an examination of the possible influence of price and incomes policies upon the GNP deflator.

In the case of the labour market discussed above, we have a ready-made proxy variable for the level of excess demand, namely the unemployment ratio. No such ready-made proxy is unfortunately available for GNP as a whole. Several authors have used indices which are based on the assumption that the productive capacity of the economy as a whole grows fairly smoothly over time.[6] The same basic assumption has been made for the purposes of the present study. It follows that an appropriate proxy variable for the level of excess demand in the economy as a whole may be deviations of GNP from some smooth path. The most convenient smooth path is a straight-line or quadratic exponential time trend. This has been assumed for the present purposes. In other words, the level of excess demand is assumed to be adequately approximated by D in the following equation:

$$\ln \text{GNP} = a_0 + a_1 t + a_2 t^2 + D \qquad (6)$$

where the a's have been estimated by ordinary least squares and a_2 is assumed to be zero when its statistical significance is low. The same method of constructing a proxy for the level of excess demand will

---

[6] See, for instance, Paish [6]. Some investigators have used the unemployment ratio as an index of the level of excess demand in the economy. It does not appear to be a very suitable index of the current level of excess demand because it lags behind output by seven months.

be used in the analysis of manufacturing wholesale prices and in the analysis of United States prices.

In addition to the proxy for the level of excess demand we have used—in accordance with the discussion in section 2—the change in import prices as a cost-push variable. The change in the GNP deflator was regressed against the independent variables with various distributed lags and the following equation gave the best fit. A log-linear structure of this equation was chosen because D is in logarithmic form.

$$\ln \frac{p_t^g}{p_{t-1}^g} = 0{\cdot}0024 - 0{\cdot}000331 D_t + 0{\cdot}000184 D_{t-1} + 0{\cdot}000203 D_{t-2}$$
$$\phantom{\ln \frac{p_t^g}{p_{t-1}^g} =} (0{\cdot}0028) \quad (0{\cdot}000112) \qquad (0{\cdot}000125) \qquad (0{\cdot}000113)$$
$$ + 0{\cdot}1021 \ln \frac{p_{t-3}^i}{p_{t-4}^i} + 0{\cdot}0075 Q_2 + 0{\cdot}0051 Q_3 + 0{\cdot}0053 Q_4$$
$$ (0{\cdot}0489) \qquad\quad (0{\cdot}0040) \qquad (0{\cdot}0039) \qquad (0{\cdot}0040)$$
$$(R^2 = 0{\cdot}40) \qquad (d = 2{\cdot}69) \tag{7}$$

In equation (7) p^g stands for GNP deflator, D for excess demand, p^i for import prices and the Q's for quarterly dummies. The sample period for this regression was 1956,II to 1965,III.

Before proceeding to the discussion of the effectiveness of incomes policy, let us briefly discuss one peculiar result of equation (7), namely the negative sign of the D_t coefficient. According to it, a *ceteris paribus* rise in D_t leads to a fall in the increase in the GNP deflator. Since D_{t-1} and D_{t-2} are also held constant, a rise in D_t represents a rise in the rate of increase in excess demand. That such a rise might have a deflationary impact upon prices, can be explained in terms of a lag in costs, particularly labour costs, per unit of output. In other words, with a given D_{t-1} and D_{t-2} a fast cyclical upswing produces a comparatively low increase in prices because wages and, hence, labour costs lag behind the excess demand for output.

Attempts have been made to isolate the influence upon the GNP deflator of the price and incomes policies in 1961–2 and 1964–5; but these attempts were unsuccessful. It is, of course, possible that the GNP deflator reacts to the price and incomes policies with a lag of some quarters. In order to be able to assess this possibility, the residuals of $\ln (p_t^g/p_{t-1}^g)$ have been plotted in Figure 2. Inspection of these residuals shows that in 1962 and, with the exception of one quarter, in 1963 the actual changes in the GNP deflator were smaller than those predicted by the regression equation. These negative deviations may have been caused by the price and incomes policy in

Figure 2

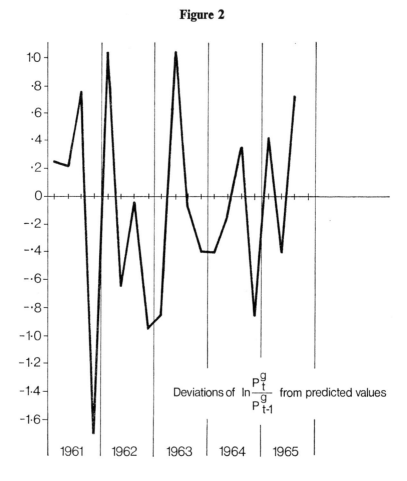

Deviations of $\ln \dfrac{P^g_t}{P^g_{t-1}}$ from predicted values

1961–2. Unfortunately, however, a good deal more evidence is necessary before this conclusion can be held with a high degree of confidence.

(iii) The last general index of inflation to be examined in this section is the change in manufacturing wholesale prices. Changes in manufacturing wholesale prices are assumed to be determined by the level of excess demand in manufacturing and by the change in import prices. Further, excess demand is again approximated by the deviations of output from its exponential time trend.

The change in manufacturing wholesale prices was regressed on the independent variables with various distributed lags and the insignificant variables were subsequently omitted. The resulting equation was as follows:

$$\ln \frac{p_t^w}{p_{t-1}^w} = 0 \cdot 0054 + 0 \cdot 0000947 D_{t-2} + 0 \cdot 2097 \ln \frac{p_t^i}{p_{t-1}^i}$$
$$(0 \cdot 0006) \quad (0 \cdot 0000198) \qquad (0 \cdot 0291)$$
$$+ 0 \cdot 00595 \ln \frac{p_{t-4}^i}{p_{t-5}^i} \quad (8)$$
$$(0 \cdot 00142)$$
$$(R^2 = 0 \cdot 80) \qquad (d = 1 \cdot 96)$$

In equation (8) p^w stands for manufacturing wholesale prices, D for excess demand in manufacturing and p^i for import prices. The sample period for this regression equation was 1950,I to 1965,IV.

Dummy variables were introduced into equation (8) in an attempt to isolate the influence of the price and incomes policies in 1961–2 and 1964–5. The coefficients of these dummies were, however, not significantly different from zero. As in the case of changes in the GNP deflator, one possible reason for the failure of manufacturing wholesale prices to react to the price and incomes policies in the regression equation is that the real reaction takes place only after a lag of some quarters. In Figure 3 the residuals of $\ln (p_t^w/p_{t-1}^w)$ from the regression equation have been plotted. Inspection of Figure 3 indicates that there was some tendency for manufacturing wholesale prices to rise at a somewhat lower rate in 1962–3 than in the preceding or succeeding quarters. This phenomenon may have been caused by the price and incomes policy in 1961–2.

The main conclusion of the examination of the British evidence can be summarized as follows: The three post-war price and incomes policies appear to have reduced the rate of increase of weekly wage rates quite markedly. By contrast the evidence of the effects of price and incomes policies upon the GNP deflator and manufacturing wholesale prices is very weak. If there are any effects at all, they appear only after a lag of three to four quarters.

4   The United States evidence
Several recent investigators have discovered that in 1961–2 a break seems to have taken place in the Phillips curve for the United States.[7] In this section of the paper some additional evidence will be

[7] As far as I am aware, none of those results have as yet been published. However, recently Professors Perry and Simler reported their findings at the M.I.T. Seminar on Applied Macro-Economics.

Figure 3

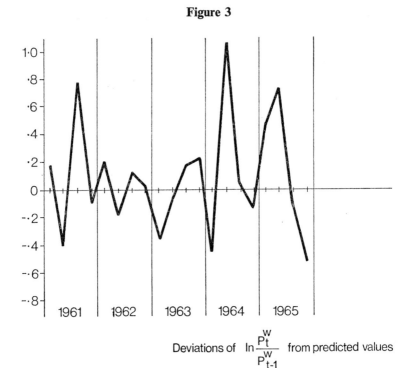

Deviations of $\ln \dfrac{P_t^w}{P_{t-1}^w}$ from predicted values

presented. According to it, not only wages but also prices appear to have risen more slowly in the present than in previous cyclical up-swings. As in the previous section we shall proceed by looking, in turn, at wages, the GNP deflator and manufacturing wholesale prices.

(i) The proportionate changes in hourly earnings in manufacturing have been regressed on the reciprocal of the (total) unemployment ratio and changes in the consumer price index with various lags.[8] Inspection of the residuals showed quite clearly, however, that the regressions tended to overpredict the changes in wages by increasing margins since about 1961. Consequently a dummy variable was included in the regressions which assumed the value of zero until 1960,IV and, thereafter, rose from 1 to 20. The equation with the most significant lagged variables turned out as follows:

[8] I am much indebted to Mr. George de Menil of M.I.T. for making the data for these regressions available to me.

$$\frac{w_t - w_{t-1}}{w_{t-1}} = 0{\cdot}0063 + 0{\cdot}1094 U_t^{-1} - 0{\cdot}0701 U_{t-1}^{-1}$$
$$(0{\cdot}0024) \quad (0{\cdot}0245) \qquad (0{\cdot}0242)$$

$$+ 0{\cdot}3146 \ \frac{p_t^c - p_{t-1}^c}{p_{t-1}^c} - 0{\cdot}000204 F_5 \qquad (9)$$
$$(0{\cdot}0870) \qquad\qquad (0{\cdot}000099)$$
$$- 0{\cdot}0083 Q_2 - 0{\cdot}0133 Q_3 - 0{\cdot}0018 Q_4$$
$$(0{\cdot}0016) \qquad (0{\cdot}0016) \qquad (0{\cdot}0016)$$
$$(R^2 = 0{\cdot}71) \qquad (d = 2{\cdot}38)$$

When overlapping changes in wages and prices were used, the equation with the most significant lagged independent variables was as follows:

$$\frac{w_t - w_{t-4}}{w_{t-4}} = 0{\cdot}0066 + 0{\cdot}1869 U_{t-1}^{-1} - 0{\cdot}0543 U_{t-4}^{-1}$$
$$(0{\cdot}0050) \quad (0{\cdot}0244) \qquad (0{\cdot}0245)$$

$$+ 0{\cdot}3513 \ \frac{p_t^c - p_{t-4}^c}{p_{t-4}^c} + 0{\cdot}1089 \ \frac{p_{t-2}^c - p_{t-6}^c}{p_{t-6}^c} \qquad (10)$$
$$(0{\cdot}0703) \qquad\qquad (0{\cdot}0613)$$
$$- 0{\cdot}000845 F_5$$
$$(0{\cdot}000198)$$
$$(R^2 = 0{\cdot}81) \qquad (d = 0{\cdot}86)$$

In equations (9) and (10), w stands for straight-time (i.e., excluding overtime) hourly earnings in manufacturing, U for the national unemployment ratio, p for the consumer price index, F_5 for the strength of incomes policy and Q for quarterly dummies.

For the present purposes the coefficients of the dummy variable F_5 are of particular interest. Both have the expected negative sign and both are more than twice their standard errors. The size of the coefficients indicates that at the end of 1965 the change in earnings was about 1·6 percentage points below the annual rate predicted by the pre-1961 experience. It would appear, therefore, that the break in the Phillips curve implied a marked reduction in the rate of increase in wages.

(ii) Next let us examine the pattern of changes in the GNP deflator. In accordance with the discussion in section 2, changes in the GNP deflator are assumed to be determined by the level of overall excess demand and changes in farm prices. As a proxy for excess demand, we again used the deviations of ln GNP from its quadratic time trend. Regressions with various distributed time lags were run. Inspection of the residuals suggested, however, that the equations tended to overpredict the change in the GNP deflator from about 1961 onwards; moreover, the size of the overprediction has tended to rise with time. Consequently, the dummy variable F_5 (described under (i)) was introduced. The regression with the most significant lagged independent variables turned out as follows:[9]

$$
\begin{aligned}
\ln \frac{p_t^g}{p_{t-1}^g} = {}& 0 \cdot 0057 + 0 \cdot 0000688 D_{t-1} + 0 \cdot 0000323 D_{t-4} \\
& (0 \cdot 0004) \quad (0 \cdot 0000149) \qquad (0 \cdot 0000131) \\
& + 0 \cdot 0492 \ln \frac{p_t^f}{p_{t-1}^f} + 0 \cdot 0160 \ln \frac{p_{t-4}^f}{p_{t-5}^f} \\
& (0 \cdot 0101) \qquad\quad (0 \cdot 0105) \\
& - 0 \cdot 0001283 \, F_5 \\
& (0 \cdot 0000440) \\
& (R^2 = 0 \cdot 66) \qquad (d = 1 \cdot 78)
\end{aligned}
\tag{11}
$$

In equation (11), p^g stands for the GNP deflator, D for excess demand, p^f for farm prices and F_5 for the dummy variable for price and incomes policy. The coefficient of F_5 has the expected negative sign and, by conventional standards, it is significantly different from zero.

(iii) Finally let is examine the pattern of changes in manufacturing wholesale prices. Changes in these prices are assumed to react only to the level of excess demand and the latter is again approximated by the deviations of ln output in manufacturing from its quadratic time trend. Various distributed lags were again tried. Inspection of the residuals indicated that the equation tended to overpredict the changes in manufacturing wholesale prices from about 1961 onwards. Since these overpredictions appeared to be more or less constant, a dummy variable was included in the regressions which assumed the value of zero until 1960,IV and of unity from 1961,I onwards. The equations with the most significant lagged independent variables for quarter-to-quarter and for overlapping changes turned out as follows:[10]

$$
\begin{aligned}
\ln \frac{p_t^w}{p_{t-1}^w} = {}& 0 \cdot 0051 + 0 \cdot 0000459 D_t + 0 \cdot 0000244 D_{t-2} - 0 \cdot 0024 Q_2 \\
& (0 \cdot 0010) \quad (0 \cdot 0000109) \qquad (0 \cdot 0000112) \qquad\quad (0 \cdot 0013) \\
& - 0 \cdot 0015 \, Q_3 - 0 \cdot 0024 Q_4 - 0 \cdot 00132 F_6 \\
& (0 \cdot 0013) \qquad (0 \cdot 0012) \qquad (0 \cdot 00092) \\
& (R^2 = 0 \cdot 55) \qquad (d = 1 \cdot 38)
\end{aligned}
\tag{12}
$$

[9] The sample period was 1954,I to 1966,I. In the first few runs, data for the period 1950 to 1966 were used. Though most coefficients were still highly significant, the general fit was worse than the one of equation (11).

[10] The sample period was 1954,I to 1966,I.

$$\ln \frac{p_t^w}{p_{t-4}^w} = 0\cdot0138 + 0\cdot000160 D_t + 0\cdot000133 D_{t-4} - 0\cdot00646 F_6 \quad (13)$$
$$(0\cdot0016) \quad (0\cdot000025) \quad (0\cdot000025) \quad (0\cdot00249)$$
$$(R^2 = 0\cdot65) \quad (d = 0\cdot55)$$

In equations (12) and (13), p^w stands for wholesale prices in manufacturing, D for excess demand and F_6 for the dummy variable described above. Though equations (12) and (13) do not seem to be very satisfactory descriptions of changes in manufacturing wholesale prices, the coefficients of the dummy variable F_6 again have the expected negative sign and the coefficient in equation (13) is a more than twice its standard error.

This concludes our survey of the United States evidence. We have found that wages, the GNP deflator and manufacturing wholesale prices have all tended to rise at a slower rate after 1961 than in comparable periods before 1961. This evidence is thus consistent with the proposition that the Administration's price and incomes policy has been effective in reducing the rate of wage and price inflation. Unfortunately, however, it is also consistent with other plausible propositions, some of which will be discussed in the next section.

5 Some alternative explanations of the United States evidence

In this section of the paper, three alternative explanations of the comparatively slow rise of wages and prices in the current cyclical upswing will be given. Most economists seem to prefer one of these explanations to the proposition that the Administration's price and incomes policy has been effective.

(i) An argument which is frequently heard is that the long period of comparative recession prior to 1961 created a general impression of price stability which has caused wage and price negotiators to suffer from money illusion in the current cyclical upswing. This money illusion is supposed to have reduced the rate of inflation. If this argument proves to be correct, then we must expect a rather vigorous inflation in the not too distant future when the money illusion will have disappeared.

(ii) According to another argument, the primary reason for the low increases in wages and prices is the gentle rate of expansion of the present cyclical upswing. Inspection of the unemployment rate or a similar index of economic activity makes it clear that the cyclical expansion since 1961 has been unprecedentedly smooth and slow. It is plausible that gentle expansions lead to fewer bottlenecks and specific shortages and, hence, to slower increases in prices than rapid expansions.[11] Consequently, this argument may be the correct explanation of the slow pace of inflation in recent years.

(iii) The most sophisticated and best documented alternative explanation of the slow growth in wages has been put forward by Professor Simler. His argument goes roughly as follows:[12] It is not the *observed* unemployment ratio which determines the change in wages but rather the proportion of people who would like to work at full employment, but currently do not have a job. Owing to changes in the participation rates, not all of the latter will appear in the unemployment statistics. In order to correct for this 'hidden' unemployment, Simler has estimated the participation rates and, hence, the labour force which would have existed, had there been full employment. From this 'full employment labour force' and the observed employment figures, Simler obtains an 'adjusted' unemployment rate. This adjusted unemployment rate was then used to re-estimate the Phillips curves. Simler obtains somewhat better fits with his adjusted than with unadjusted unemployment rates. Moreover, the tendency of the Phillips curve to overpredict wage changes after 1961 is much reduced by Simler's adjustments. But the overprediction does not disappear entirely: the coefficients of Simler's dummy variables still have negative signs and some are more than twice their standard errors. Thus Simler's ingenious adjustments have reduced but not eliminated the negative residuals from the Phillips curves.

There are undoubtedly other plausible explanations of the comparatively slow pace of inflation since 1961. Whether they are valid or whether the Administration's price and incomes policy has been responsible for it, cannot (unfortunately) be answered with a high degree of confidence.

6   Summary

In this paper an attempt has been made to present and to analyze the evidence which might suggest that the price and incomes policies in the United Kingdom and the United States have been effective in retarding the *general* level of wages and prices. According to our

[11] I find this argument particularly appealing because Wolfe and I found that in Britain rapid cyclical expansions seem to cause more severe balance of payments difficulties than gentle cyclical expansions. See [1].
[12] I am much indebted to N. J. Simler for making his, as yet unpublished, results available to me.

theoretical framework, changes in wages and prices are normally determined by demand-pull elements (i.e., excess demand) and various cost-push elements (i.e., consumer prices, import prices and farm prices). A successful price and incomes policy is defined as one which reduces the change in wage and/or prices with given demand-pull and cost-push elements.

In the statistical part of the present investigation, we have examined changes in wages, in the GNP deflator and in manufacturing wholesale prices in both the United Kingdom and the United States. The most positive result was obtained for wages in the United Kingdom; in all three periods of price and incomes policy, increases in wages were markedly lower than at other times. In the case of changes in the GNP deflator and in manufacturing wholesale prices in the United Kingdom, the evidence is very weak; but prices may have been retarded somewhat by the price and incomes policy.

In the United States, wages, the GNP deflator and manufacturing wholesale prices have all risen more slowly in recent years than they did in similar circumstances in earlier years. This slow pace of inflation has coincided with the Administration's price and incomes policy. Hence, the latter may have been the cause of the former, but there are other plausible explanations of the slow rise in wages and prices.

References

[1] F. Brechling and J. N. Wolfe, 'The End of Stop-Go', *Lloyds Bank Review*, January, 1965.
[2] L. A. Dicks-Mireaux, 'The Interrelationship between Cost and Price Changes, 1946–1959', *Oxford Economic Papers*, October, 1961.
[3] S. F. Kaliski, 'The Relation between Unemployment and the Rate of Change of Money Wages in Canada', *International Economic Review*, January, 1964.
[4] L. R. Klein, R. J. Ball, A. Hazlewood and P. Vandome, 'An Econometric Model of the United Kingdom', Basil Blackwell, 1961.
[5] R. G. Lipsey, 'The Relation between Unemployment and the Rate of Change of Money Wage Rates in the United Kingdom, 1862–1957: A Further Analysis', *Economica*, February, 1960.
[6] F. W. Paish, 'Studies in an Inflationary Economy', MacMillan and Co., 1962.
[7] G. L. Perry, 'The Determinants of Wage Rate Changes and the Inflation-Unemployment Trade-off for the United States', *Review of Economic Studies*, October, 1964.
[8] A. W. Phillips, 'The Relation between Unemployment and the Rate of Change in Money Wage Rates in the United Kingdom, 1861–1957', *Economica*, November, 1958.

David C. Smith[1]

Chapter 3 Incomes policy[2]

Difficulties in meeting national economic goals have led governments in many countries to search for new or remodelled policy tools to supplement monetary and fiscal policies. One area of exploration has been into the possibility of developing criteria for individual economic decisions that would reduce apparent conflicts among national goals if people could be persuaded to follow them. Within the group of moral suasion policies, as they are sometimes called, considerable attention has been given to incomes policy.

The major purpose of incomes policy has been to try to solve a universal riddle of modern economies: how to avoid inflation at full employment. The policy has also been linked to other economic, social and political objectives such as raising productivity, changing the distribution of incomes, or securing greater support for other government programmes. Generally, incomes policies have attempted to introduce into wage, non-wage income and price decisions criteria which, if followed, would produce greater price stability without sacrificing employment objectives. Primary emphasis has been placed on gaining voluntary adherence to these criteria, but some government intervention has usually been needed. The policy may take the form of a short-run curb on the rise of money incomes and prices (usually instigated in the United Kingdom by a balance-of-payments crisis), or it may seek to secure a longer-run change in economic behaviour. It may focus primarily on wages or, as in the forms more popular recently, on the broader set of incomes, prices and productivity.

[1] Queens University.
[2] Abridged from Chapter 3 of *Britain's Economic Prospects*, edited by R. E. Caves; © 1968 The Brookings Institution, Washington, D.C., U.S.A. Reprinted by permission of the author and publisher.

Despite some apparent successes, British incomes policy has been beset by difficulties on each occasion, and its longer-run effectiveness remains an open question. Proponents feel that it has been worth the effort and that an appropriate longer-run form of the policy is emerging that will yield greater benefits in the future. Others, however, suggest that the costs of an incomes policy may outweigh the benefits or make it less attractive than alternatives.
. . .

Influences on British incomes policy

Interest in incomes policy extends over much of the post-war period. At the end of the 1940's there was a serious attempt to restrain directly the rise in money incomes in excess of the average rise in physical output and thus to prevent a rise in the general price level. This policy was dissolved in 1950. A proposal early in 1952 to revive some form of a national wage policy did not get anywhere, but in 1956 the government sought a halt to general price increases and called for wage restraint. In the summer of 1961 a pay pause was initiated, followed, between 1962 and the autumn of 1964, by the publication of a set of criteria or 'guiding lights' for wages and salaries and by the establishment of a National Incomes Commission to review pay claims. After the election of a Labour government in the autumn of 1964, agreement was obtained from business and labour leaders on the need for an incomes policy; criteria to guide wage and price decisions were published; a National Board for Prices and Incomes was established to review the conformity of income and price changes to these criteria; and steps were taken to develop an 'early warning system' that would permit review of key wage and price decisions before they took effect. In July 1966 the government announced a standstill on money incomes and prices to the end of the year, followed by a period of severe restraint during the first six months of 1967 when only minor exceptions to the freeze on wages and prices would be allowed. Statutory powers were passed to enforce the policy, if necessary. In the summer of 1967 a new stage of incomes policy began. Apart from those already agreed upon but deferred during the previous year's freeze, wage increases were to be allowed only if they could be justified by a list of criteria which emphasized direct contributions to increased productivity and the relative income position of low-paid workers. The government also passed legislation permitting it to stop a wage or price increase for a period of up to seven months. But, concerned about the subsequent rise in earnings, the government announced in the budget in March 1968 a ceiling on annual income increases (including dividends) of $3\frac{1}{2}\%$, except for increases justified by the productivity criterion; and it indicated its intention to introduce legislation to permit a deferral or suspension of wage, salary or price rises for up to twelve months.

Pressures for additional policy instruments
The timing of incomes policy measures has been closely related to efforts to overcome balance-of-payments difficulties. The major steps have generally followed a deterioration in the international balance on current and long-term capital account. During four periods when a form of freeze or pause was attempted—1948–50, 1956, 1961–2 and 1966–7—a variety of measures was brought to bear on an adverse balance-of-payments position. The sustained interest in incomes policy since the early 1960's has reflected, in part, a belief that the policy would reduce the extent to which 'go' policies to promote domestic prosperity would have to be shifted to a 'stop' position occasionally to remedy a loss of international reserves.

There has appeared to be a shortage of policy instruments to meet national goals, particularly when balance-of-payments difficulties are encountered, and the attractiveness of an incomes policy has increased. From 1949 to November 1967 exchange rate adjustments were not used because of prevailing arguments about their ineffectiveness in dealing with sources of British economic difficulties, political views on the benefits of an unchanged external value of the pound and the hope that incomes policy would prove effective in lowering British prices relative to foreign prices. A reliance on direct measures to curb imports or expand exports, such as import quotas, higher tariffs and export subsidies, were not regarded as desirable. Each period of payments difficulties brought about deflationary monetary and fiscal policies, but protests against the resulting unemployment led each time to strong political pressures for a quick reversal.

The case for an incomes policy has thus depended on the case against the alternatives. If inflation and balance-of-payments problems are encountered at desired employment levels and if acceptable measures to regulate the balance of payments are limited, incomes policy promises at least to reduce the need for deflationary monetary and fiscal policies and for a devaluation. Further, the persistence of inflation at high employment levels and the recurrence of balance-of-payments difficulties have gradually come to be viewed as symptoms of an economic disease which orthodox remedies are inadequate to treat.

An important feature of post-war British economic policy has been the commitment to maintain low unemployment rates. A number of factors have influenced the weight given to the full employment goal.

There have been the longer-term effects of high unemployment between the world wars. Although both the United Kingdom and the United States suffered high unemployment rates in the 1930's, high unemployment was more prolonged in the United Kingdom during the inter-war years. Unemployment rates in the United Kingdom were substantially higher in the 1920's than before World War I, while any difference was less noticeable in the United States. The high degree of economic insecurity through the inter-war period; the fears, frequently expressed in post-war political debates, that a modest short-run rise in the unemployment rate could signal the beginning of a return to such conditions; and the pervasive influence of the ideas of J. M. Keynes and his followers on the reponsibilities of governments for determining general employment levels—all of these factors contributed to the great political unpopularity of increases in the unemployment rate.

In addition, regional disparities in unemployment rates have reduced the tolerable national average. During the period 1960–6 the average annual unemployment rate for Britain was 1·7%, but it ranged from a low of 1·1% in London and Southeastern England to 3·6% in Scotland and 6·9% in Northern Ireland. Although a small rise in the national unemployment rate may be accepted more easily in tight labour markets, it produces an outcry about its effects in areas where unemployment rates are already excessively high.

. . .

The weight that has been attached to a low unemployment rate in the short run in the formulation of British economic policies, and the meaning of the full employment goal over the longer run, may change with the dimming of memories of the inter-war period, the greater emphasis on regional employment policies that has been emerging, and expanded financial support and training programmes for the unemployed. Yet, the question would remain of the economic costs of restraining rises in the general price level and improving the international competitive position through more restrictive monetary and fiscal policies. A short-run loss of employment and output has been associated with the 'stop' policies, along with some short-term gains to the balance-of-payments position and to greater wage and price stability. But these experiences do not demonstrate the effects on unemployment, growth of output and price stability of a more moderate longer-term expansion of monetary demand. The timing of steps with incomes policy has been dominated by practical short-run policy problems of combining high employment levels with a reasonable degree of price stability and external balance; the longer-run survival of the policy will depend on ideas about economic relationships affecting wages, prices, employment and productivity.

Incomes policy and causes of inflation
Prescriptions for an incomes policy are influenced by prevailing views on the sources of inflationary pressures as well as by judgements about its side effects on other national goals. Some approaches to an explanation of post-war inflation in the United Kingdom have pointed to factors which incomes policy might be expected to change; other approaches have been much less favourable to an incomes policy.

Particularly popular in recent economics literature has been the idea of a fairly stable relationship—often referred to as a trade-off relationship—between the rate of increase of the general price level and the unemployment rate, the latter being interpreted as a reflection of general demand conditions. Since the government, through its monetary and fiscal plicies, can affect general demand conditions, it is frequently argued that policy makers must choose between a lower rate of average price increases at the expense of a higher unemployment rate or a lower unemployment rate at the expense of a higher rate of average price increases. According to this approach, the persistent inflation in post-war years is an inevitable result of the greater emphasis on maintaining socially preferred high employment levels.

Not all who acknowledge the existence of a trade-off relationship conclude that monetary and fiscal policies are the only weapons against inflation. The conflict between low unemployment and price stability has been ascribed in significant measure to imperfections in economic adjustment processes which can and should be removed. This conflict, it is sometimes suggested, has become more serious in post-war years because of structural changes in labour and product markets. In addition to policies affecting general demand conditions, policies that would shift the trade-off relationship to a more favourable position have been proposed including measures to improve the mobility of labour and capital, more vigorous competition policies in product and factor markets and incomes policy. Here, incomes policy becomes a supplementary instrument to monetary and fiscal policies attempting to secure a better price performance at given employment levels than demand policies could secure alone.

Proponents of incomes policy have not tied their case to the fate of this approach to inflation. Other approaches have also been relevant. The attractions of a trade-off approach have been the emphasis on the short-run dynamics of wage and price changes, which were so often neglected in equilibrium analyses of inflation, and its expression in a form especially amenable to statistical tests. But serious doubts have been raised about the adequacy of the work for understanding the causes of inflation and for the setting of economic policies. An observed relationship in time-series data between price changes and the unemployment rate does not necessarily provide much insight into their economic determinants. The effects on the price level of holding unemployment at a given rate for a considerable length of time or the effects on the unemployment rate of keeping price increases at a fairly steady rate cannot be predicted simply from observations of past relationships between these series when both have been changing.

There are two different approaches which reject the idea of a trade-off as a basis for longer-run policy decisions. One approach is that the generation of inflation is much more determined by cost than demand factors and that, through the exercise of economic power by unions and businesses, wages and prices are set largely independently of monetary demand conditions. In this case there would be no guarantee that, if the unemployment rate were stabilized at a higher rather than a lower level, the rate of increase of wages and prices would be much different. To combat the causes of the inflationary pressures it would be necessary to break up the sources of economic power in wage and price decisions or to adopt measures to control its exercise. Although the policy implications of this approach differ, it could lead to a much stronger role for incomes policy than in the preceding case. The other approach, which bears a close affinity to traditional monetary analysis, weakens the

5

case for incomes policy. It argues that the movements in the general
price level are determined by monetary factors and the longer-run
unemployment rate is determined by characteristics of the function-
ing of the labour market. Again, there would be no reason to expect
a consistently stable relationship between price changes and the
unemployment rate. Although attempts to curb the expansion of
monetary demand in the short run could lead to some fall in employment, a more moderate expansion of monetary demand, particularly as determined by the money supply, could be expected to
reduce the rate of increase of prices with little effect on the longer-
term unemployment rate.

Many studies in the United Kingdom have attempted to test the
empirical relationships distinguishing these approaches. Most of
these investigations have attempted to determine whether the inflation has been a consequence of an upward push on costs or an
upward pull of demand on prices.

. . .

These statistical studies have been viewed as confirming a trade-off
approach in which the rate of increase of general prices, with given
productivity and import price movements, depends on the rate of
increase of wages. In turn, the rate of increase of wages is related to
the unemployment rate because both are dependent on demand
conditions. While the evidence is consistent with the form of the
relationship being influenced by cost-push factors, it has not pointed
to conditions for a continuous wage-price spiral. Thus, a trade-off
between inflation and unemployment has been suggested.

It is indicative of the difficulties of establishing the causes of
inflation empirically that other interpretations of these findings
could be made. With a monetary view of inflation, it may be argued
that further consideration of the role of expectations and monetary
factors is necessary. Expectations of future wage and price changes
influence current decisions, and when monetary demand conditions
change, expectations about the future wage and price movements
will not adjust fully to the new conditions in the short run. Thus,
variations of monetary demand in the sequence of time periods
examined in the studies will have less impact on actual money wages
and prices and a greater impact on output and employment than
would occur if there were a more stable, longer-run change in
monetary demand conditions. It could be misleading to derive the
choices to be made in setting policies that bear on monetary demand

conditions simply from present statistical evidence of an inverse relation between inflation and unemployment.[3]

Economic studies in the United Kingdom have generally assigned a substantial role to cost inflation factors. The valid point that a sustained rise in prices requires a sustained expansion of the money supply, since there is unlikely to be an accommodating, prolonged decline in the quantity of cash balances demanded, has not been a serious barrier to cost-push arguments on inflation. It has been pointed out that, instead of money wages tending to adjust towards an equilibrium level within a given or autonomously determined set of monetary conditions, the authorities, in the pursuit of full employment policies, have tended to adjust the equilibrium level of wages and prices towards the actual levels by altering monetary demand conditions. As Hicks has stated:

So long as wages were being determined within a *given* monetary framework, there was some sense in saying that there was an 'equilibrium wage', a wage that was in line with the monetary conditions that were laid down from outside. But the world we now live in is one in which the monetary system has become relatively elastic, so that it can accommodate itself to changes in wages, rather than the other way about. Instead of actual wages having to adjust themselves to an equilibrium level, monetary policy adjusts the equilibrium level of money wages so as to make it conform to the actual level. It is hardly an exaggeration to say that instead of being on a Gold Standard, we are on a Labour Standard.[4]

Thus, within a monetary environment that permits a sustained rise in prices it is possible to focus on other explanations of the determinants of wages and prices.

In British discussions of inflation, much emphasis has been placed on the process of collective bargaining leading to an upward push on wages. Reference has frequently been made to the apparent rigidity of the wage structure,[5] and this rigidity has been viewed as a product of a system of wage bargaining characterized by a clustering of similar wage increases, referred to as wage rounds. The problem of what determines the size of these increases has been difficult to

[3] There are still doubts, however, about the existence of a trade-off even in the short run between inflation and unemployment. See, for example, Bernard Corry and David Laidler, 'The Phillips Relation: A Theoretical Explanation', *Economica*, Vol. 34 (May 1967), pp. 189–97.

[4] J. R. Hicks, 'Economic Foundations of Wage Policy', *Economic Journal*, Vol. 65 (September 1955), p. 391.

[5] See, for example, L. A. Dicks-Mireaux and J. R. Shepherd, 'The Wages Structure and Some Implications for Incomes Policy', *National Institute Economic Review*, No. 22 (November 1962), pp. 38–48.

resolve. An explanation based on the growth of trade union organizations has been suggested.[6] It has also been argued that a few key wage settlements have regularly acted as bellwethers for settlements in other sectors. But analysis of British post-war wage rounds has failed to reveal a few key leaders that have regularly or predictably influenced general wage increases.[7] Generally, the view now is that rounds of increases are influenced by particular wage settlements, but that it is not possible to identify these settlements in advance. The implication for an incomes policy is that instead of focusing on a few key sectors—an approach which enjoyed perhaps even greater popularity in the United States than in Britain during the first few years of the wage-price guideposts—it is necessary to have a comprehensive review of wage increases.

The economic significance of negotiated wage increases in the United Kingdom is complicated by the phenomenon of wage drift.[8] There are often substantial differences between the changes in wages agreed upon in the industry wage negotiations and the actual change in earnings as they are determined at the plant level. Although there are many definitions of the term, wage drift generally means the difference between the increase in earnings and the increase determined in wage negotiations. Differences of view persist but it appears, on the basis of studies in the United Kingdom, that while demand conditions for labour have affected the size of wage drift, movements of earnings have been substantially influenced by the terms of wage settlements, rather than being independent of them.

The present evidence on the causes of inflation in the United Kingdom does not support an extreme position on either the demand versus cost inflation arguments or on the extent of the conflict between inflation and unemployment, particularly for making longer-run policy decisions. The trade-off approach has relevance for discussions of problems facing decisions on the use of monetary and fiscal policies for economic stabilization. Evidence that a curtailment of monetary demand reduces employment as well as the rate of increase of wages and prices, and that rigidities in economic adjustment processes complicate the problem, adds to

[6] A. G. Hines, 'Trade Unions and Wage Inflation in the United Kingdom, 1893–1961', *Review of Economic Studies*, Vol. 31 (October 1964), pp. 221–52.
[7] See, for example, Kenneth G. J. C. Knowles and D. Robinson, 'Wage Rounds and Wage Policy', *Oxford University Institute of Statistics Bulletin*, Vol. 24 (May 1962), pp. 269–329.
[8] See Chap. 8 of R. E. Caves (editor), *Britain's Economic Prospects* (1968).

the attractiveness of efforts to develop supplementary policies such as incomes policy to affect wages and prices more directly. The trade-off approach appears to be a less useful way of thinking about longer-run policy choices, but where monetary expansion is to a considerable extent induced by employment policy there is also an argument for trying to curb inflation over time by measures that would reduce the upward push on wages and prices. These measures may be directed to structural reform in the operation of economic markets, including attacks on restrictive practices and changes in commercial policy, but may also include a longer-run form of incomes policy.

What is it that an incomes policy is supposed to affect? Wages and prices can be controlled and an inflation suppressed even in conditions of pure demand inflation, but the bases for recent interest in incomes policy have rested on securing a largely voluntary adherence to the policy rather than on using compulsion. What causes of inflation might it treat?

It may have some effect on expectations about future wage and price changes. Deflationary monetary and fiscal policies have a smaller impact on the rate of increase of prices because wage and price decisions are influenced by expectations of the future. If the authorities can successfully supplement a change in direction of monetary and fiscal policies with measures that more quickly and smoothly adjust expectations to the new conditions, the effect on general price movements will be greater and the effect on employment and output will be less. Also, where the deflationary policies have been implemented because of balance-of-payments difficulties and where these difficulties have been caused partly by speculation against the country's currency on the assumption that domestic inflation will lead to a devaluation, announcements of new guides for money incomes and prices may work to change the views of speculators. These arguments do not assign a very large or permanent role to incomes policy. They may merely signify that statements of intentions can have temporary importance but may soon appear to be a bluff if not backed by other policies.

A much stronger argument is that incomes policy will affect rules of behaviour in making wage and price decisions. In the Keynesian explanation of high unemployment, workers resist a cut in money wage rates partly because the relation between a fall in money wage rates and a fall in general prices is not seen. Similarly, in discussions of inflation it is often argued that workers press for higher money wages and do not see that the associated rise in prices will leave real wages unaffected. It is suggested by many that by showing the interconnections on a national level of movements in money wages, productivity and prices an incomes policy will have an important educational function and will modify the inflationary bias in wage bargaining. Others remain sceptical of a significant effect here, particularly where wage bargaining remains decentralized. A more centralized system of wage negotiations, according to this argument, would make an incomes policy more effective, but it would probably also increase the need for one. While the British system has not been highly centralized in comparison to some European countries, the development of slightly stronger central powers of the Trades Union Congress in recent years has been viewed both as a product of the intense interest in incomes policy and as a means of improving the opportunities for the policy's success.

A related argument is that incomes policy can change somewhat the balance of power underlying wage and price decisions. This argument can be expressed simply as follows: post-war commitments to a national full employment policy have strengthened the employee side in wage bargaining, and businesses feel freer to pass on increased costs in the form of price increases because the government is committed to maintain the necessary demand (often on a sectoral level) to avoid greater unemployment of economic resources. An incomes policy may thus be viewed as a means to offset this change by strengthening the employer's side in wage decisions and the consumer's side in price decisions.

There is also the point, made perhaps more frequently in discussions of the United States wage-price guideposts, that there are a number of specific, important areas of the economy with a high concentration of market power. In these areas the timing and size of wage and price changes tend to bear little relation to movements in economic conditions, and the task of stabilization policies would be eased if a more flexible response could be induced in these areas.

Finally, if the policy works through channels that curb money wage rates in relation to prices, and the resulting lower real wage rate per unit of labour makes it attractive to hire more labour, a higher level of employment would occur at a given price level. This is a possible route for a shift of the trade-off relationship. Central to Keynes' argument for reducing high unemployment levels was a reduction in the real wage rate which could be accomplished by an increase in prices in relation to money wage rates or a fall of money wage rates in relation to prices. This argument can be used in support of an incomes policy. To the extent that a policy restrains the rise in money wage rates in relation to prices, an inducement to expand employment would be provided. However, this argument does not mean that the ratio of total profits to total wages will necessarily rise.

Productivity, income distribution and planning
Enthusiasts have seen in British incomes policy not simply a means of restraining the rise of money incomes but also a means of raising productivity and achieving a greater social accord on a fair distribution of incomes. The policy has also been linked to recent interest in economic planning.

Inflation can be slowed by a smaller rise in money incomes at given rates of productivity increase or by a larger rise in productivity at given rates of increase of money incomes. The lack of international competitiveness and the degree of inflation have been blamed partly on an unnecessarily poor performance of productivity.

. . .

To a great extent, incomes policy in the United Kingdom has been viewed as part of a broader effort to increase productivity. Restlessness with restrictive practices by unions and businesses and the difficulties of developing and applying specific policies to curb such practices, particularly in the labour market, have raised hopes that national guides for wages and prices will at least help to expose and moderate such barriers to economic change. There is a widely held view that excessive flabbiness in economic markets has perpetuated inefficiencies and that it can be trimmed through a national programme of economic fitness based on a set of guidelines for economic behaviour. Thus, the agreement on an incomes policy signed by representatives of the government, the Trades Union Congress and various employer organizations in December 1964 was called 'The Joint Statement of Intent on Productivity, Prices and Incomes'. In the reports of the National Board for Prices and Incomes opportunities for productivity improvements have been viewed as an integral part of judgements on the merits of particular wage and price changes.

Guidelines to promote economic growth have developed along with guidelines to curb the rise in incomes and prices. But much of the discussion of the former has taken place under the name of economic planning. As with incomes policy, economic planning has not implied the left-wing political complexion it held in pre-World War II years, and it has been part of the new faith in moral suasion techniques of economic policy. The first step, taken under a Conservative government, was the establishment of the National Economic Development Council in 1962. Its principal objectives were to examine the future potential performance of the British economy, to point out the obstacles to its economic growth, and to seek agreement on ways to increase economic growth. Among its initial tasks was the preparation of a set of projections of growth in the economy to 1966. Following the election of the Labour government in the autumn of 1964, some of the broader functions of the Council were shifted to the newly created Department of Economic Affairs, and in 1965 the government published a National Plan.[9] The purpose of the plan was to develop a coordinated, internally consistent set of projections of how the economy might develop to 1970 and thereby create expectations that would induce private economic decisions to conform to the projections. The work of the National Economic Development Council was directed more to the establishment and operation of consultative bodies for particular industries: economic development committees, of which there are now over twenty. The function of these committees is to explore problems at the industry level and to suggest ways to reduce them.

The projections of the National Economic Development Council and those of *The National Plan* have influenced incomes policy. The report of the council in 1963 that a rate of growth of about $3\frac{1}{4}\%$ in output per worker was a feasible target for the economy through to 1966 was taken as a basis for deriving a norm for a non-inflationary rise in money incomes. *The National Plan*'s call for an annual rise in output per head of about 3.4% (it had averaged around 2% in the 1950's and nearly $2\frac{3}{4}\%$ 1960 to 1964) supported optimistic expectations of the extent to which money incomes could rise without inflationary consequences. A problem of combining indicative planning and incomes policy is thus that the attempt to raise expectations of average productivity increases may make more difficult the attempt to lower expectations of average money income increases.

In turn, the targets and guides for economic growth have been influenced by views on the effectiveness of incomes policy. It was

[9] Department of Economic Affairs, *The National Plan*, Cmnd. 2764 (London: H.M. Stationery Office, 1965).

soon apparent that *The National Plan* had been based on incorrect assumptions about the degree of success in containing price increases and avoiding balance-of-payments difficulties. The move to deflationary policies shortly after the publication of the plan thwarted its expected impact.

A serious interest in incomes policy is unlikely to be confined to technical economic criteria for price stability or for greater productive efficiency. People are concerned about whether their present wage is fair in relation to that of others. Economic interest groups cannot be expected to leave to a body of experts the proper relationship among wages, salaries, profits and rent. The distribution of income and wealth involves social valuations about equity, opportunity and economic power. Thus, as a practical matter for its survival over time, incomes policy 'must stand ready to include in the bargain a wide range of issues concerned with the ordinary man's notions of social justice.'[10] These problems are less serious where there is already a wide measure of agreement in the society on income distribution issues. In earlier postwar years (greater difficulties have now emerged) Dutch incomes policy and the Swedish move to centralized private wage negotiations were both made easier by workers' beliefs in the importance of centralized policies for achieving a more desirable wage structure. There was greater agreement on the features of such a wage structure than has existed in the United Kingdom. But in the next section it will be pointed out that efforts to achieve a greater accord in this area have not been unimportant in recent British incomes policy.

Criteria and machinery
The characteristics of British incomes policy have changed substantially. Difficulties have emerged in each experience with it, and important modifications have been introduced successively. To some people, such variation is a reflection of the will-o'-the-wisp nature of an incomes policy; to others, each experience has provided some benefits at the time and has provided lessons for the construction of a more enduring and endearing policy in the future.

There are two principal areas in which problems arise in implementing an incomes policy. The first is in determining the appropriate criteria for guiding incomes. These criteria must be consistent with

[10] Andrew Shonfield, *Modern Capitalism* (London: Oxford University Press, 1965), p. 219.

the general targets set for the policy and can be quite different, for example, if incomes policy is to help overcome a short-run balance-of-payments crisis or if it is to modify economic behaviour over a much longer period. Because of changes in economic conditions, the criteria require flexibility if they are to retain their credibility and relevance to the economy. The criteria must make economic sense if they are to improve upon the workings of economic markets. They must also be sufficiently simple to be easily understood by the public. Particularly if the criteria are to be accepted for long, they must take into account social considerations about fairness in relative incomes. These are demanding conditions. The function of the criteria, however, is not to achieve a perfect system but to improve an existing imperfect one.

The second problem area is in securing agreement on, and adherence to, the criteria. It is usually argued that an incomes policy should or could only be largely voluntary. There has been little interest so far in making it similar to a tax law which provides well-defined automatic penalties to non-compliers or in making legal compulsion a basis for compliance, except possibly in conditions of national emergency. Few, however, would expect purely spontaneous conformity to the criteria. For the promotion of general support for the criteria there is the question of the role that private institutions— labour and employer organizations—will play. For the identification of non-compliers, some form of a review procedure may be proposed. Although sometimes referred to as a 'jawbone', 'ear-stroking' or 'open-mouth' approach to economic policy, incomes policy—and moral suasion policies in general—are not distinguished from other economic policies by the absence of sanctions against non-compliers. But the sanctions usually are less certain, more implied, and more indirect.[11] There is the possibility of exposure and public censure of offenders, the danger of unfavourable treatment in the administra-ministration of other government policies, and perhaps the threat of legislation.

. . .

It has not been possible to maintain a fixed set of criteria in British incomes policy. A specific norm for wages and salaries which is determined by a trend in productivity and around which only a few limited exceptions should occur has not, despite its general appeal,

---

[11] See J. T. Romans, 'Moral Suasion as an Instrument of Economic Policy,' *American Economic Review*, Vol. 56 (December 1966), pp. 1220–26.

proved to be suitable for all circumstances. The balance-of-payments situation, changes in domestic economic conditions, and a fear that the norm may have perversely raised expectations of minimum wage increases have been important in bringing about revisions to the norm. Recently, the four criteria permitting limited exceptions to the norm have been elevated in importance in judging all pay increase proposals, giving a somewhat greater emphasis to differentiation than to uniformity in pay increases. Further, two of the criteria, for productivity and low-paid workers, have emerged at this time as more important than the relative labour shortage or comparability criteria in the reports of the National Board for Prices and Incomes.

Too much resort to these two criteria as sole grounds for justifying any pay increase could undermine the general credibility of the policy. It has not been the intention, nor does it make economic sense,[12] for relative wage changes to be determined by relative productivity movements among occupations or industries. The productivity criterion is intended to provide an incentive for changes in labour practices which would make a direct contribution to greater productivity.[13] Its purpose is to help reduce restrictive practices and promote adjustments to economic change in labour markets. Thus, a high proportion of pay decisions in a year are not supposed to be affected by this criterion. Also, the low-paid worker criterion is to be limited in coverage, although its effect could be weakened by institutional links of other wages to wages of the low-paid workers or by increasing unemployment among those with low pay, if a higher relative wage reduces their employment. This criterion reflects social aspects of incomes policy and makes less distinct the difference between incomes policy, on the one hand, and minimum-wage legislation and the variety of government policies to help those with low incomes, on the other hand. Relative demand and supply conditions are not covered in either of the criteria; in a situation of general upward pressure on money wages, incentives to evade the confines of the two criteria will be particularly strong. Therefore, more attention has been given to these two criteria but they have been asked to bear a greater weight in relative and absolute wage movements than is sustainable.

Similarly, with prices there have been some difficulties in deriving

---

[12] See Kelvin Lancaster, 'Productivity-Geared Wage Policies', *Economica*, Vol. 25 (August 1958), pp. 199–212.

[13] See Chap. 8 of R. E. Caves (editor), *Britain's Economic Prospects* (1968).

a simple set of criteria that would be appropriate for all circumstances. The 1965 criteria did not call for any shift in the relationship between wage and salary incomes and profits, and changes in prices were to be determined primarily by changes in costs per unit of output. At that time, the norm for wages and salaries was linked to a national productivity trend, and the change in output per employee in relation to that of national productivity provided a guide (with allowance for some exceptions) to whether individual prices should rise or fall. Changes in the criteria for wages affect the criteria for prices, and both wage and price criteria were affected by the terms of the freeze and the decision to maintain a nil norm for wages following the end of the freeze. If indeed a zero norm for wages and salaries were held successfully with only minor exceptions, prices in general would be expected to fall, but few have contemplated this degree of effect on the wage side. The price criteria have been criticized by economists for the excessive emphasis on costs, for the neglect of relative demand conditions, and for introducing, if adhered to, 'a most unhealthy rigidity'.[14] But the criteria have not been rigidly applied in the reports of the National Board for Prices and Incomes, and these reports have tended to take the form of broad investigations of particular industries and recommendations concerning their operations.[15] Thus, on the side of prices, incomes policy has recently been extended into broader areas of public policy in the field of industrial organization.

Voluntary support for the criteria of an incomes policy has not been easily attained. People have to be convinced that the criteria serve individual as well as national interests. Along with the campaign for a voluntary acceptance of, and adherence to, the criteria, the British government has moved, particularly in recent years, to a greater exercise of governmental powers to implement the policy.

Three factors have influenced the extent to which voluntary support for the criteria could be expected. First, in a national economic crisis, such as the balance-of-payments crisis in 1966, there is likely to be a greater awareness of the national interest in curbing inflation and of the importance of 'all pulling together' to surmount the crisis.

[14] E. V. Morgan, 'Is Inflation Inevitable?' *Economic Journal*, Vol. 76 (March 1966), p. 14.
[15] For example, the board's report on bank charges involved a wide review of and general proposals for improving the competitive structure of British banking. National Board for Prices and Incomes, *Bank Charges*, Report No. 34 (HMSO, 1967).

The four post-war attempts with a freeze or pause have tried to draw on the common interest in overcoming serious balance-of-payments difficulties.

Second, the support of union and business leaders and the extent to which they can influence members of their organizations are important. The more centralized the private economic decisions are, the more easily these leaders are convinced of the effect of their actions on the general price level. But the existence of highly central-ized wage negotiations does not necessarily ease the implementation of an incomes policy if decisions at the plant level on earnings—the determinants of wage drift—are to a considerable extent independent of the terms of the central wage agreements. Similarly, commitments given by business leaders on prices may lack force where actual prices can differ from quoted prices and where the quality of products can be varied.

The acceptance by unions of wage restraint in 1948–50 in part came through the influence of several strong trade union leaders, but unrest over the policy built up among individual unions, ending the policy. The Joint Statement of Intent on Productivity, Prices and Incomes, signed in December 1964 by representatives of the Trades Union Congress as well as employer organizations, the support given to the freeze of 1966–7, and the recent development of a system of review of wage proposals in the Trades Union Congress have en-couraged supporters of an incomes policy, but the strong tradition of autonomy of unions in the United Kingdom leaves the future of voluntary support in doubt.

Third, the degree of unity within the labour movement on the criteria of an incomes policy and the relations between the labour movement and the political party in power can be important. Agreement among workers on a fair wage structure has not been a notable feature of the British scene, but the political party in power has clearly made a difference. Union support for an incomes policy was strongest in 1948–50 and after 1964, periods when there was a Labour government. During the period of a Conservative govern-ment, from October 1951 to October 1964, several attempts to develop an incomes policy ran into opposition from the Trades Union Congress. Both the proposal in 1952 for a national advisory council to keep wages in line with the growth of productivity and the appeal for wage restraint in 1956 were rejected by the unions. The pay pause of 1961–2 also failed to win the support of the Trades

Union Congress, and the unions refused to participate in the formulation of the 1962 criteria for a longer-run incomes policy or to support the National Incomes Commission.

It is usually agreed that a campaign for voluntary adherence to incomes policy needs to be supported by direct governmental action, but British governments have had to move cautiously since collective bargaining in Britain has been more decentralized and characterized by less involvement of the state than in many other countries. As an employer, the government has faced the difficult task of setting an example by conforming to the policy criteria in its own wage negotiations without resisting for long pay changes determined in private markets. For example, the attempt to apply the pay pause in 1961–2 to the civil service produced considerable unrest in the public sector over its discriminatory impact, and, afterwards, governments were more wary of this approach.

Another area of government action has been to establish a body to review the application of the criteria in specific cases; even if the body has no powers to enforce its findings, such reviews can encourage compliance through public exposure and censure of noncompliance. To be publicly exposed in this manner is not entirely unlike being put in the stocks in earlier days for misdemeanours against society. Thus, in 1962 the National Incomes Commission was established to review retrospectively pay settlements referred to it by the government and to review pay claims in advance of a settlement if they were submitted by both parties. The work of the commission was slow and plagued with difficulties. The commission was to focus on wages and salaries, arousing opposition from those who felt other incomes and prices should be included. From the outset the Trades Union Congress failed to support it; its public stature was thus reduced, and the number of references to it was small.

With the establishment in 1965 of the National Board for Prices and Incomes, which included representatives of unions and businesses, it was hoped that many of these weaknesses would be removed. Prices as well as incomes were to be examined. The government was responsible for referring cases for review to the board, and the reports were to be issued more quickly. In its first two years—from April 1965 to April 1967—thirty-one reports were issued. They probed a wide range of issues in the cases examined and provided important interpretations to such criteria as those for productivity and low-paid workers. But it was soon felt that the impact of the reports on public opinion and on affecting wage and price decisions would be greater if proposals for wage and price changes could be reviewed before coming into force.

In the autumn of 1965 the government announced its intention to develop an early warning system which would mean notification in advance of wage and price changes,[16] and the Trades Union Congress responded by deciding to establish its own system of review of proposed wage changes. In the Prices and Incomes Act, 1966, the government was given the power to introduce a statutory early warning system. As a result, the government could, by an order in council, require advance notice of thirty days for increases of prices and wages, and provision was also made for notification within one week of decisions to increase dividends. If the government referred a case to the National Board for Prices and Incomes, a further delay would be required until the board made a report on it, or until three months had elapsed. This part of the act was subject to the provisions of the price and wages freeze during 1966–7 which permitted the government to enforce a standstill for a longer period. The Prices and Incomes Act of 1967 also extended stronger powers of the government in this area until August 1968. In addition to the possibility of a four-month delay on wage or price increases to give the board an opportunity to report, the government was given the powers under the act to require a further delay of three months if the report of the board on a proposed increase was adverse, permitting a total delay of seven months. In the spring of 1968 the government indicated it would seek legislation to permit a deferral or suspension of pay or price increases for up to twelve months.

Problems of gaining compliance to the criteria have led to statutory powers which a few years ago would have been generally regarded in the United Kingdom as undesirable, unnecessary and politically impossible. But legal compulsion has been more a deterrent than a weapon for use. During the 1966–7 freeze only fourteen orders were issued enforcing the standstill in particular cases. The powers now are unlikely to mean much if there is widespread dissatisfaction with the policy. In addition, compared to the experience of the United States with wage-price guideposts, there has not been the same resort to a threatened use of other government measures to penalize non-compliers, such as shifts in government spending or stockpile policies,

---

[16] The government's position at this time was set out in *Prices and Incomes Policy: An 'Early Warning' System*, Cmnd. 2808 (HMSO, 1965).

changes in tariffs or export subsidies, and investigations under the antitrust laws. Nevertheless, some government intervention has long been part of British incomes policy and can take many forms. For example, in 1948 the government stated that if the criteria were violated this would be taken 'into account in settling controlled prices, charges or margins or other financial matters requiring government action.'[17] Also, since incomes policy has led to a substantial amount of consultation among government officials, business executives and union leaders (some see dangers and others benefits to this), it is not easy to determine the role that less formal political pressures play. Hopes for the policy have remained pinned on a voluntary change in economic behaviour to conform to the criteria even if at times the meaning of the word 'voluntary' has to be stretched a bit.

Effects of incomes policy
Common to all the experiments in the post-war period has been the belief that incomes policy would reduce the rate of price increases at given employment levels. In assessing the effects of the policy the empirical evidence of effects on prices, incomes and other less direct results must be examined. Such an examination involves the problems of costs as well.

Effects on prices and incomes
Evidence that the actual movement of prices and incomes was greater than that aimed for in the policy does not mean the policy had no effect, for without the policy other factors might have raised prices and incomes even more. Likewise, a movement of prices and incomes in line with the aims of the policy is not necessarily proof that the policy had any effect, for other factors might have been responsible for this movement. Thus, to isolate the effects incomes policies have had on the rate of increase of prices, it is necessary to specify how prices would have behaved in the absence of the policies. The conceptual and statistical difficulties of doing this obviously leave room for doubt about the exact effects. In addition, it would be useful to have answers to a number of supplementary questions. Did the form the policy took in different periods make a difference? Was there an effect on incomes which in turn influenced prices or was there also an independent effect on pricing decisions? Did the

[17] *Statement on Personal Incomes, Costs and Prices*, p. 4.

factors affecting wage drift mean that it was easier to influence wage rates, determined in major wage negotiations, than earnings?

A growing body of research throws light on some of these questions. . . . Taken together, these various studies suggest that weekly wage rates were affected in the expected direction during three periods of an incomes policy, but it was not established that the general price level was affected in the expected direction in the two periods examined. Since it is usually argued that the main objective of an incomes policy is to moderate increases in the general price level and that a push on wages has been partly responsible for inflation, the results are somewhat puzzling and not very encouraging.

A number of further points need to be examined. It is possible that the effect on weekly wage rates was not reflected in labour costs. At the beginning of the 1960's, and again in 1965, there was a significant fall in the normal or standard hours of work per week, which might mean that a series of hourly wage rates would have given different results than the series for weekly wage rates. In addition, because of wage drift, earnings might have moved differently from wages. In considering price effects, it is important to allow for other influences on price movements; to take into account periods when incomes policy might have been more effective than in 1961–2 and 1964–5; and to recognize the impact on prices of special factors, such as a rise in indirect taxes, at the time an incomes policy was introduced. There is now more evidence on incomes policy, although a longer time perspective will be necessary to assess fully the effect of recent measures.

To explore these points it is necessary to know how wages, earnings and prices would likely have changed in the absence of an incomes policy. The statistical techniques employed in this study are similar to those in the studies of aggregate wage and price relationships in the United Kingdom previously noted. The variables in the wage and price relationships used are, likewise, similar to those used by Dicks-Mireaux.[18] Demand conditions in the labour market, for which the unemployment rate is assumed to be a proxy, and changes in prices were used for predicting changes in wages or earnings. For predicting changes in prices, the variables were changes in wages or earnings, changes in import prices, and changes in productivity. In addition, estimates of the relationship between output and capacity to represent the direct influence of demand conditions on prices were

[18] Dicks-Mireaux, 'Cost and Price Changes'.

6

included in some tests.[19] Also, it was necessary to question whether wage rates, earnings rates and prices behave differently in the various periods of an incomes policy than at other times.

Four series for wages and earnings were examined over the period 1948–67: weekly wage rates, compiled from wage settlements, the variable most frequently used in studies of British aggregate wage movements; hourly wage rates, derived by dividing the weekly wage rate series by the normal or standard hours worked per week; hourly earnings including overtime, taken from a survey conducted only twice a year, in the last week of April and the last week of October; and hourly earnings excluding overtime, based on the same survey. For both hourly earnings series, the two observations each year were assumed to represent the half years in which they fell. For these earnings series, tests were made on a half-yearly basis, while for weekly and hourly wage rates the tests were on a quarterly as well as on a half-yearly basis. Three price series were examined: an index of retail prices since 1948, an index of wholesale prices since 1948, and an implicit price index for gross domestic product at factor cost since 1957.

There may not always be complete agreement on the precise dates when the various experiments with incomes policy took place, but the following were used in this study: first quarter 1948 to the third quarter 1950 inclusive; 1956; third quarter 1961 to the second quarter 1962; third quarter 1962 to the third quarter 1964; first quarter 1965 to the second quarter 1966; third quarter 1966 to the second quarter 1967. Various assumptions were made about the timing of the impact of incomes policy in each period: that its impact was the same in each quarter within a period of incomes policy, that it was greater in the early quarters than in the late quarters, and that its impact became progressively greater within each period. The statistical methods and some results of the tests are given in the appendix.

Depending on the series, the tests indicate successes and failures in influencing wages and earnings and different effects on wages and earnings. In 1948–50 the evidence is consistent with an annual rate of increase of weekly wage rates below that expected in the absence of an incomes policy, by over 2 percentage points. It is not clear whether the impact on hourly earnings was equally large. For 1956

[19] For a measure of capacity utilization, see W. A. H. Godley and J. R. Shepherd, 'Long-Term Growth and Short-Term Policy', *National Institute Economic Review*, No. 29 (August 1964), pp. 26–38.

the evidence does not point to a lower rate of increase of the wages or earnings series. In 1961–2 the expected annual rise of weekly wage rates was slowed by over $1\frac{1}{2}$ percentage points. The rates of increase of hourly wage rates and of both earnings series were also below the expected, but whether the lower rates are statistically significant is more doubtful than in the case of weekly wage rates. In 1962–4 the tests do not indicate that any one of the series was affected by incomes policy.

The importance of the series used is revealed clearly in the 1965–6 period of an incomes policy. The rate of increase of weekly wage rates was significantly below the expected by about 1 percentage point. This was a period during which normal hours worked per week declined. The rate of increase of hourly wage rates was not below that predicted in these tests in the absence of an incomes policy. The rate of increase of both hourly earnings series was greater than expected, supporting the claims some have made that the policy had a perverse effect. Two interpretations of this experience are possible. It might be argued that the reduction in normal hours worked per week was an independent phenomenon which happened to occur in this period and which would have pushed up hourly wages and earnings even faster if it had not been for the incomes policy. This argument would point to weaknesses in the hourly wage rate and earnings relationships used here. Another argument might be that the policy, in focusing on wage increases in major wage negotiations, induced a greater rise in other forms of economic returns, such as a shortening of normal hours at this time and a rise in wage drift. In addition, it might be suggested that workers were attempting to get into a better relative earnings position in anticipation of a stronger and more permanent incomes policy. Since the policy in this period was introduced in a longer-run form there is a question of whether the effects, if any, became greater as the period wore on. However, a separate test to allow for a gradual taking hold of incomes policy from the end of 1964 to mid-1966 did not support this possibility.

For the 1966–7 standstill and period of severe restraint the tests indicate a lowering of the annual rate of increase of weekly wage rates by about $1\frac{1}{4}$ to $1\frac{1}{2}$ percentage points. The other wages and earnings series were affected in a similar direction, in some tests by more than this amount. But no adjustment was made for the pay claims agreed upon before the freeze and deferred until the summer of 1967.

To be successful, an incomes policy should have an effect on the rate of increase of average prices, although, as noted, a greater effect on wage rates in relation to prices is not necessarily inconsistent with the objectives of such a policy. The restraint on prices may be direct and independent of the effect on labour costs, or it may result wholly or partly from restraining labour costs. Statistically significant decreases in both retail and wholesale price changes did not occur in any period, although several, but not all, tests indicated a smaller rise in retail prices in 1956 and 1965–6. When the indirect effects of labour costs are also considered, some of the tests indicate a fractionally lower rate of increase of retail prices in 1948–50 which, in turn, would feed back on wage claims. During the three periods of an incomes policy from the summer of 1961 to the summer of 1966, the statistical work does not point to a significant reduction in the rate of increase of prices, with the possible exception of a slight restraining effect in 1965–6.

The case for the impact of incomes policy is strong in the 1966–7 experience. It is important to recognize that the freeze was accompanied by the introduction of the Selective Employment Tax. According to estimates of the National Institute of Economic and Social Research, this tax could be expected to add about 0·6% to retail prices.[20] When adjustments are made for this tax, a significant reduction in the expected rate of increase of prices appears to have occurred. Some further support for this point was found in the changes in the implicit price index for gross domestic product at factor cost, an index which excludes indirect taxes. As in 1948–50, however, the policy seems to have borne more heavily on wages than on prices.

These tests must be interpreted with great caution. Knowledge of how wages, earnings and prices might have behaved in the absence of an incomes policy is highly imperfect. The complexity of economic factors affecting incomes and prices calls for more complete models of economic relationships. The effects of incomes policies may appear to be weaker in these tests because the policies were introduced during periods when special factors, not considered in the tests, were increasing wages, earnings and prices more quickly. Also, when some direct control over the prices of products and labour is attempted, such as in 1966–7, opportunities for adjusting the quality

[20] 'The Economic Situation, The Home Economy', *National Institute Economic Review*, No. 36 (May 1966), p. 19.

of products or of labour services may make the prices and wages reported in official series a less accurate reflection of the true prices and wages and may lead to an overestimation of the effects of incomes policy.

A different kind of test for the effects of an incomes policy can be developed from the proposition that a norm or guidepost for average wage increases, with criteria to permit some limited exceptions to it, should produce a close bunching of wage-rate increases around the norm. In addition, it has been suggested that the effects of wage-price guideposts in the United States will be greater on the visible or more nationally significant wage settlements than on the average wage settlements.[21]

Table 1 presents the distribution of percentage changes of weekly wages for 179 groups of male manual workers for twelve-month periods from April 1961 to April 1967. To the extent that incomes policy has been effective there should have been a greater effect in the first and last two twelve-month periods shown in the table than from April 1962 to April 1965. In the periods containing the pay pause of 1961–2 and the freeze of 1966–7 a higher proportion of wage increases occurred in the lower classes of percent increases than in other periods, but the lowest proportion was in the period 1965–6. In this latter period only about 15% of the wage groups were in the range which included the official wage norm of 3–3½%, and less than 7% were below it. Both of these figures were smaller than in the other periods, but demand conditions, reflected in the unemployment rates shown for the twelve-month periods, were particularly strong at this time.

The dispersion of wage increases around the average increase, which is measured in the table by the standard deviation, was highest in 1961–4, third highest in 1966–7, and lowest in 1965–6. This evidence is not conclusive that incomes policy generally reduced the dispersion of weekly wage-rate increases. Assuming that the 179 wage groups selected for publication by the Ministry of Labour were regarded as of somewhat greater national importance than others, average weekly wage increases of these groups can be compared with those of the national average to test for the effect of 'exposure'. As the table indicates, the ratio of average wage increases in the selected wage groups to the national average wage increase was highest in

[21] See George L. Perry, 'Wages and the Guideposts', American Economic Review, Vol. 57 (September 1967), pp. 897–901.

Table 1   Percentage distribution of annual rates of weekly wage changes for 179 groups of male manual workers, April 1961 to April 1967

Item	Percentage of workers receiving changes, by year					
	April 1961 to April 1962	April 1962 to April 1963	April 1963 to April 1964	April 1964 to April 1965	April 1965 to April 1966	April 1966 to April 1967
Classes of percentage changes						
Wage cut	0·0	0·0	0·0	0·0	0·0	1·1
0–0·99	29·0	17·3	20·1	20·7	2·8	53·6
1–1·99	0·6	1·1	0·0	1·1	0·6	0·6
2–2·99	7·3	8·9	0·0	7·8	3·3	3·4
3–3·99	15·1	14·5	14·0	14·5	151	11·2
4–4·99	9·5	15·1	27·4	16·8	20·7	10·6
5–5·99	10·6	14·5	17·9	16·2	11·2	11·2
6–6·99	6·7	11·2	6·7	12·3	25·1	5·0
7–7·99	5·0	10·1	3·3	2·2	12·3	2·2
8–8·99	4·5	5·0	5·0	4·5	2·2	0·0
9–9·99	6·1	0·0	2·8	1·7	4·5	0·0
10–10·99	1·7	1·1	1·7	0·6	0·6	0·0
11 and over	3·9	1·1	1·1	1·7	1·7	1·1
Total[1]	100·0	99·9	100·0	100·1	100·1	100·0
Average wage increases	4·2%	4·4%	4·4%	4·2%	5·6%	2·3%
Standard deviation	3·53	2·70	2·81	3·11	2·46	3·01
National average unemployment rate	1·58%	2·45%	2·15%	1·55%	1·36%	1·80%
National average increase in weekly wages	3·62%	3·88%	4·11%	4·17%	5·45%	2·35%
Ratio of average wage increase of the 179 wage groups to the national average increase	1·16	1·13	1·07	1·01	1·03	0·98

Sources: Ministry of Labour, *Statistics on Incomes, Prices, Employment and Production*, No. 21 (HMSO, 1967); Central Statistical Office, *Monthly Digest of Statistics*, various issues.

[1] Because of rounding, percentages may not add up to 100.

1961–2, lowest in 1966–7 and third lowest in 1965–6. While the evidence seems to point to a downward trend in the ratio, independent of incomes policy, the lower ratios in the last periods could also reflect a greater impact of more recent incomes policies on wage settlements in these groups in relation to the national average.

Tests such as the previous ones are based on the past and do not provide evidence for the future if the environment in which future policies are conducted changes. It is not at all clear from the previous tests what long-run effects incomes policy could have. Because of the special difficulties in each case, the earlier postwar experiments may not be a very reliable guide to the future. In 1948–50 the criteria and machinery were not well developed for a longer-run policy, and problems of maintaining the policy were increased by the effects of devaluation in 1949 and the outbreak of the Korean war in 1950. The policies of 1956 and 1961–2 were not cast in a longer-run form, and the attempt in 1962–4 to achieve a more durable form failed, as in 1956 and 1961–2, to gain the support of trade unions. The policy, starting at the end of 1964 and early 1965, was launched in a period of strong inflationary demand pressures and at a time when wage and price expectations, based on past experience, were not easily reversible. The 1966–7 freeze was supported, however, by legal compulsion. Uncertainties about the future course of wages and prices after the end of the war probably made it easier to affect expectations in the late 1940's than it has been after a period of sustained peacetime inflation. A serious problem of comparing the impact of the United States wage-price guideposts during 1962–6 and British incomes policy since the early 1960's is that the former followed a period, at the end of the 1950's and beginning of the 1960's, when there had been excess capacity, relatively high unemployment, and a high degree of price stability. The job of keeping expectations of average income increases roughly in line with average productivity trends is likely to be easier in such a case than when for some time incomes have been rising well in excess of productivity and expectations have adjusted to these conditions.

Other effects and costs

Attempts to measure the direct effects of incomes policy on wage and price changes neglect other benefits imputed to an incomes policy as well as the economic, social and political costs that may be incurred. Difficulties of making statistical tests for other benefits and costs and the great variations possible in the meaning and form of an incomes policy ensure continuing controversy about it.

Along with restraint on the growth of money incomes, some have expected that British incomes policy would increase productivity and thus permit a faster growth of real incomes. No measurements of its net contribution have been made, but arguments exist for both positive and negative effects. On the positive side, public attention was undoubtedly drawn to the relationships among money wages, productivity, prices and real incomes and encouraged more interest in productivity bargaining. In public discussions and in the reports

of the National Board for Prices and Incomes, the borderline between incomes policy and policies to promote competition and
adjustments to economic change has become less clear than in other
western countries; incomes policy has been viewed as part of a
broader approach to reducing barriers to change in economic markets,
modernizing the structure of labour and management institutions,
and improving the coordination of public policies. On the other hand,
it can also carry dangers to productivity performance. There has
been the concern that the criteria do not make sufficient allowance for
relative demand and supply conditions and that they may impose
new rigidities that hamper some economic adjustments. A strict
application of the criteria to price increases reduces the incentives for
individual price decreases and encourages quality deterioration where
market forces permit it. If the criteria are applied too strictly to
incomes, without allowance for changes in income differentials in
other countries, pressures rise in some occupations for emigration.
However, it is not clear that the overall effects on economic growth
have been significant one way or the other.[22]

Incomes policy has also been viewed as an instrument for achieving
a greater social accord on the distribution of incomes. The plight
of low-paid workers has received special attention in the last few
years in the announced criteria and in the reports of the National
Board. But it is too early to know whether the board's solicitude for
the position of low-paid workers and the encouraging steps towards
a wage policy within the Trades Union Congress will have lasting
effects. There is the danger that opposition, particularly to strong
forms of the policy, will cause serious discontent and industrial strife.
Incomes policy involves discrimination as some forms of income and
some prices are easier to affect than others. Also, instances of price
increases are more likely to be publicly examined than instances that
call for price decreases. In addition, in the selection of the limited
number of cases for public review there may be considerations of the
propaganda effects. But, among public policies, discrimination is not
peculiar to incomes policy.

There is, finally, the effect on political processes. The policy has
fostered consultation among government, business, and labour
leaders on economic matters. It has served to reassure the public

---

[22] See Chaps. 7 and 8 of R. E. Caves (editor), *Britain's Economic Prospects*,
1968, for a fuller assessment of the relation of incomes policy to productivity
bargaining and to industrial organization policies.

(and also at times speculators on the fate of the pound) that something was being done about inflation. At the same time, it has opened more opportunities for political pressures to influence wage and price decisions. The stronger the policy the more it can interfere with economic freedom. Overly optimistic views of the effectiveness of incomes policy could divert attention and public support from improvements in other policies and create disillusionment with the nation's ability to manage its economic affairs when the policy fails to achieve its goals. The social and political costs and benefits are outside the main focus of this study but must be part of a more general assessment of the policy's value and appropriate form.

The policy's prospects
Judged on the basis of post-war experiments, incomes policy has not been very effective in contributing to greater price stability and did not prove to be a substitute for exchange rate changes in 1949 and 1967. But the nature of the policy has changed substantially, and its greater effects after mid-1966 have been noted. The move to stronger statutory powers for enforcing the policy increases its potential for holding down inflation but also raises the possible political, social and economic costs.

The policy has been dominated so far by freezes, pauses or ceilings, initiated in response to balance-of-payments problems; thus conclusions about its form and value in the long run are difficult to derive from these experiences. Instead of being used to tackle a serious balance-of-payments situation quickly and almost single-handedly, its task now is to help preserve the advantages of a devaluation by moderating the subsequent pressures on domestic costs and prices. In this supporting role the chances for some success have been improved by recent developments. There is a stronger commitment by the government to maintain the policy, which has been reflected in legislation, in a larger role of the state in wage negotiations, and in the development of institutions such as the National Board for Prices and Incomes. Recently, the greater slack in the economy has perhaps also lowered expectations of future wage and price increases, although they would rise sharply again if strong demand pressures were allowed to build up. Nevertheless, past difficulties in maintaining the policy and unrest about some of its impacts and costs warn against a heavy reliance on it in planning the mix of future economic policies.

The principal uncertainty is whether enough is known now about how to make the policy survive for long in a healthier economic environment. A review of post-war attempts to move from short-run curatives for a crisis to a long-run policy has pointed to a number of serious problems. Norms and criteria for incomes and prices, appropriate for short-run restraint, become less credible over time unless they can be made to accommodate shifts in demand and supply conditions. Voluntary support and endorsement of strong govern-ment powers to back up the policy have been easier to obtain when the national economic interest seems seriously threatened. Under more settled conditions there is greater concern about the fairness of the policy's impacts on relative income positions. Curbs on incomes and prices can be gradually eroded through man's ingenuity to circumvent restrictions not in his self-interest. Yet much depends on the form of the policy. It has also become more closely linked to broad investigations of particular economic markets and to reform of the processes of collective bargaining. It is in moving beyond con-trols on wage and price decisions to policies dealing with the causes underlying these decisions that the more enduring contributions are likely to be found. Thus, in the long run, incomes policy tends to merge with other economic policies—complicating further the trouble-some problem of identifying what is and what is not an incomes policy.

Appendix   Regressions for wages, earnings and prices
The following wage and price equations were used to test for the effects of British incomes policies.

$$\dot{W}(t) = a + bU^{-1}(t) + c\dot{P}_r(t) + e\dot{P}_r(t - 1) + f_1 I_1 + f_2 I_2 + f_3 I_3 \\ + f_4 I_4 + f_5 I_5 + f_6 I_6 + u(t)$$

$$\dot{P}_r(t) \text{ or } \dot{P}_w(t) = g + h\dot{W}(t) + j\dot{P}_m(t) \text{ [or } \dot{P}_m(t - 1)] + k\dot{R}(t) \\ + m_1 I_1 + m_2 I_2 + m_3 I_3 + m_4 I_4 + m_5 I_5 + m_6 I_6 + v(t)$$

In all cases a dot ($\cdot$) over a variable indicates a rate of change. For tests on quarterly data, where t refers to a three-month period, it indicates a rate of change from four quarters ago. Thus, $\dot{W}(t)$ would be $W(t) - W(t - 4)/W(t - 4)$. For tests on half-yearly data, where t refers to a six-month period, it indicates a rate of change from two six-month periods ago. Thus, in this case, $\dot{W}(t)$ would be $W(t) - W(t - 2)/W(t - 2)$.

The following notation was used:

W: wages or earnings, for which there were four different series
W_w: weekly wage rate
W_h: hourly wage rate
W_{ei}: hourly earnings including overtime
W_{ex}: hourly earnings excluding overtime
U^{-1}: reciprocal of a four-quarter average unemployment rate
P_r: index of retail prices
P_w: index of wholesale prices
P_m: index of import prices
R: industrial output per industrial employee; $\dot{R}(t)$ is the change in R during a twelve-month period over the previous twelve-month period
$I_1 \ldots I_6$ = dummy variables at the time of incomes policies. The following periods were used: IQ 1948–3Q 1950 (I_1); 1956 (I_2); 3Q 1961–2Q 1962 (I_3); 3Q 1962–2Q 1964 (I_4); 1Q 1965–2Q 1966 (I_5); 3Q 1966–2Q 1967 (I_6).

In line with other studies cited earlier, the dummy variables were initially given the value of 1 when the policy was in effect and 0 at other times. This is referred to as a regular value (reg. I). Since wages and prices are examined as rates of change over a year the regular value of the dummy assumes a greater effect from the policy at the beginning than at the end of each experiment. In addition, therefore, values of the dummies were used that were proportional to the length of time the policy was in force. We shall refer to this as a proportional value (prop. I). For example, in a quarterly equation it would take the value of $\frac{1}{4}$ in 3Q 1966, $\frac{1}{2}$ in 4Q 1966, $\frac{3}{4}$ in 1Q 1967, and 1 in 2Q 1967. Since the average value would not be 1 in this period, the proportional dummy would tend to raise the value of the coefficient in comparison to that of a variable which averaged 1.

Interpretations of the tests require the usual cautionary notes; also, the quarterly and half-yearly equations which use a twelve-month change in the dependent variable were found to fit better— although still not too well in many cases—and to imply generally stronger effects of incomes policy on wages and earnings than when no moving averages of the changes were used. Table 2 presents results of some of the regressions for wages and earnings. The t-values are

Table 2 Wages and earnings regressions, coefficients of explanatory variables

Explanatory variable	Weekly wages (W_w) Quarterly 1Q 1948–2Q 1967		Hourly wages (W_h) Quarterly 1Q 1948–2Q 1967		Hourly earnings including overtime (W_{ei}) Half-yearly 1H 1948–1H 1967		Hourly earnings excluding overtime (W_{ex}) Half-yearly 1H 1948–1H 1967	
	Reg. I	Prop. I	Reg. I	Prop. I	Reg. I	Prop. I	Reg. I	Prop. I
Constant	−0·0006	−0·0017	0·0094	0·0119	0·0223	0·0120	0·0163	0·0075
U^{-1}	0·0433	0·0460	0·0348	0·0342	0·0349	0·0556	0·0351	0·0538
	(4·607)	(4·803)	(2·392)	(2·681)	(1·158)	(2·032)	(1·300)	(2·261)
$\dot{P}_r$	0·3128	0·2724	0·4642	0·4411	0·6780	0·5412	0·6628	0·5432
	(4·352)	(3·687)	(4·176)	(4·486)	(3·415)	(2·954)	(3·723)	(3·407)
$\dot{P}_{r-1}$	0·2284	0·2545	0·0570	0·0768	−0·2318	−0·0906	−0·1410	−0·0207
	(3·411)	(3·760)	(0·551)	(0·853)	(1·252)	(0·541)	(0·850)	(0·142)
$I_1(1948-50)$	−0·0213	−0·0238	−0·0152	−0·0234	−0·0061	−0·0192	−0·0080	−0·0215
	(8·157)	(8·302)	(3·760)	(6·150)	(0·753)	(2·573)	(1·101)	(3·306)
$I_2(1956)$	0·0085	0·0083	0·0107	0·0071	0·0087	−0·0174	0·0125	−0·0104
	(1·760)	(1·407)	(1·425)	(0·906)	(0·599)	(1·075)	(0·962)	(0·739)
$I_3(1961-2)$	−0·0166	−0·0184	−0·0044	−0·0098	−0·0091	−0·0229	−0·0061	−0·0176
	(4·138)	(3·694)	(0·717)	(1·476)	(0·751)	(1·744)	(0·562)	(1·539)
$I_4(1962-4)$	0·0059	0·0072	0·0040	0·0018	0·0028	0·0068	0·0044	0·0069
	(1·815)	(2·020)	(0·791)	(0·377)	(0·292)	(0·724)	(0·514)	(0·845)
$I_5(1965-6)$	−0·0099	−0·0112	0·0085	0·0108	0·0255	0·0236	0·0236	0·0228
	(2·936)	(2·770)	(1·620)	(2·005)	(2·533)	(2·159)	(2·619)	(2·402)
$I_6(1966-7)$	−0·0127	−0·0143	−0·0074	−0·0206	−0·0124	−0·0358	−0·0066	−0·0275
	(3·168)	(2·386)	(1·200)	(2·579)	(1·036)	(2·222)	(0·618)	(1·965)
R^2	0·86	0·85	0·68	0·76	0·55	0·65	0·62	0·73

in parentheses. According to these findings the annual rate of change of weekly wage rates was lower during the 1948–50 incomes policy by over 2 percentage points. The effect on hourly earnings appears to have been smaller, but in this case it makes a greater difference whether the regular or proportional dummy is used. There was no statistically significant reduction in wages or earnings in 1956. In 1961–2 weekly wage rates were slowed in their annual rate of increase by over $1\frac{1}{2}$ percentage points, but it is doubtful if there was a similar impact on hourly wages and earnings. Neither wage nor earnings increases were reduced in 1962–4. In 1965–6 the annual rate of increase of weekly wages was lower by about 1 percentage point, but the importance of the wages and earnings series is particularly clear in this period. Increases in hourly wage rates did not decline, and hourly earnings rose by over $2\frac{1}{4}$ percentage points a year faster than would have been predicted in the absence of the policy. In 1966–7 the annual rate of change of weekly wages was lower by a little over $1\frac{1}{4}$ percentage points, and there is a case for a similar and perhaps greater impact on hourly wages and earnings.

Some tests on prices are reported in Tables 3 and 4. The policies might be expected to affect prices directly as well as indirectly through labour costs. But the evidence does not point to a statistically significant direct effect on both retail and wholesale prices in any of the periods of incomes policies; only in 1956 and 1965–6 might there have been a direct restraint on retail prices. In fact, the direct effects are positive and significant in a number of cases, particularly where weekly wage rates are used as a measure of labour cost in the price equations. The policy has had a more predictable impact on weekly wage rates, but the tests raise doubts about their being the best measure of labour costs for price decisions. When the indirect effects of wages and earnings are also considered, 1948–50 and 1966–7 are the two periods when the strongest argument can be made for an impact of incomes policies. The case for an impact in 1966–7 is strengthened if an adjustment, which was discussed earlier, is made for the influence of the selective employment tax on prices.

The regressions in Tables 2 to 4 were estimated by the method of ordinary least squares. Since a wage variable appears in a price equation and a price variable in a wage equation there is the statistical problem of bias in the coefficients. In studies by Dicks-Mireaux[23]

[23] Dicks-Mireaux, 'Cost and Price Changes'.

Table 3 Retail price index regressions, coefficients of explanatory variables

Explanatory variable	Quarterly 1Q 1948–2Q 1967		Quarterly 1Q 1948–2Q 1967		Half-yearly 1H 1948–1H 1967		Half-yearly 1H 1948–1H 1967	
	Reg. I	Prop. I	Reg. I	Prop. I	Reg. I	Prop. I	Reg. I	Prop. I
Constant	−0.0127	−0.0106	0.0006	−0.0038	0.0080	0.0102	0.0066	0.0076
$\dot{W}_w$	1.0433 (9.240)	1.0204 (8.042)	—	—	—	—	—	—
$\dot{W}_h$	—	—	0.775 (7.177)	0.870 (7.217)	—	—	—	—
$\dot{W}_{ei}$	—	—	—	—	0.5600 (4.618)	0.5394 (4.420)	—	—
$\dot{W}_{ex}$	—	—	—	—	—	—	0.5941 (5.278)	0.5892 (5.012)
$\dot{P}_{m-1}$	0.0618 (3.272)	0.0644 (2.974)	0.0900 (4.469)	0.0791 (3.593)	0.1294 (5.518)	0.1381 (5.898)	0.1232 (5.561)	0.1280 (5.599)
$\dot{R}$	−0.0682 (1.579)	−0.0553 (1.136)	−0.1724 (3.7536)	−0.1670 (3.609)	−0.2955 (5.194)	−0.2859 (5.484)	−0.2590 (5.153)	−0.252 (5.363)
$I_1(1948\text{--}50)$	0.0190 (3.648)	0.0156 (2.300)	0.0089 (1.630)	0.0105 (1.537)	0.0030 (0.502)	−0.0042 (0.627)	0.0036 (0.654)	−0.001 (0.153)
$I_2(1956)$	−0.0196 (2.721)	−0.0279 (3.177)	−0.0125 (1.575)	−0.0230 (2.532)	−0.0051 (0.587)	−0.0090 (0.944)	−0.0082 (0.998)	−0.0121 (1.324)
$I_3(1961\text{--}2)$	0.0214 (3.160)	0.0231 (2.616)	0.0060 (0.809)	0.0087 (0.975)	0.0083 (1.024)	0.0145 (1.504)	0.0076 (0.999)	0.0132 (1.450)
$I_4(1962\text{--}4)$	−0.0030 (0.641)	−0.0052 (0.986)	−0.0044 (0.842)	−0.0027 (0.477)	−0.0015 (0.269)	−0.0056 (0.942)	−0.0021 (0.415)	−0.0052 (0.920)
$I_5(1965\text{--}6)$	0.0108 (1.984)	0.0070 (1.073)	−0.0036 (0.557)	−0.0126 (1.756)	−0.0088 (1.125)	−0.0136 (1.560)	−0.0091 (1.255)	−0.0147 (1.794)
$I_6(1966\text{--}7)$	0.0121 (1.804)	0.0146 (1.415)	0.0044 (0.587)	0.0167 (1.521)	0.0053 (0.658)	0.0128 (1.005)	0.0026 (0.353)	0.0110 (0.944)
R^2	0.77	0.76	0.71	0.73	0.82	0.84	0.84	0.86

Table 4 Wholesale price index regressions, coefficients of explanatory variables

Explanatory variable	Half-yearly 1H 1948–1H 1967		Half-yearly 1H 1948–1H 1967	
	Reg. *I*	Prop. *I*	Reg. *I*	Prop. *I*
Constant	−0.0029	−0.0161	−0.0036	−0.0169
$\dot{W}_{ei}$	0.4214	0.6023	—	—
	(2.815)	(3.653)	—	—
W_{ex}	—	—	0.4367	0.6186
	—	—	(3.074)	(3.962)
$\dot{P}_m$	0.3554	0.3280	0.3576	0.3294
	(11.865)	(9.408)	(12.362)	(9.850)
$\dot{R}$	−0.0780	−0.0341	−0.0508	0.0045
	(0·905)	(0·383)	(0·621)	(0·053)
I_1(1948–50)	0·0257	0·0256	0·0257	0·0271
	(2·942)	(2·281)	(3·005)	(2·469)
I_2(1956)	0·0271	0·0404	0·0250	0·0373
	(2·074)	(2·418)	(1·938)	(2·293)
I_2(1961–2)	0·0036	0·0080	0·0034	0·0066
	(0·284)	(0·475)	(0·273)	(0·404)
I_4(1962–4)	−0·0106	−0·0110	−0·0111	−0·0110
	(1·242)	(1·072)	(1·335)	(1·109)
I_5(1965–6)	−0·0029	−0·0126	−0·0026	−0·0123
	(0·250)	(0·904)	(0·238)	(0·918)
I_6(1966–7)	0·0024	0·0177	0·0038	0·0140
	(0·191)	(0·847)	(0·031)	(0·706)
R^2	0·86	0·86	0·87	0·86

and by Klein and his colleagues [24] in which wage and price equations for the United Kingdom were estimated both by ordinary least squares and by simultaneous methods the latter method did not greatly affect the size of the coefficients. Table 5 on the next page presents the results of a two-stage least squares test. While there are some important changes in the coefficients, the general picture is much the same as with the ordinary least squares tests.

[24] Klein, Ball, Hazlewood and Vandome, *Econometric Model of the United Kingdom.*

Table 5 Wage and price regressions: method of two-stage least squares, coefficients of explanatory variables[1]

Explanatory variable	Quarterly 1Q 1948–2Q 1967				Half-yearly 1H 1948–1H 1967			
	Weekly wages	Retail prices	Hourly wages	Retail prices	Hourly earnings including overtime	Retail prices	Hourly earnings excluding overtime	Retail prices
Constant	0·0008	-0·0291	0·0110	-0·0312	0·0182	-0·0034	0·0106	-0·0034
U^{-1}	0·0404 (3·539)	—	0·0311 (2·019)	—	0·0434 (1·349)	—	0·0460 (1·571)	—
$\dot{P}_r$	0·3774 (2·835)	—	0·5670 (3·157)	—	0·5875 (2·412)	—	0·5485 (2·474)	—
$\dot{P}_{r-1}$	0·1778 (1·610)	—	-0·0233 (0·156)	—	-0·1890 (0·903)	—	-0·0758 (0·398)	—
$\dot{W}$	—	1·350($\dot{W}_w$) (9·344)	—	1·3560($\dot{W}_h$) (8·060)	—	0·8070($\dot{W}_{el}$) (3·840)	—	0·8137($\dot{W}_{ex}$) (4·238)
$\dot{P}_{m-1}$	—	0·0304 (1·419)	—	0·0306 (1·238)	—	0·0934 (2·894)	—	0·0906 (3·006)
$\dot{R}$	—	-0·0104 (0·223)	—	-0·1046 (2·117)	—	-0·3966 (5·670)	—	-0·3313 (5·608)
$I_1(1948–50)$	-0·0233 (9·023)	-0·0293 (4·877)	-0·0203 (5·843)	0·0272 (4·033)	-0·0133 (1·594)	0·0035 (0·464)	-0·0141 (1·860)	0·0042 (0·595)
$I_2(1956)$	0·0096 (1·843)	-0·0273 (3·556)	0·0121 (1·722)	-0·0270 (3·071)	0·0067 (0·470)	-0·0130 (1·300)	0·0098 (0·754)	-0·0161 (1·653)
$I_3(1961–2)$	-0·0168 (4·404)	0·0262 (3·717)	-0·0048 (0·938)	-0·0066 (0·858)	-0·0079 (0·682)	0·0047 (0·554)	-0·0046 (0·434)	0·0043 (0·541)
$I_4(1962–4)$	0·0057 (1·756)	-0·0006 (0·131)	0·0038 (0·863)	0·0005 (0·093)	0·0037 (0·405)	0·0012 (0·210)	0·0057 (0·680)	-0·0001 (0·017)
$I_5(1965–6)$	-0·0097 (2·998)	0·0115 (2·065)	0·0088 (1·998)	-0·0126 (1·829)	0·0252 (2·637)	-0·0176 (1·777)	0·0231 (2·663)	-0·0166 (1·846)
$I_6(1966–7)$	-0·0125 (3·284)	0·0167 (2·392)	-0·0071 (1·379)	0·0103 (1·319)	-0·0121 (1·069)	0·0086 (0·983)	-0·0062 (0·602)	0·0044 (0·557)
R^2	0·87	0·77	0·78	0·69	0·58	0·80	0·65	0·82

[1] Using regular values of policy dummies only.

Richard G. Lipsey
and Michael Parkin[1]

Chapter 4 Incomes policy: a reappraisal[2]

In this paper we examine the effects of the policies of wage and price restraint that have at various times been employed in Britain since 1945. We have taken the two-equation model that has been studied extensively in the context of data for both the United Kingdom and the United States,[3] and have assumed that, although far from perfect, this model will be a good enough statistical description of wage and price inflation to allow it to catch any major influence of wage and price restraints. In order to see how the potential effects of incomes policies should be specified in this two-equation model, we are forced to examine the derivation of the equations in some detail. In this process we discover that shift dummies which have been used by other investigators[4] to catch the effects of incomes policies are inappropriate and that their use can give rise to misleading results. After conducting tests more satisfactory than those employing shift dummies, we conclude that the data are not inconsistent with the view that wage and price restraints have usually been ineffective in restraining inflation, and also that the restraints have sometimes actually had the effect of raising the rate of inflation above what it would otherwise have been. This perverse effect is very noticeable in the most recent periods of 'restraint' since 1966.

1 The two-equation inflation model and the effects of incomes policy

Virtually all two-equation models of wage and price inflation have been variants of the following prototype model:

[1] Formerly at the University of Essex, currently at Queen's University, Ontario and the University of Manchester, respectively.
[2] Reprinted from *Economica*, May 1970, by permission of the authors and publisher. An earlier version of this paper was presented in April 1969 to the Conference of the Association of University Teachers of Economics.
[3] For a survey of this work, see Bodkin [1]. References in square brackets are listed on pp. 110–11.
[4] See e.g., Smith [2] and PIB Annual Report [7].

7

$$\dot{p} = a_1 + a_2\dot{w}_{-r} + a_3\dot{m}_{-s} + a_4\dot{q}_{-t}, \tag{1}$$

$$\dot{w} = a_5 + a_6[\psi(U)]_{-u} + a_7\dot{p}_{-v} + a_8S_{-w}, \tag{2}$$

where $\dot{p}$ = the proportionate rate of change of an index of prices;[5]
$\dot{w}$ = the proportionate rate of change of wages or earnings;
$\dot{m}$ = the proportionate rate of change of import prices;
$\dot{q}$ = the proportionate rate of change of output per head;
$\psi(U)$ = some function of the percentage of the labour force unemployed (often taken as U or as U^{-1}, but other transformations have been used); and
S = some measure of the aggressiveness of the trade unions. r, s, t, u, v and w are lags in quarters.

A.   *The derivation of the equations*

Our task in this section is to derive equations (1) and (2) from underlying assumptions that are sufficiently well specified for it to be clear how to alter the equations to take account of various hypothesized effects of incomes policy. First, consider the price equation. We start with an identity that relates the market value of final output to the value of measured costs, the value of unmeasured costs and residual profits, all expressed as amounts per unit of output:[6]

$$P \equiv WL + MT + CD + \Pi, \tag{3}$$

where P = market price of final output;
W = price per unit of labour;
L = quantity of labour used per unit of output;
M = price per unit of imported materials;
T = quantity of imports per unit of output;
C = price per unit of other inputs (called unmeasured inputs);
D = quantity of unmeasured inputs per units of output;
Π = profit per unit of output.

In order to make the transition from equation (3) to an *ex ante* price decision function which will yield equation (1), we make the

---

[5] Throughout this paper we use a dot over an upper-case letter to refer to the time derivative of the variable and a dot over a lower-case letter to refer to the time derivative of the logarithm of the variable, i.e., to its proportionate rate of change (thus e.g., $\dot{L}/L \equiv \dot{l}$.)
[6] We could also have included taxes but, since our empirical studies were unable to identify any significant effect arising from tax changes, we have omitted taxes from our analysis.

following assumptions: (1) the quantity of imports per unit of output (T) is constant; (2) unmeasured costs (CD) are a constant fraction μ of measured costs ($WL + MT$); (3) firms aim for a constant proportionate unit mark-up β, and hence aim for $\Pi = \beta P$; and (4) firms' expectations of W, L and M, (W^*, L^* and M^* respectively) are generated by the simplest possible scheme $W^* = W_{-r}$; $M^* = M_{-s}$; and $L^* = L_{-t}$. Using these assumptions with equation (3) yields the price decision equation

$$P = \frac{(1 + \mu)}{(1 - \beta)}(W_{-r}L_{-t} + M_{-s}T), \qquad (4)$$

where μ, β and T are constants, r, s and t are constant lags, and P, W, L and M are variables. Differentiating (4) with respect to time, dividing the resultant equation by P, multiplying the terms on the right-hand side by L_{-t}/L_{-t}, W_{-r}/W_{-r} and M_{-s}/M_{-s} respectively, replacing $\dot{L}/L$ by $-\dot{Q}/Q$ ((minus the proportionate rate of change of output per head), and using lower-case letters for proportionate rates of change (e.g., $\dot{p} = \dot{P}/P$), yields:

$$\dot{p} = \left\{ \frac{(1 + \mu)}{(1 - \beta)} \frac{W_{-r}L_{-t}}{P} \right\} \dot{w}_{-r} + \left\{ \frac{(1 + \mu)}{(1 - \beta)} \frac{M_{-s}T}{P} \right\} \dot{m}_{-s}$$
$$- \left\{ \frac{(1 + \mu)}{(1 - \beta)} \frac{M_{-r}L_{-t}}{P} \right\} \dot{q}_{-t}, \qquad (5)$$

which, for simplicity, we write as

$$\dot{p} = a_1 \dot{w}_{-r} + a_2 \dot{m}_{-s} + a_3 \dot{q}_{-t}. \qquad (6)$$

This is equation (1) with the constant set at zero. Examination of equation (1) in terms of the coefficients of equation (5) gives us two further theoretical restrictions on the parameters: the coefficient on $\dot{q}$ should be minus the coefficient on $\dot{w}$, and the coefficients on $\dot{w}$ and $\dot{m}$ should not be equal to the share of wages and imports in final price but should be larger by a factor $(1 + \mu)/(1 - \beta)$.

Now consider the derivation of the wage equation. The relation between wage changes and unemployment has been outlined by Lipsey [6],[7] and we do not need to repeat the theory here but merely outline

[7] The relation has recently been subjected to some more elaborate and rigorous theorizing, e.g., Holt [5]. This later work confirms that it is possible to derive a Phillips curve from simple and widely acceptable assumptions. For our analysis we will rely on the simpler derivation in Lipsey [6].

its main features. A linear reaction function relating excess demand for labour to the rate of change of money wages in each labour market is postulated. This reaction function is kinked at the origin so that a given amount of excess demand for labour produces a larger absolute change in money wages than does the same amount of excess supply. Aggregation over all markets produces a non-linear macro-relation between aggregate excess demand and the rate of change of an index of money wages. This macro-relation has a positive $\dot{w}$ intercept at zero aggregate excess demand, and this intercept will be larger the greater the dispersion of individual-market excess demands when aggregate excess demand is zero. It is further postulated that a stable relation holds between the percentage of the national labour force unemployed and aggregate excess demand for labour. This is assumed to be a non-linear relation with U approaching zero (or some small positive number) as excess demand approaches infinity. These two relations together produce a non-linear relation between $\dot{w}$ and U—the 'Phillips curve'.

Next consider the relation between wages and prices. *Unanticipated* changes in prices affect wages through excess demand. An *unanticipated* rise in the price level lowers the real wage, raises the excess demand, and, through the mechanism outlined above, leads to a rise in wages. *Anticipated* changes in prices lead to an increase in wages independently of excess demand for labour. Hence, in common with previous studies, we enter the rate of change of prices in the wage equation as a proxy for the *anticipated* rate of change of prices.

Lastly we examine the relation between money wages and union aggressiveness. In such non-competitive situations as bilateral monopoly there is a substantial range over which wages can be determined independently of economic variables, and such considerations as bargaining strength, strategies adopted and possibly union aggressiveness become important. The main problem is how to measure aggressiveness. Hines [4] has suggested that when unions become more aggressive not only do they push harder on money wages but also they raise the rate at which they recruit new members so that the rate of increase of the percentage of the labour force unionized, $\dot{N}$, can be taken as an index of aggressiveness.[8]

[8] Hines [4] also used N, but we have confined ourselves to $\dot{N}$ for two reasons: first, $\dot{N}$ is usually the more significant variable, and, second, the relation between $\dot{w}$ and N contains a very large constant with a very high standard error so that its inclusion makes it impossible to estimate with any precision the intercept of the linear approximation to the Phillips curve.

B   *The representation of incomes policies in the model*

We now ask how we would specify within the model embodied in equations (1) and (2)[9] the various possible effects of price and wage restraint policies, and also examine whether shift dummies, as employed by others, will adequately capture these effects. The policy variable with which we are concerned is the rate of change of the price level.

We distinguish two main policies for controlling the price level: aggregate demand policies and income policies. Aggregate demand policies seek to control $\dot{p}$ by controlling aggregate demand (using fiscal or monetary measures) without attempting to change the links by which aggregate demand affects prices. In our model a fall in aggregate demand would raise U and lower $\dot{w}$ and thus lower $\dot{p}$. We use the term incomes policy to refer to a wide range of alternatives to aggregate demand policy. These alternatives are shown in the 2×3 matrix of Table 1. The two-fold division concerns the equation the policy seeks to work through, while the three-fold division concerns the way in which the policy is supposed to affect the equation. These distinctions may at first sight seem unnecessarily cumbersome, but they are made necessary because there has been so much ambiguous discussion about the way in which various incomes policies are supposed to work, and hence confusion as to where to observe their possible effects.

Wages policies attempt to reduce $\dot{w}$ below what it would otherwise have been, given the level of aggregate demand and hence the level of U. Pure wages policies do not attempt to change the price formation equation but rely on the reduction in $\dot{w}$ to reduce $\dot{p}$ according to the existing price formation relation. Prices policies, on the other hand, seek to work directly through equation (1). They try to affect the level of prices independently of varying $\dot{w}$. The three-fold division relates to the way in which wages and prices policies could affect the relevant

---

[9] In the model described by equations (1) and (2), changes in prices are fully determined by changes in costs. The model can, none the less, handle demand-pull inflations as well as cost-pull ones. Let us see how these work out. A typical full-cost pricing firm will have an equilibrium output where its demand curve cuts its full cost line. An increase in aggregate demand shifts the firm's demand function to the right, thus increasing desired output. This causes an increase in demand for labour which reduces unemployment and raises the money wage rate. This raises the firm's costs and so, following a constant mark-up policy, the firm raises prices. Changes in the price level not necessarily associated with aggregate demand are allowed for in the model through $\dot{m}$, $\dot{q}$ and $\dot{N}$.

Table 1   Incomes policies to reduce $\dot{p}$

	Wages policies	Prices policies
Changing independent variables other than U	1. Reduce S	4. Raise $\dot{q}$ Reduce effective $\dot{m}$
Changing coefficients attached to independent variables	2. Reduce a_6, a_7, a_8	5. Temporarily reduce a_2 or a_3 (while Π is being reduced)
Substituting new relations (new variables or constants) for those existing	3. E.g., a constant wage norm, or making $\dot{w}$ vary, e.g., with the balance of payments position	6. Difficult in the long run, but for short periods margins could be changed in response to many variables other than costs

equations: by varying the value of any of the independent variables other than U, by changing the coefficients attached to some or all of the independent variables, or by breaking the existing relation.

We must now consider how all of these various policies would show up in our model. We distinguish two basic situations: 'policy-off' —no active attempts at incomes policy are being pursued; and 'policy-on'—some active form of incomes policy is being pursued.

(a) *Wages Policies:* We consider each of the cells in Table 1. In cell 1, the only available policy is that of reducing union aggressiveness. If we could measure it directly, we would see a reduction during the policy-on period of the average value of S. Problems arise because of the use of a proxy variable for S. There are two possibilities. First, the decline in S is a general decline in all dimensions of union aggressiveness and the proxy falls with S. Second, the decline in S may be only in respect of aggressiveness in wage bargaining but nothing else. In this case there will be a decline in the coefficient attached to the proxy for S although no change in the coefficient attached to S. Since we use a proxy in our equation, this second case will fall into cell 2. Clearly a shift dummy will not catch either of these effects since the first changes the value taken by an independent variable and the second changes the coefficient attached to that variable.

In cell 2 we have a number of important effects. One goal of incomes policy may be to reduce or to eliminate the response of wages to price changes and so to eliminate any wage-price spiral that would otherwise have existed. This would be shown by a fall in the coefficient attached to $\dot{p}$. With a completely successful policy the coefficient would become zero. We have already seen that the coefficient attached to the proxy for union aggressiveness would fall if unions could be persuaded to channel their militancy in directions other than that of obtaining wage increases. Both the change in the union-aggressiveness and $\dot{p}$ relations could be caught by slope dummies but not by shift dummies.

Now consider a policy that changes the relation linking U to $\dot{w}$. Figure 1 shows the postulated reaction function for a single micro-labour market. A wages policy that reduces, by exhortation or force, the rate of increase of wages associated with any given amount of excess demand will flatten the reaction function in the positive quadrant.

Figure 1

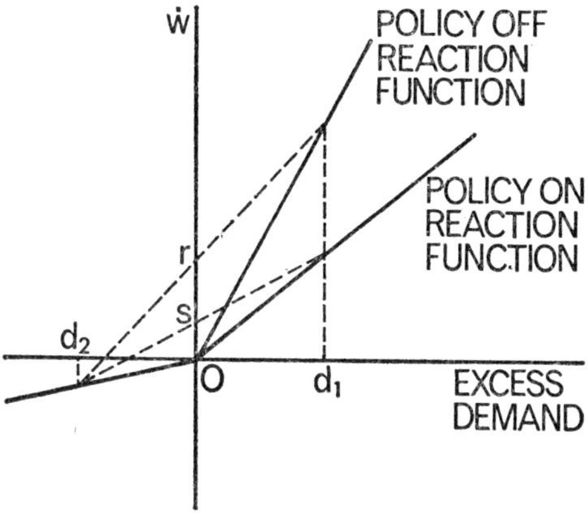

Now consider aggregation over a number of labour markets whose reaction functions are flattened by the wages policy. The effect of this wage restraint policy can be seen by considering aggregation over only two markets equal in size and with identical reaction functions. Suppose (in Figure 1) that the two markets have excess demands of d_1

and d_2 when aggregate excess demand is zero. The average rate of wage rise for the two markets is Or. With the policy-on function and the same micro-levels of unemployment, the average $\dot{w}$ is Os. Only when every market is in the range of excess supply will the average $\dot{w}$ be the same for policy-on as for policy-off. Now assume that the relation between excess demand and unemployment is unchanged. The wages policy thus has the effect of shifting the aggregate Phillips curve downwards except where aggregate U is so high that there is excess supply in every significant micro-labour market.[10]

Next consider cell 3 in Table 1. Here the policy-makers seek to break the relations described by equation (2) and to substitute something in its place. We first consider the case in which they seek to substitute a constant, and then the case in which new variables replace those in equation (2) as the determinants of $\dot{w}$.

In the first case the policy-makers seek to substitute a constant, usually called a 'wages norm', for the relationships described by equation (2). We assume that some norm, $\dot{w}^*$, has been decided upon and is fully enforced. If the norm is a minimum as well as a maximum and the reaction function, in Figure 2, which was ROR, now becomes $\dot{w}^*$

Figure 2

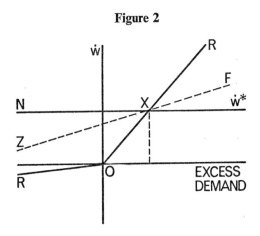

[10] A further change in the relation between $\dot{w}$ and U may result from wage restraint policies. The Phillips relation (as derived in Lipsey [6]) has two components: a reaction function and a relation between excess demand for labour and U. The position of this second relation depends in part on the labour turnover rate. If, as is sometimes believed, incomes policy has increased the amount of labour turnover associated with any given level of excess demand, this will have the effect of shifting the Phillips curve in the 'wrong' direction, i.e., to the right.

throughout, then the Phillips curve becomes, in Figure 3, the broken horizontal line $P'\dot{w}^*$ instead of PP. If, on the other hand, the norm is only a maximum, the reaction function, in the same diagram, becomes $ROX\dot{w}^*$ and the Phillips curve shifts from PP to $PvxP'$.[11] Clearly no combination of shift and slope dummies will catch this basic change in the shape of the Phillips curve.

Figure 3

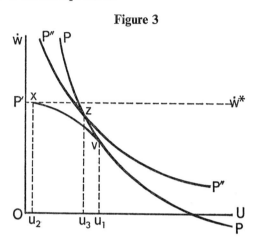

Next consider the more realistic case in which the norm is meant as a maximum only but where also two other influences are at work. First, some sectors of the economy, e.g., nationalized industries, regard the norm as a minimum as well as a maximum. Their reaction curves become $N\dot{w}^*$ in Figure 2. Other sectors may now be forced to give higher wage increases than they otherwise would have done so as not to fall too far behind in relative wages. Their reaction functions may become something like $ZX\dot{w}^*$.[12] The second influence is that the norm is no longer a fully effective ceiling but that it does exert some restraining effect where wage rises would otherwise have exceeded the norm. This makes the reaction curve to the right of X become say XF rather than $X\dot{w}^*$. Thus, in this mixed case, the reaction function for some industries becomes ZXF and for others NXF. If we now map

[11] The point v occurs at a level of overall unemployment where excess demand for labour first reaches Oq (in Figure 2) in at least one micro-labour market. At levels of unemployment below u_1 (in Figure 3) the wages policy begins to take effect. The point x, where the Phillips curve becomes horizontal at $\dot{w}^*$, occurs at a level of over-all unemployment u_2, where excess demands equals or exceeds Oq (in Figure 2) in all micro-labour markets in the economy.
[12] The slope of ZX may bear any relation to the slope of XF, and merely for convenience they are shown the same.

from excess demand to unemployment, assuming the relation between these two variables to be unchanged, we find that the Phillips curve pivots (say at u_3) from PP to $P''P''$ in Figure 3.

Such a pivoting of the Phillips curve cannot be caught either by a slope or by a shift dummy in isolation. To try to catch the change by means of either a slope or an intercept dummy alone would be to obscure the central issue of the location of the point of intersection of the new and the old curve, *which point determines the dividing line between incomes policies that reduce, and those that increase, the rate of inflation*.[13]

So far in cell 3 (in Table 1) we have considered the case in which the policy administrators try, with more or less success, to replace equation (2) by a constant wages norm, $\dot{w}^*$. It is possible, however, to introduce new variables with which $\dot{w}$ is allowed to vary. The administrators of the wage policy could, for example, grant wage increases that varied from year to year according to the state of the balance of payments or the political climate. It is also possible that the authorities might exert some general downward pressure on $\dot{w}$ that varied from year to year, but not systematically in respect to any small number of determining variables. A successful downward pressure that was not systematic with respect to any known variables could be tested for by fitting equation (2) to the policy-off period and then using it to predict $\dot{w}$ into the policy-on period. The prediction errors should generally be positive if the policy were operating as described, but *the effect would not be fully caught by any combination of shift and slope dummies*.

(b) *Prices Policies:* In cell 4 of Table 1 we have policies designed to raise $\dot{q}$. This was certainly one of the hopes of governments in the United Kingdom since the war, but no significant success seems to have been achieved to date. Indeed, average $\dot{q}$ for the 1960's, since active growth policies have been attempted, has been lower than in

---

[13] The potentially misleading effects of shift dummies can be seen by considering a case in which incomes policy completely breaks the relation between $\dot{w}$ and U and substitutes a constant $\dot{w}^*$, and in which the point Z in Figure 3 is at a level of U well above the mean level for the whole period. Fitting an equation with separate shift dummies for each policy-on period will have the following results: (i) the estimated slope of the policy-off Phillips curve will be less than the true slope; (ii) the overall estimated goodness of fit will be lower than the true one; (iii) the shift dummies will have larger and statistically more significant coefficients the further away is the mean U during the particular policy-on period from the U at which the policy-off Phillips curve cuts the $\dot{w}^*$ line. Point (iii) implies that some dummies may appear statistically significant, some statistically insignificant, and some even have positive coefficients in spite of the fact that incomes policy was *completely successful in every case* in breaking the relation between $\dot{w}$ and excess demand.

the 1950's when such policies were not in vogue. The price of imports, on the other hand, can generally be taken as exogenous and so is not available as a policy tool.

Cell 4 refers to cases in which the policy-makers attempt to change the coefficients of the price equation. Since as long as Π is constant the coefficients attached to $\dot{w}$ and $\dot{m}$ should sum to unity, it follows that any change in one variable must be offset by an equal and opposite change in the other. If, however, Π is being reduced, the coefficient will be less than unity *during the transition period.* A shift dummy implies a steady shift in the relation between $\dot{p}$ and $\dot{w}$ and $\dot{m}$, and hence a permanent downward absolute decline in Π. Clearly we cannot take seriously any specification which implies that, as a result of an incomes policy, profit margins will fall continuously and eventually become negative. A temporary downward trend in Π can, however, be checked for by using the price equation fitted to the policy-off period to predict into the policy-on period, and by looking for negative prediction errors during the transition period. (Prediction errors are defined as actual minus predicted values.)

There is a second possibility that is often taken as a justification of a separate prices policy. Assume that a successful wages policy reduces $\dot{w}$ but that, in the face of heavy demand, firms raise their profit margins and thus at least partially frustrate the policy of reducing $\dot{p}$. In this case, the coefficients attached to $\dot{w}$ and $\dot{m}$ will temporarily rise as profit margins are increased. This possibility would show up as positive prediction errors when the policy-off $\dot{p}$ equation was used to predict the policy-on results.

The above discussion reveals two possibilities for a prices policy. First, a wages policy alone may lead to a widening of profit margins and positive prediction errors on $\dot{p}$. Thus a prices policy may be necessary merely to prevent margins from widening. In this case an effective wages and prices policy will lead to no systematic prediction errors on the price equation. Second, our basic pricing hypothesis that Π is a constant may be correct, in which case a wages policy alone will reduce $\dot{p}$ but only by as much as is predicted by the policy-off price equation. In the case of a wages policy alone, there will be no systematic prediction errors when the policy-off $\dot{p}$ equation is used to predict the policy-on results. If there is both a wages policy and a prices policy, profit margins may be narrowed, and we will get systematic negative prediction errors on the price equation while profit margins are being narrowed.

One final effect in this category arises from a possible mis-specification of the labour cost variable when there is wage drift. Assume that a wages policy succeeds in reducing $\dot{w}$, and that, nevertheless, the true cost of labour rises just as it would have done, as a result of wage-drift phenomena that raise earnings without raising rates. If we used earnings in the price equation, we would see no change in price formation behaviour; but, instead, we are using rates which now understate the rise in labour costs. In this case (assuming that $\dot{w}$ is correlated with but understates the true change in unit labour costs) the coefficient on $\dot{w}$ will rise and the sum of the coefficients on $\dot{w}$ and $\dot{m}$ will exceed unity because some of the cost increases that cause P to rise will not be measured by W and M. Thus an $x\%$ rise in W and M will be associated with a more than $x\%$ rise in P.

None of these possible effects leads to the prediction of a downward shift in the constant term in the price equation such as would be picked up by a shift dummy. Indeed, since the theory on which the equation is based predicts that there should not be a significant constant in the equation, it is hard to give any economic meaning to a test that depends on the presence or absence of a significant downward shift in a number that should be zero—except for transitional periods.[14]

2   The model tested empirically

We now define the basic model leaving specific lags to be determined empirically. The model is:

$$\dot{p} = a_1 + a_2\dot{w}_{-r} + a_3\dot{m}_{-s} + a_4\dot{q}_{-t} + \varepsilon, \qquad (7)$$

$$\dot{w} = a_5 + a_6 U_{-u} + a_7\dot{p}_{-v} + a_8\dot{N}_{-w} + \delta. \qquad (8)$$

All level variables are defined in the Appendix and all the proportionate rate-of-change variables $\dot{x}$ are defined as follows:[15] $\dot{x} = X_{+2} - X_{-2}/[\frac{1}{2}(X_{+2} + X_{-2})].100$, where time is measured in quarters. $\dot{N}$ is the first difference of N.

---

[14] On page 87 we assumed that unmeasured costs were perfectly correlated with measured costs. If this is not so and if unmeasured costs have a positive mean rate of change, then some of the influence of unmeasured costs will show up as a positive constant in the price equation. If the mean value of the rate of increase of unmeasured costs were to fall, for any reason whatsoever, during policy-on periods, the constant will fall and a dummy variable will take on a negative value for reasons unrelated to incomes policy.

[15] The reason for defining the rate of change variables as in the text is spelled out in Lipsey [6], pp. 2 and 3, n. 2.

Problems of specification and estimation

A. *Choice of Variables.* The variables are defined in the Appendix and here we mention only special problems concerned with their choice. For our wage variable we chose average weekly rates rather than earnings in spite of wage-drift considerations. The main reason for this choice is that rates are available quarterly while earnings are available only semi-annually, and that we required a quarterly model if it was to discriminate adequately between policy-on and policy-off periods.[16]

According to the theory spelled out in section 1, the data for output per head should cover the same sectors as are covered by the price series. In fact, in order to obtain quarterly observations, we had no choice but to use the index of industrial production and an index of employment in comparable industries.

For two reasons the unemployment variable is entered linearly and not transformed as it is in the Phillips model. First, over the range of variations of U in the post-war period, the linear approximation is empirically a very good one.[17] Second, it was more convenient to have the constant in the wage equation as the intercept of the Phillips curve on the $\dot{w}$ axis rather than as the asymptotic value approached by $\dot{w}$ as U approached infinity.

The series for the percentage of the labour force unionized, required to calculate $\dot{N}$, is reported semi-annually, and we obtained our quarterly observations by taking mid-points between the reported semi-annual figures.

B. *Choice of lags:* Every rate-of-change variable was tried with lags from zero to four quarters. The best lag on unemployment was searched for in a slightly more involved way. Unemployment was first defined as average U over one quarter, and lags from zero to eight quarters were tried. We then defined U as a two-quarters average, and tried lags from zero to seven quarters. Then U was defined as a three-quarters average, and lags up to six quarters tried, and this process was continued until U was defined as an eight-quarters average, and no lags tried.

[16] It is arguable that, even if incomes policy is shown to affect wage *rates*, earnings and prices may continue to behave in the same way as they would have done in its absence. Our findings on the effects of incomes policy on wage rates are, however, that rates rise on average by more than they would have done in the absence of incomes policy, the higher is the level of unemployment. It would have to be shown, therefore, that drift behaved perversely when incomes policies were being operated to offset this result.

[17] We tried U^{-1}, $U^{-3/4}$, $U^{-1/2}$, $U^{-1/4}$, and the fits, both in terms of R^2 and t statistics on the U variable and other variables, were inferior (sometimes only slightly so) to the linear form.

The definition of U and the combinations of lags on each variable that combined to give the highest R^2 was then selected. The U variable so selected is defined as follows: $U = (U' + U'_{-1} + U'_{-2})/3$, where U' represents the average level of unemployment in the ith quarter.[18] For the rate-of-change variables, a zero-quarter lag appears to be the best, except for the import price index. Here, as has been found in earlier studies (e.g., Dicks-Mireaux [3]), a one-quarter lag performs best.

C. *Selection of policy-on and policy-off periods:* When dividing our data into policy-on and policy-off periods, we used the criterion, 'when in doubt include the observation in the policy-on period'. This procedure ensured that our equations describing price and wage formation in policy-off conditions were as free from policy-on influences as we could make them. At the outset we also wanted to make our results as comparable as possible with those of Smith [2]; and when we decided that he seemed also to have followed our principle of classification, it seemed appropriate to use his definition of periods. The policy-on periods selected are as follows:

Period 1: 1947(3)–1950(3). This period started in September 1948 with Cripps' appeal to the unions for wage restraint and to the Federation of British Industries for dividend restraint. It ended with the Trades Union Congress announcing in October 1950 that it was not prepared to pursue wage restraint any longer.

Period 2: 1956(1)–1956(4). There is room for disagreement about the appropriate starting and ending dates of this period of incomes policy. It was not started neatly and ended by clear government announcements. There was, however, evidence throughout 1956 of attempts to establish wages and prices restraint. Activity reached a peak in July 1956 when the Prime Minister had discussions with the TUC and the FBI, and appealed for restraint on both wages and prices. Our primary reason for choosing the whole of 1956 as a policy-on period was to conform to Smith's choice of periods.

Period 3: 1961(3)–1964(3). This period began in 1961(3) with the introduction of traditional restraint policies. The National Incomes Commission was set up in October 1962. The period ended with the election of the Labour government in September 1964.

---

[18] This definition for U raises the possibility of seasonality in the relation. To test for this we ran regressions both with and without seasonal dummies. The seasonal dummies were wholly insignificant in every case, and the other coefficients were insensitive to the introduction of the seasonal dummy.

Period 4: 1964(4)– . This period is a mixed one. It started in the fourth quarter of 1964 with the Labour government dismantling the National Incomes Commission and pledging itself to a more thorough-going prices and incomes policy. In the early part of 1965 the Prices and Incomes Board was established and subsequently the government took legislative power to delay wage and price increases. The way in which the policy has operated in this latest phase since 1965 is for the government to refer to the Board a selection of wage and price increases which exceed the allowable norm. The Board decides, in terms of criteria laid down in the statute which established the Board, whether there is a case for an increase in excess of the norm. The government may then delay the increase in prices or wages if it is judged to violate the criteria for an increase of more than the norm. This situation would seem to correspond closely to the theory of the pivoting Phillips curve. (See the discussion of the curve *XZF* in Figure 2 and $P''P''$ in Figure 3.)

D. *Choice of estimating procedure:* The ordinary least-squares method was used to estimate each of the two equations separately. Ideally we would have liked to use a simultaneous equation estimator such as two-stage least-squares. However, there is a data problem which makes it impossible to use such an estimator. If we could treat all the variables in the two equation sub-system, except $\dot{p}$ and $\dot{w}$, as exogenous and as the only exogenous variables in the entire economy, then two-stage least-squares could be used. However, such two-stage least-squares estimates would rest on the assumption that U, $\dot{q}$, $\dot{m}$ and $\dot{N}$ are exogenous. We think it more reasonable to suppose that $\dot{p}$ and $\dot{w}$, along with U, $\dot{q}$ and $\dot{N}$ (but not $\dot{m}$), are all jointly determined endogenous variables the values of which depend on such exogenous variables as government expenditures, taxes, exports, bank rate and a large number of other exogenous and pre-determined variables. To obtain the two-stage least-squares estimates of the coefficients in the wage and price equations would require (a) that we specify the complete macro model and (b) that quarterly data are available for the time period covered by our study. It would probably be safe to specify a quite crude macro model; however, most macro series in the United Kingdom are not available on a quarterly basis before 1955. We therefore could not estimate even approximately the appropriate reduced forms. Hence two-stage least-squares estimators are not available to us. It follows even more strongly that other simultaneous-equation estimators could not be used.

The model fitted to the whole period

Fitting the equations by ordinary least squares and choosing the lags that maximized the R^2 for each equation[19] gives the following results for the whole period (t statistics in parentheses throughout):

$$\dot{p} = 1{\cdot}374 + 0{\cdot}562\dot{w} + 0{\cdot}085\dot{m}_{-1} - 0{\cdot}145\dot{q}$$
$$\quad [2{\cdot}51] \quad\ [5{\cdot}53] \qquad [4{\cdot}60] \qquad\quad [3{\cdot}48] \qquad\qquad (9)$$
$$R^2 = 0{\cdot}697 \qquad DW = 0{\cdot}946$$

$$\dot{w} = 4{\cdot}147 - 0{\cdot}891U + 0{\cdot}482\dot{p} + 3{\cdot}315\dot{N}.$$
$$\quad [4{\cdot}26] \quad\ [1{\cdot}77] \qquad [5{\cdot}76] \qquad [2{\cdot}09] \qquad\qquad (10)$$
$$R^2 = 0{\cdot}616 \qquad DW = 0{\cdot}742$$

The fit shows the characteristics of the existing state of knowledge on the subject. In the wage equation, the unemployment variable hovers near the conventional margin of significance, the price variable is highly significant with a coefficient of just less than 0·5, and the unionization variable also is significant. The R^2 is significantly greater than zero but much less than we would hope to obtain from a fully satisfactory model, and the Durbin-Watson statistic (DW) indicates, as in the earlier studies, the presence of significant positive serial correlation in the residuals.

The price equation differs somewhat from results of earlier studies fitted to shorter time-periods. This can be illustrated by comparing our results with those obtained by Dicks-Mireaux [3].[20] Our constant, although significantly different from zero, is smaller than Dicks-Mireaux's. Our coefficient on $\dot{w}$, although still too low, is closer to its theoretically expected value than was Dicks-Mireaux's. Our import coefficient is much smaller than Dicks-Mireaux's and further from the theoretical expectation than his. Finally, our coefficient on $\dot{q}$ is further

[19] In order to be able to perform tests for changes in the coefficients between policy-off and policy-on, we employ the same lags in the results reported in the text for policy-off, policy-on and the entire period. The lags reported are those which maximize R^2 in policy-off. The R^2 maximizing lags for policy-on and the entire period are reported in footnotes. The R^2 maximizing lags in the price equation for the entire period are those reported in the text. For the wage equation the maximum R^2 result over the entire period is

$$\dot{w} = 4{\cdot}649 - 1{\cdot}200U_5 + 0{\cdot}473\dot{p} + 3{\cdot}412\dot{N},$$
$$\quad [4{\cdot}85] \quad\ [2{\cdot}35] \qquad [5{\cdot}95] \quad\ [2{\cdot}18]$$
$$R^2 = 0{\cdot}792$$

where U_5 is the average of unemployment in quarter t and the preceding four quarters.

[20] Using our notation, the price equation from Dicks-Mireaux [3, p. 272] is (standard errors in parentheses):

$$\dot{p} = 2{\cdot}47 + 0{\cdot}27\dot{w} + 0{\cdot}21\dot{m}_{-1} - 0{\cdot}54\dot{q}.$$
$$\quad (1{\cdot}39) \ (0{\cdot}04) \qquad (0{\cdot}04) \qquad (0{\cdot}16)$$

away from the negative of the coefficient on $\dot{w}$ than was Dicks-Mireaux's.

The model fitted to the policy-off period

When the equations are fitted solely to the policy-off periods, the changes are dramatic:

$$\dot{p} = -0\cdot140 + 0\cdot851\dot{w} + 0\cdot073\dot{m}_{-1} - 0\cdot092\dot{q},$$
$$[0\cdot16] \quad [5\cdot52] \quad\quad [2\cdot93] \quad\quad\quad [1\cdot90] \tag{11}$$
$$R^2 = 0\cdot843 \quad\quad DW = 1\cdot274$$

$$\dot{w} = 6\cdot672 - 2\cdot372U + 0\cdot457\dot{p} + 0\cdot136\dot{N}.$$
$$[5\cdot79] \quad [3\cdot64] \quad\quad [6\cdot25] \quad\quad [0\cdot07] \tag{12}$$
$$R^2 = 0\cdot856 \quad\quad DW = 1\cdot231$$

Consider the wage equation first. As compared with equation (10), the intercept of the (linear approximation to the) Phillips curve rises, the slope increases substantially, and the whole unemployment fit becomes significant at the 1% level. The price variable retains its significance and the coefficient is virtually unchanged. The Hines' unionization variable becomes totally insignificant with a t statistic of $0\cdot07$. The R^2 rises substantially as does the Durbin-Watson statistic

Table 2   Estimated effects of incomes policies on the rate of wage inflation

Incomes policy years	No. of positive prediction errors	No. of negative prediction errors	Mean prediction error, % p.a.
1. 1948(3)–1950(3)	1	8	−1·778
2. 1956(1)–1956(4)	2	2	+0·290
3. 1961(3)–1964(3)	9	4	+0·220
4. 1964(4)–1968(2)	7	8	+0·322
5. All Labour (1 and 4)	8	16	−0·465
6. All Conservative (2 and 3)	11	6	+0·236
7. All Periods	19	22	−0·174

Standard deviation of residuals for policy-off equation: $0\cdot774$

(although the latter remains unsatisfactorily low, indicating the presence of positive serial correlation in the residuals, significant at the 5% level).

The substantial differences between the fit of the wage equation to the whole period and the fit to the policy-off period only are consistent with the hypothesis that incomes policy has some effect on the system, and that any equation would have to allow for this explicitly or else would have to be fitted solely to the data for the policy-off period. The magnitude of the changes is sufficient to cast doubt upon the validity of all those previous fits for the whole post-war period which have not attempted to allow systematically for the effects of incomes policy.[21]

The changes in the price equation [equation (11) compared with equation (9)] are equally dramatic. The constant satisfactorily conforms to the theoretical expectation that it should be zero. The coefficient on $\dot{w}$ is highly significant and is in reasonable correspondence with the theoretical expectation that it should be $[(1 + \mu)/(1 - \beta)]$ (LW/P). The sum of the two cost coefficients is 0·924 close to its

Table 3   Extimated effects of incomes policies on influencing the rate of price inflation

Incomes policy years	No. of positive prediction errors	No. of negative prediction errors	Mean prediction error, % p.a.
1. 1948(3)–1950(3)	6	3	+0·745
2. 1956(1)–1956(4)	0	4	−1·922
3. 1961(3)–1964(3)	6	7	+0·222
4. 1964(4)–1968(2)	6	5	+0·289
5. All Labour (1 and 4)	12	8	+0·495
6. All Conservative (2 and 3)	6	11	−0·283
7. All Periods	18	19	+0·138

Standard deviation of residuals for policy-off equation: 1·265

[21] Of course, any finite set of observations is always consistent with an infinite set of theoretical explanations. All we can say is that the observations are consistent with the theory that incomes policy does disturb the system. Many other explanations of our results are possible and other studies will no doubt set up and test alternative theories to account for what we have observed.

theoretical expectation. The coefficient on $\dot{q}$, however, remains unsatisfactorily low.

We may now ask how the behaviour of wages and prices differed during policy-on periods from what it would have been if prices and incomes policies had not been employed. To answer this question we used equations (11) and (12) to predict $\dot{p}$ and $\dot{w}$ in the policy-on periods and then compared these predictions with the actual behaviour of wages and prices. The results of this exercise are summarized in Tables 2 and 3 and Figures 4 and 5.

It seems that only in one period of incomes policy did policy exert a significant average downward pressure on wages. This was the policy operated by Cripps from 1948(3) to 1950(3). The average prediction error expressed on an annual basis is -1.8%, which is approximately

Figure 4 The proportionate rate of change of wages: residuals from equation fitted to policy-off periods and prediction errors of that equation for policy-on periods. (The shaded areas are for policy-off and the unshaded for policy-on.)

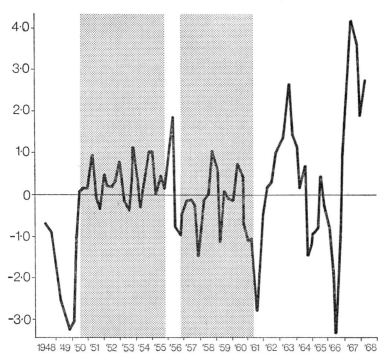

$2\frac{1}{2}$ times the standard deviation of the residuals of the policy-off equation from which the predictions were made. For the other three periods the prediction errors are positive, but all lie within one standard deviation of the residuals of the policy-off equation.

We now look at prices. In the last two periods of incomes policy the average predictions of the policy-off price equation conform very closely to the actual average results. In the first two periods there is a substantial discrepancy. During the Cripps period prices rose an average of 0·75% more than expectation, given the changes in costs and productivity. This suggests that something between a third and a half of the potential anti-inflationary effect of the successful wage restraint was lost. However, this is not significant at the 5% level. During the 1956 policy-on period there is a mean prediction error of almost 2%.

Figure 5 The proportionate rate of change of prices: residuals from equation fitted to policy-off periods and prediction errors of that equation for policy-on periods. (The shaded areas are for policy-off and the unshaded for policy-on.)

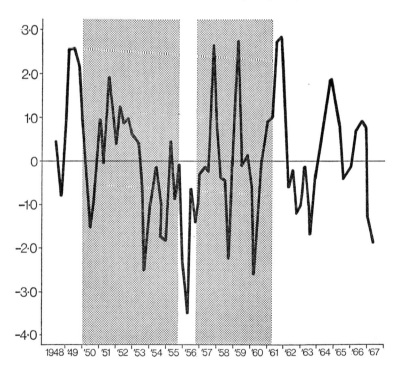

The surface interpretation is that the inflation was temporarily restrained by direct action on price setting. The fact that the price equation was over-predicting throughout the whole period from mid-1953 to the end of 1955 (see Figure 5) suggests that some other forces may have been operating during that period.

A glance at Figure 4 suggests that, although the mean prediction errors for most of the incomes policy periods are not large, some of the individual errors are very large. Indeed, if we divide the latest incomes policy period into two sub-periods, 1964(3) to 1966(4) and 1967(1) to 1968(2), we find that wages rose by 1·16% less than expected in the first sub-period and by 2·53% more than expected in the second sub-period.

The model fitted to the policy-on period

In order to see if the price and wage formation relations had changed in at least some of the possible ways outlined in section 1, we fitted our equation to the policy-on data, and obtained the following results.[22]

$$\dot{p} = 3\cdot874 + 0\cdot014\dot{w} + 0\cdot001\dot{m}_{-1} - 0\cdot198\dot{q},$$
$$[5\cdot65] \quad [0\cdot10] \quad\quad [0\cdot04] \quad\quad\quad [2\cdot68] \quad\quad\quad\quad (13)$$
$$R^2 = 0\cdot241 \quad\quad DW = 1\cdot088$$

$$\dot{w} = 3\cdot919 - 0\cdot404U + 0\cdot227\dot{p} + 3\cdot764\dot{N}.$$
$$[2\cdot27] \quad [0\cdot56] \quad\quad [0\cdot93] \quad\quad [1\cdot61] \quad\quad\quad (14)$$
$$R^2 = 0\cdot138 \quad\quad DW = 0\cdot724$$

Consider, first, the wage equation. Incomes policy seems to have been dramatically successful in weakening the relation between wage changes and unemployment and replacing it by a constant, the size of which we shall study later. It also seems to have weakened the feedback effect from price changes to wage changes. On the other hand, the union-aggressiveness term, which was utterly insignificant during the policy-off periods, has its significance greatly increased. Thus incomes policy seems to create a relation between wage rises and union aggressiveness where none existed before! The R^2 does not differ significantly from zero; an unexplained component in wage changes,

---

[22] The price equation is the R^2-maximizing one, but the wage equation is not. The R^2-maximizing wage equation is

$$\dot{w} = 3\cdot986 - 0\cdot684U_5 + 0\cdot178\dot{p} + 3\cdot419\dot{N},$$
$$[2\cdot94] \quad [1\cdot10] \quad\quad [0\cdot98] \quad\quad [1\cdot69]$$
$$R^2 = 0\cdot162$$

where U_5 is the average of unemployment of the five quarters t to $t - 4$ inclusive.

is, however, significantly serially correlated. Apparently, there is some systematic variability in policy-on wage changes which is not caught by the present model. In summary, it would appear that income policy has to a great extent succeeded in replacing the forces expressed in the wage equation by a constant upward pressure on wages,[23] and has introduced some degree of sensitivity of wage changes to the aggressiveness of unions.

We performed an F test to establish whether the wage equation is structurally different between the policy-off and policy-on periods. On the basis of this test, the wage equations are significantly different at the 5% level.[24] We thought it interesting to establish whether the structural change in the wage equation could be accounted for by an intercept change only, and so we fitted the wage equation to the entire period with a dummy variable (D_p) taking the value of zero for policy-off and unity for policy-on. This equation is

$$\dot{w} = 4\cdot274 - 0\cdot623D_p - 0\cdot774U + 0\cdot481\dot{p} + 3\cdot045\dot{N}.$$
$$[4\cdot50] \quad [2\cdot21] \quad [1\cdot57] \quad [5\cdot89] \quad [1\cdot96] \qquad (15)$$
$$R^2 = 0\cdot640 \qquad DW = 0\cdot780$$

We performed a further F test for the stability of the slope coefficients only. On the basis of this test, the policy-on slope coefficients in the wage equation are not significantly different from their policy-off counterparts at the 5% level, although they are significantly different at the 10% level.[25] This is an impressive result in view of the poor fit of the policy-on equation.

The failure of the policy-on price formation equation to explain more than 25% of the variance in $\dot{p}$ is at first sight rather surprising.

[23] Although the residuals are serially correlated, indicating some systematic variability, the absolute amount of variation in $\dot{w}$ is substantially lower during policy-on periods than during policy-off periods. The standard deviations of $\dot{w}$ are 1·96% policy-off and 1·27% policy-on.

[24] The F test was done to test the null hypothesis, $\beta_1 = \beta_2 = \beta_3$, where β_1, β_2 and β_3 are the vectors of regression coefficients for 'policy-off', 'policy-on' and 'entire' periods, respectively. The calculated value of F is 3·275 with (4·68) degrees of freedom. Hence the null hypothesis is rejected at the 5% level of significance. Full details of this test can be found in Rao [8] pp. 199–200. All these tests should be treated with some caution in view of the low Durbin-Watson statistics.

[25] The F test was carried out on the wage equation to test the null hypothesis: $\beta_1 = \beta_2 = \beta_3$, where β_1, β_2 and β_3 are the vectors of *slope coefficients* for 'policy-on', 'policy-off' and 'entire periods', respectively [the 'entire' being estimated with a shift dummy (equation 15)]. The calculated F is 2·70 with (3·68) degrees of freedom; the critical $F_{3,68}$ at the 5% level of significance is 2·76, so that the null hypothesis is not rejected at that level. The critical $F_{3,68}$ at the 10% significance level is 2·18, so that the null hypothesis is rejected at that level.

One of the possible reasons for this result is important. It seems that the wages norm produces an approximately constant $\dot{w}$ with much of the remaining variation in $\dot{w}$ being random. Thus the significant influence exerted by wages on prices will be for prices to rise by a constant amount equal approximately to 85% of the constant rise in wages. Since variations in $\dot{w}$ around the wages norm are partly random, we would not expect variations in $\dot{p}$ to be significantly associated with these variations in $\dot{w}$. Thus the genuine relation between $\dot{w}$ and $\dot{p}$ would show up as a highly significant constant in the price formation equation and as a non-significant regression coefficient on $\dot{w}$. This is roughly the relation shown in equation (13). Whether or not this provides the correct explanation of the insignificant regression coefficient on $\dot{w}$ is a question which requires further study. We have no explanation for the collapse of the coefficient on $\dot{m}$.

We applied an F test for the structural stability of the price equation as between policy-off and policy-on. The result of this test[26] was that the policy-off price equation coefficients are significantly different from the policy-on coefficients at the 1% level. We also fitted the price equation to the entire period with an intercept dummy (D_p) so that we could perform an F test for the stability of the slope coefficients only. The fitted equation is

$$\dot{p} = 1{\cdot}660 - 0{\cdot}240 D_p + 0{\cdot}528\dot{w} + 0{\cdot}090\dot{m} - 0{\cdot}152\dot{q}.$$
$$[2{\cdot}44] \quad [0{\cdot}71] \qquad [4{\cdot}67] \qquad [4{\cdot}57] \qquad [3{\cdot}54] \qquad (16)$$
$$R^2 = 0{\cdot}702 \qquad DW = 0{\cdot}936$$

On the basis of the test, the policy-on *slope* coefficients only are significantly different from the policy-off coefficients at the 5% level.[27]

3   Conclusion

To consider the effects of incomes policy on wage inflation, we may now compare the policy-on and the policy-off Phillips curves. To do this we let $\dot{N}$ and $\dot{m}$ take on their average values over the whole period

[26] The F test was done to test the null hypothesis, $\beta_1 = \beta_2 = \beta_3$, where β_1, β_2 and β_3 are the vectors of regression coefficients for 'policy-off', 'policy-on' and 'entire' periods, respectively. The calculated value of F is $6{\cdot}37$ with $(4{\cdot}68)$ degrees of freedom. Hence the null hypothesis is rejected at 1% level of significance.

[27] The F test was carried out on the price equation to test the null hypothesis, $\beta_1 = \beta_2 = \beta_3$, where β_1, β_2 and β_3 are the vectors of *slope coefficients* for 'policy-on', 'policy-off' and 'entire' periods, respectively [the 'entire' being estimated with a shift dummy (equation 16)]. The calculated F is $8{\cdot}27$ with $(3{\cdot}68)$ degrees of freedom; the critical $F_{3,68}$ at the 0·1% level of significance is $6{\cdot}17$, so that the null hypothesis is rejected at that level.

and substitute the relation between $\dot{p}$ and $\dot{w}$ from the price formation equation into the wage equation: consequently our Phillips curve allows not only for the initial rise in $\dot{w}$ associated with any level of U but also for the fact that this rise in wages raises prices and thus will cause a further rise in wages. We calculate this reduced-form Phillips curve on two alternative assumptions about $\dot{q}$; (i) $\dot{q} = 2\%$ p.a. (ii) $\dot{q} = 3\%$ p.a. The indirect reduced-form Phillips curves are:

$$\dot{w} = 10\cdot984 - 3\cdot980U \quad \text{Policy-off: } \dot{q} = 2\%$$
$$\dot{w} = 10\cdot911 - 3\cdot980U \quad \text{Policy-off: } \dot{q} = 3\%$$
$$\dot{w} = 4\cdot639 - 0\cdot405U \quad \text{Policy-on: } \dot{q} = 2\%$$
$$\dot{w} = 4\cdot593 - 0\cdot405U \quad \text{Policy-on: } \dot{q} = 3\%$$

Regardless of the $\dot{q}$ assumption made, the policy-off curve cuts the policy-on curve at about $1\cdot8\%$ unemployment. This suggests that incomes policy tends to reduce the rate of wage inflation at levels of unemployment below $1\cdot8\%$, but to increase the rate of inflation above what it would otherwise have been when unemployment is above $1\cdot8\%$.

Figure 6 plots the two relevant reduced-form Phillips curves and the partial scatter diagram for policy-on. This illustrates an important general possibility that is suggested by our analysis. The successful incomes policy that substitutes a wage norm (possibly plus a weak relation between $\dot{w}$ and U) for a normal Phillips curve will have the

Figure 6

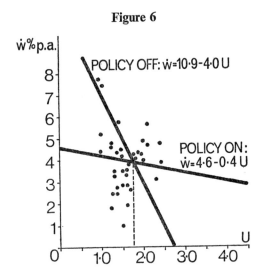

effect of pivoting the reduced-form Phillips curve at a level of $\dot{w}$ *well above the wage norm*. Assuming that the wage norm is chosen to be the non-inflationary wage increase, then the Phillips curve pivots at a level of $\dot{w}$ well above the non-inflationary increase in wages. In these circumstances, a policy that combines an incomes restraint with the depression of aggregate demand sufficient to remove all inflation will require a much higher level of unemployment than will a policy that relies solely on depressing aggregate demand without wage restraint. According to the relations we have estimated for the United Kingdom and illustrated in Figure 6, if the non-inflationary wage increase is 3% p.a., this will require about 2·1% unemployment if no incomes policy is in operation, but approximately 4% unemployment if an incomes policy is used as well as an aggregate demand policy. The divergence is even more marked if the non-inflationary wage increase is as low as 2% p.a. To achieve this would require about 2·3% unemployment without an incomes policy, and about 6·8% unemployment with an incomes policy.

On the other hand, a policy that accepts a moderate-to-large rate of inflation and seeks to reduce unemployment to the lowest possible level may be more successful with an incomes policy than without it. This will be true if the accepted rate of inflation is greater than that which results from the $\dot{w}$ occurring at the point where the policy-on and policy-off Phillips curves intersect. To illustrate with the relations that we have estimated for the United Kingdom and which are shown in Figure 6, a policy that accepts a $\dot{w}$ of $4\frac{1}{4}\%$ p.a. can allow unemployment to fall as low as 1·1% if an incomes policy is operated, but only as low as 1·7% if there is no such policy.[28]

It is true, of course, that all the above remarks must be subject to a wide range of error in view of the poor fit of the policy-on wage equation. However, inspection of the partial scatter, in Figure 6, of the policy-on behaviour of $\dot{w}$ and U indicates that, whenever unemployment has been above 1·8% (the pivot point), wages have risen by more than would have been predicted by the policy-off equation. On the other hand, when unemployment has been less than 1·8%, wages have risen by less than the policy-off prediction in all but four cases.

---

[28] We are aware of the many theoretical arguments that these curves cannot remain stable in the long run once expectations adjust to them. Those who find these arguments compelling can regard our statements as statements about short-term relations when incomes and aggregate demand policies are used to affect $\dot{w}$ and $\dot{p}$ over periods of not more than a few years.

The moral of this story is that to break the existing relation between excess demand and wage rises and to replace it by a constant (plus a very much weakened association with excess demand) is not an un-mixed blessing. It has most to recommend it if the economy is to be run at a very high level of demand and some inflationary price rises accepted. If an attempt is to be made to *reduce demand* sufficiently to keep increases down to the level of increases in productivity (so that an approximately stable price level is achieved), then a reasonably successful incomes policy (with a wage norm) would seem to make the achievement of the goal very much more difficult than if no such policy were operated.

Appendix   Definitions of variables and sources of data [See equations (7) and (8)]

  P: Index of Retail Prices, MDS, 'all items' index. Quarterly figures are obtained by averaging monthly data.

  W: Index of weekly wage rates as in the MDS in 'all industries and services' table and 'male and female' column. Quarterly figures are again obtained by averaging monthly data.

  U: Percentage of registered labour force wholly unemployed as a percent of total in civil employment as in the *Ministry of Labour Gazette* (now *Employment and Productivity Gazette*), or MDS. The figures used seasonally unadjusted and quarterly figures were obtained as averages of monthly data.

  N: Percentage of labour force unionized. Source: *Ministry of Labour Gazette*. Quarterly data obtained by interpolation.

  M: Import unit value index as in the Index of Import Prices in the MDS.

  R: Index of industrial production in the MDS. Quarterly data obtained by averaging three monthly entries.

  E: Index of industrial production employees as in the *Ministry of Labour Gazette*, consisting of total manufacturing plus mining and quarrying plus construction plus gas, electricity and water. Quarterly data obtained by averaging three monthly entries.

  Q: R/E.

  'MDS' refers to the *Monthly Digest of Statistics* published by the Central Statistical Office.

References

[1] R. G. Bodkin, *The Wage, Price, Productivity Nexus*, Philadelphia, 1966.
[2] D. C. Smith, 'Income Policy', Chapter III in R. E. Caves, (ed.), *Britain's Economic Prospects*, 1968. Abridged as Chapter 3, above.
[3] L. A. Dicks-Mireaux, 'The Interrelationship between Cost and Price Changes, 1946–1959. A Study of Inflation in Post-War Britain', *Oxford Economic Papers*, vol. 13 (1961), pp. 267–92.
[4] A. G. Hines, 'Trade Unions and Wage Inflation in the United Kingdom, 1893–1961', *Review of Economic Studies*, vol. 31 (1964), pp. 221–52.
[5] C. C. Holt, 'Improving the Labor Market Trade-off between Inflation and Unemployment', *American Economic Review: Papers and Proceedings*, vol. LIX (1969), pp. 135–46.

[6] R. G. Lipsey, 'The Relation between Unemployment and the Rate of Change of Money Wage Rates in the United Kingdom, 1862–1957: A Further Analysis', *Economica*, vol. XXVII (1960), pp. 1–31.
[7] National Board for Prices and Incomes, *Third General Report*, Report No. 77, Cmnd. 3715, 1968. Appendix A: A Preliminary Study of the Effects of Incomes Policy, pp. 63–7.
[8] C. R. Rao, *Linear Statistical Inference and its Applications*, New York, 1965.

Michael Parkin[1]

Chapter 5 Incomes policy: some further results on the rate of change of money wages[2]

1

In an earlier paper, Lipsey and Parkin[3] reported that the rate of change of money wages in the United Kingdom is closely related inversely to the level of unemployment in times when income restraint policies are not being operated, and that it is approximately constant and independent of the level of unemployment when these policies are being operated.[4] If the Lipsey-Parkin analysis is correct, there is a crucial level of unemployment *below* which restraint policies will, on the average, be successful and *above* which such policies will, on the average, fail. That crucial level of unemployment was calculated to be 1·8%. There is, of course, a considerable range of error on this point estimate. The equations on the basis of which this conclusion was reached are:[5]

'Policy off' $\dot{w} = 6·672 - 2·372U + 0·475\dot{p} + 0·136\dot{N}$
$\quad\quad\quad\quad [5·79]\quad [3·64]\quad\quad [6·25]\quad\quad [0·07]$
$\quad\quad\quad\quad\quad R^2 = 0·856 \quad\quad DW = 1·231$

[1] Ann Dowden and Rodney Barrett collected the data and Rodney Barrett supervised the calculation of the regressions reported. Robyn Kemmis modified the non-linear estimation programme BMDX85 used for some of the regressions.
    Valuable comments were made on an earlier version of this paper presented at a seminar organized by the National Institute for Economic and Social Research and PhD Labour Workshop at the University of Essex. Professors Christopher Archibald, David Laidler and Richard Lipsey have supplied much-needed criticism and stimulation.
    [2] Reprinted from *Economica*, November 1970, by permission of the publisher.
    [3] Chapter 4 above [3].
    [4] References in square brackets are listed at the end of this chapter.
    [5] The policy-off equation was estimated using quarterly data for the period 1950(4) to 1955(4) and 1957(1) to 1961(2), and the policy-on equation, using quarterly data for 1948(3) to 1950(3), 1956(1) to 1956(4) and 1961(3) to 1967(2). The data definitions and sources for these and all the other regressions reported can be found in the appendix to this paper.

'Policy on'[6] $\dot{w} = 3\cdot919 - 0\cdot404U + 0\cdot227\dot{p} + 3\cdot764\dot{N}$
$\quad\quad\quad\quad\quad$ [2·27] [0·56] [0·93] [1·61]
$\quad\quad\quad\quad\quad R^2 = 0\cdot138 \quad\quad DW = 0\cdot724$

where $\dot{w}$ = the proportionate rate of change of weekly wage rates.
$\quad\quad \dot{p}$ = the proportionate rate of change of retail prices,
$\quad\quad U$ = the percentage of the labour force unemployed, measured
$\quad\quad\quad$ as the average of the current and preceding two quarters,
and $\dot{N}$ = the change in the percentage of the labour force
$\quad\quad\quad$ unionized.

These equations speak for themselves. In the policy-off equation, all the coefficients other than that on $\dot{N}$ are well determined and have appropriate signs. In the policy-on equation there is, in effect, no relationship between $\dot{w}$ and the 'independent' variables.

Three criticisms may be made of this Lipsey-Parkin work. The first criticism concerns the estimation procedures and statistical tests employed. There are two causes for concern here: (a) The independent variables used are stochastic and jointly determined with the dependent variable; this suggests the desirability of using a simultaneous equation estimator. (b) There appears to be some auto-correlation in the residuals of the model, as seen from the Durbin-Watson statistic. In the case of the policy-on wage equation, it seems that the auto-correlation might be very serious.

It is felt that the problems connected with the stochastic simultaneity of the variables in this system are too large to be tackled, given the present state of our knowledge of the structure of the United Kingdom economy. Even the use of two-stage least-squares would involve a quite arbitrary reduced-form specification to which the resultant structural parameters estimated could be quite sensitive.

However, the second statistical problem, that of auto-correlated residuals, is handled fairly readily. It is particularly important that an attempt be made to remove such auto-correlation so that the

[6] The equation in the text is that reported in Lipsey-Parkin and is based on the time period noted in footnote 3, above. The equation has been re-estimated adding the observations from 1967(3) to 1969(1) and gives the following results:

$$w = 2\cdot313 + 0\cdot332U + 0\cdot376\dot{p} + 1\cdot053\dot{N}$$
$$\quad [2\cdot00] \quad [0\cdot63] \quad\quad [2\cdot03] \quad\quad [1\cdot06]$$
$$\quad R^2 = 0\cdot157 \quad\quad DW = 0\cdot678$$

Although the unemployment slope is now positive, it is not well determined. However, the price-change coefficient is now bigger and much better determined.

hypotheses about the differences in the wage-determining process in policy-off and policy-on periods can be tested in a formally correct manner.[7] A clue to a potential source of the auto-correlation problem is found in the work of Phelps [4]. The rate of price inflation variable, $\dot{p}$, used in the Lipsey-Parkin wage equation is the *actual* proportionate rate of change of retail prices. The coefficients on that variable are 0·475 and 0·227 for policy-off and policy-on, respectively.[8] Now *actual* $\dot{p}$ is being used as a proxy for *expected* $\dot{p}$. Those who emphasize the importance of inflation expectations argue that the coefficient on *expected* $\dot{p}$ should be unity. It seems sensible, therefore, to modify the way in which $\dot{p}$ enters the model and to specify an explicit scheme for the generation of expectations. This procedure will enable us both to introduce a (potential) way of removing auto-correlation in the residuals and to give a further and perhaps fairer test of the hypothesis that the coefficient on expected $\dot{p}$ is unity.

The second criticism of the earlier Lipsey-Parkin work basically is to the effect that the findings are consistent with the hypothesis that the inflation-unemployment trade-off has worsened for reasons other than the effects of wage restraint policies. In particular, it has been suggested that changes in redundancy and unemployment benefits in the United Kingdom, and especially those introduced at the end of 1966, have shifted the relation between unemployment and the excess demand for labour so that any given amount of excess demand for labour will be associated with a higher level of unemployment. Earlier work by Corry and Laidler [1] suggests a way in which this can be tested: we can test separately the wage-rate reaction function and the mapping from unemployment to excess demand for labour. If it is the reaction function which shifts between policy-off and policy-on periods and if the excess-demand/unemployment mapping is stable, there will be a presumption in favour of the original Lipsey-Parkin results. If the excess-demand/unemployment mapping has shifted, the original results will require modification.

The third criticism concerns the choice of wage variable to be used. It would be useful to examine the effects of incomes policy on *earnings* as well as on *wage rates*. This paper, like that by Lipsey and Parkin, examines only the rate of change of weekly wage rates. Explorations of the behaviour of earnings will require a more sophisticated model,

---

[7] The F tests employed in Lipsey-Parkin were, of course, only approximate: see Chapter 4, note 23, above.

[8] It is 0·376 for the extended policy-on period. See note. 6, above.

and its formulation has not yet been attempted. Such a model would have to explain normal hours and overtime hours as well as the underlying wage rates. To the extent that Smith's results[9] can be relied upon, they indicate that earnings are less disturbed by policies of income restraint than are wage rates.[10]

This paper deals, then, with two of the three criticisms. In section 2, price-inflation expectations are introduced into the wage equation and the effects on both the wage inflation process and the previous Lipsey-Parkin results are explored. In section 3 the wage reaction function and the excess-demand/unemployment mapping are investigated.

The conclusions reached are: (1) the introduction of expected $\dot{p}$ (with adaptive expectations) into the wage equation overcomes the problem of auto-correlation in the residuals; but (2) the coefficient on *expected $\dot{p}$* is less than 1, and does not differ much from that estimated on *actual $\dot{p}$* (3.) The wage reaction function is well determined in policy-off periods but is flat in policy-on periods, and (4) the mapping from excess demand to unemployment has been remarkably *stable* over the entire period investigated. The broad conclusions of the previous Lipsey-Parkin work stand, but with some aspects of those conclusions strengthened. There is, apparently, even in the long run, a trade-off between inflation and unemployment. That trade-off has, however, been broken by policies of incomes restraint to give a rate of inflation which appears to be independent of the level of unemployment.

2

The hypothesis about wage determination which was employed in Lipsey and Parkin [3] was, in effect:[11]

$$\dot{w} = \alpha_1 + \beta_1 U + \gamma_1 \dot{p}^e + \varepsilon, \tag{1}$$

$$\dot{p}^e = \dot{p}, \tag{2}$$

where $\dot{p}^e = $ *expected* proportionate rate of change of retail prices, and the other variables are as defined on p. 113.

The estimating equation is simply $\dot{w} = \alpha_1 + \beta_1 U + \gamma_1 \dot{p} + \varepsilon$. It is

[9] See Chapter 3 above [5].

[10] We do not mean to imply that Smith's results are inaccurate, but that the use of a shift dummy to capture the effects of incomes policy can be misleading; see Chapter 4 above [3].

[11] The separate introduction of $\dot{p}^e$ was implicit, though it was not introduced formally. $\dot{N}$ has been dropped in this study since it was not significant in the earlier work.

this equation which displays positive auto-correlation in the residuals. The modification which is explored in this section is to specify $\dot{p}^e$ as the outcome of an adaptive expectations generation scheme, i.e.,

$$\dot{p}^e = \lambda\dot{p} + (1 - \lambda)\dot{p}^e_{-1}, \qquad 0 \le \lambda \le 1. \tag{3}$$

Combining equation (1) with equation (3), and applying a Koyck transformation, yields

$$\dot{w} = a_0 + a_1 U + a_2 U_{-1} + a_3\dot{p} + a_4\dot{w}_{-1} + v, \tag{4}$$

where $a_0 = \alpha_1\lambda$, $a_3 = \gamma_1\lambda$,
$\quad\ \ a_1 = \beta_1$, $a_4 = (1 - \lambda)$,
$\quad\ \ a_2 = -\beta_1(1 - \lambda)$ and where $v = \varepsilon - (1 - \lambda)\varepsilon_{-1}$.

The error term, v, will be a first-order moving average of ε. We approximate this by specifying a first-order auto-correlation scheme for v,[12] i.e.,

$$v = \rho_1 v_{-1} + z, \tag{5}$$

where $E[z] = 0$, and $E[zz'] = \sigma_z^2 I$.

A further transformation of equations (4) and (5) yields

$$\dot{w} = b_0 + b_1 U + b_2 U_{-1} + b_3 U_{-2} + b_4\dot{p} + b_5\dot{p}_{-1} \\ + b_6\dot{w}_{-1} + b_7\dot{w}_{-2} + z \tag{6}$$

where $b_0 = \alpha_1\lambda(1 - \rho_1)$, $b_4 = \gamma_1\lambda$,
$\quad\ \ b_1 = \beta_1$, $b_5 = -\gamma_1\lambda\rho_1$,
$\quad\ \ b_2 = -\beta_1(1 - \lambda + \rho_1)$, $b_6 = (1 - \lambda + \rho_1)$,
$\quad\ \ b_3 = \beta_1(1 - \lambda)\rho_1$, $b_7 = -(1 - \lambda)\rho_1$.

The parameters in the two models in equations (4) and (6) may be estimated by non-linear constrained least squares.[13] The results obtained[14] are set out in Tables 1 and 2. (The asymptotic standard errors are shown in parentheses; and $\hat{\sigma}^2$ is the variance of residuals.)

[12] There is some evidence from a Monte Carlo study that the parameter estimates will not be biased as a result of this approximation. I am indebted for this point to David Hendry of the London School of Economics and Pravin Trivedi of Southampton University. See [2].
[13] The programme used was BMDX85, written by the Health Services Computing Facility, University of California, Los Angeles, and converted to CDC 3600 by the Data and Programme Library Service, University of Wisconsin. This was further converted to operate on an ICL 1900 by Miss Robyn Kemmis of the University of Essex.
[14] All the results in this paper are based on the following data periods— policy-on: 1948(3) to 1950(3), 1956(1) to 1956(4), and 1961(3) to 1969(1); policy-off: 1950(4) to 1955(4), and 1957(1) to 1961(2).

Table 1 Model 1, $\rho_1 = 0$, equation (4)

	α_1	β_1	γ_1	λ	$\hat{\sigma}^2$
Policy off	6·967	−2·542	0·472	0·554	0·605
	(1·587)	(0·869)	(0·100)	(0·141)	
Policy on	−0·098	1·701	0·347	0·240	0·788
	(2·632)	(0·891)	(0·471)	(0·083)	
Entire	2·097	0·069	0·650	0·282	0·815
	(1·480)	(0·666)	(0·168)	(0·076)	

What emerges from these results is very clear. The policy-off wage equation with a distributed-lag function generating expected $\dot{p}$ improves considerably the over-all fit as compared with the use of actual $\dot{p}$.

The first-order auto-correlation in the residuals seems to be taken care of by this modification. The coefficient on expected $\dot{p}$ remains less than one half. Expectations adjust quite rapidly, with the weight on current actual $\dot{p}$ being in the region of 0·6. The alternative estimates of the parameters in the $\dot{w}$ equation are summarized in Table 3.

Regardless of the precise specification, the intercept in the linear Phillips curve is about 7, the unemployment coefficient about $-2·5$, and the $\dot{p}$ coefficient a little under 0·5. All these coefficients are well determined. In all three alternative estimates of the policy-off $\dot{w}$ equation, the only non-significant coefficient (at the 0·05 level) is the auto-regression parameter ρ_1. This suggests that the employment of an adaptive formulation of price-inflation expectations is sufficient to remove all the significant auto-correlation in the residuals of the $\dot{w}$ equation.

Table 2 Model 2, $\rho \neq 0$, equation (6)

	α_1	β_1	γ_1	λ	ρ_1	$\hat{\sigma}^2$
Policy off	7·283	−2·629	0·421	0·609	0·277	0·582
	(1·845)	(1·001)	(0·127)	(0·216)	(0·238)	
Policy on	1·223	1·390	0·166	0·475	0·516	0·707
	(2·728)	(0·949)	(0·500)	(1·275)	(1·319)	
Entire	3·007	0·005	0·440	0·439	0·483	0·701
	(1·674)	(0·762)	(0·202)	(0·203)	(0·229)	

Table 3   Policy-off wage equations

Parameter	OLS[1] ($\lambda = \rho_1 = 0$)	NLCLS[2] ($\lambda \neq 0; \rho_1 = 0$)	NLCLS[2] ($\lambda \neq 0; \rho_1 \neq 0$)
α_1	6·672	6·967	7·283
β_1	−2·372	−2·542	−2·629
γ_1	0·475	0·472	0·421
λ	—	0·554	0·609
ρ_1	—	—	0·277

[1] Ordinary least squares.
[2] Non-linear constrained least squares.

The policy-on equations reported in Tables 1 and 2 display odd characteristics. The parameter estimates which emerge are extremely sensitive to specification changes and lend general confirmation to the non-existence of a $\dot{w}$ to U trade-off during periods of incomes policy. For ease of comparison, the alternative policy-on equations are set out in Table 4. Although these parameters move around a good deal

Table 4   Policy-on wage equations

Parameter	OLS[1] ($\lambda = \rho_1 = 0$)	NLCLS ($\lambda \neq 0; \rho_1 = 0$)	NLCLS ($\lambda \neq 0; \rho_1 \neq 0$)
α_1	2·313	−0·098	1·223
β_1	0·332	1·701	1·390
γ_1	0·376	0·347	0·166
λ	—	0·240	0·475
ρ_1	—	—	0·516

[1] These parameters are based on the equation reported in note 6, above, and relate to the same time period as the non-linear constrained estimates.

depending upon specification, hardly any of them are significant at the 5% level, with the exception of the intercept in the first equation and λ in the second equation.

In order to test for the stability of the $\dot{w}$ equation between policy-off and policy-on periods, an F test was performed for the hypothesis that, in equation (4) (i.e., Model 1), the vector of policy-off coefficients is equal to those for policy-on. The computed value of F is 4·160. The

Figure 1

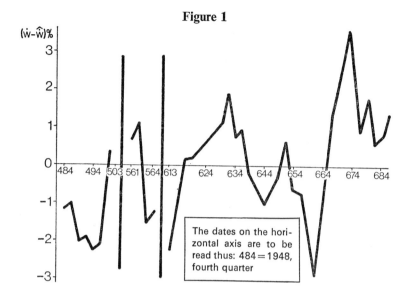

The dates on the horizontal axis are to be read thus: 484 = 1948, fourth quarter

critical value of F (with 4, 75 degrees of freedom) is 2·51. Hence the hypothesis is rejected, and it is concluded that the $\dot{w}$ function is different between the two sub-periods.

Further, in order to establish *which* coefficients are different between policy-off and policy-on, t tests were performed on the individual parameters. The calculated t statistics are: constant, α, 2·300; unemployment slope, β, 3·409; price slope, γ, 0·260, and the price expectation parameter, λ, 1·919. Hence at the 5% level, the only parameters which differ between policy-off and policy-on are the constant and the unemployment slope.

In order to check for the effects of incomes-restraint policy, the policy-off wage equation reported in Table 1[15] has been used to calculate what $\dot{w}$ would have been had there been no such policy. The results of this exercise are set out in Figure 1 and summarized in Table 5. The mean effect of income policy is nil. The Cripps period [1948(3) to 1950(3)] resulted in a gain of more than 1% per annum, while other periods of policy had no significant effect. The pattern of residuals is almost identical to that revealed by the simpler $\dot{w}$ equation. Thus, the broad findings of the Lipsey-Parkin study are confirmed and strengthened by this more refined analysis of the $\dot{w}$ equation.

[15] This equation was used in preference to that in Table 2 on the grounds that ρ_1 is estimated as a small and non-significant parameter.

Table 5   Estimated effects of incomes policies in influencing the rate of wage inflation

Incomes policy years	Number of positive prediction errors	Number of negative prediction errors	Mean prediction error, % p.a.
1. 1948(3)–1950(3)	2	6	−1·154
2. 1956(1)–1956(4)	2	2	−0·230
3. 1961(3)–1964(3)	9	4	+0·164
4. 1964(4)–1969(1)	10	8	+0·400
5. All Policy Years	23	20	+0·019

Standard deviation of residuals for policy-off equation: 0·778.

3

In the preceding section it has been established that the wage inflation-unemployment trade-off is effectively broken during periods of incomes policy. This section attempts to unravel whether it is restraint policies or some other factors which have led to the breaking of that trade-off. The way in which this is done is to examine separately the wage-rate reaction function and the excess-demand/unemployment mapping.

The reaction function may be written as

$$\dot{w} = \alpha_2 + \beta_2 E + \gamma_2 \dot{p}^e + \varepsilon_1, \tag{7}$$

where E = percentage excess demand for labour (defined as Vacancies minus Unemployment).

The unemployment excess demand mapping may be written as

$$E = \alpha_3 + \beta_3 U + \varepsilon_2. \tag{8}$$

The linear specification of this equation is, of course, only an approximation. However, since the Phillips curve with which we are working is linear, it seems appropriate to specify linear forms for the two underlying relationships from which that curve is constructed.

Equations (7) and (8) may be combined to give

$$\dot{w} = (\alpha_2 + \beta_2\alpha_3) + \beta_2\beta_3 U + \gamma_2\dot{p}^e + (\varepsilon_1 + \beta_2\varepsilon_2), \text{ or} \tag{9}$$
$$\dot{w} = \alpha_1 + \beta_1 U + \gamma_1\dot{p}^e + \varepsilon,$$

which is the (linearized) Phillips-curve version of the $\dot{w}$ equation estimated in section 2. If the reaction function, equation (7), is broken by
incomes policy, and the excess-demand/unemployment mapping,
equation (8), is stable, there is a presumption in favour of the original
Lipsey-Parkin result. If, on the other hand, it is the excess-demand/
unemployment mapping which collapses during periods of incomes
policy, then Lipsey-Parkin could have picked up some effects of the
$(\dot{w} - U)$ relation which are unrelated to incomes policy. A further
possibility has to be investigated. It may be the case that the excess-
demand/unemployment mapping is stable but that it depends on
additional variables omitted from the original study, such as, for
example, unemployment and redundancy benefits. If this is the case,
the mapping in the $E - U$ space may have shifted in such a way as to
have *worsened* the $\dot{w} - U$ trade-off, and thus weakening the Lipsey-
Parkin conclusions about the adverse effect on inflation of the most
recent phases of incomes policy.

We begin by looking at the reaction function, equation (7). If we
assume that $\dot{p}^e = \dot{p}$, we can estimate the parameters in this model by
ordinary least squares. The results are set out in Table 6. (The t values
are in square brackets.)

Table 6   Ordinary least squares estimates of the $\dot{w}$ reaction function

	α_2	β_2	γ_2	R^2	DW
Policy-off	3·619	1·607	0·388	0·872	1·249
	[10·96]	[4·53]	[5·37]		
Policy-on	2·621	−0·462	0·422	0·174	0·622
	[3·92]	[1·71]	[2·40]		
Entire	2·260	−0·023	0·628	0·548	0·659
	[7·17]	[0·11]	[8·90]		

It is evident that these $\dot{w}$ reaction functions display the same characteristics as the Phillips-curve version of the $\dot{w}$ equation. The coefficient
on excess demand is appropriately positive and quite well determined
in the policy-off equation, but it is negative (and statistically insignificant) in the policy-on equation. This agrees with the perverse slope
found on the $\dot{w}$-unemployment relation for policy-on. The coefficient
on $\dot{p}$ is slightly lower than in the unemployment variant of the equation
for policy-off. Also, just as in the unemployment version, the Durbin-

Watson statistic indicates the presence of positive first-order auto-correlation in the residuals. In order to try to eliminate the auto-correlation, the modification embodied in equation (3) is incorporated. That is, it is assumed the $\dot{p}$ expectations are adaptive. Using equation (3) with equation (7) yields models identical to those in equations (4) and (6) except that excess demand replaces unemployment. That is, if we ignore auto-correlation in v,

$$\dot{w} = c_0 + c_1 E + c_2 E_{-1} + c_3 \dot{p} + c_4 \dot{w}_{-1} + v, \qquad (10)$$

where $c_0 = \alpha_2$, $c_3 = \gamma_2 \lambda$,
$c_1 = \beta_2$, $c_4 = (1 - \lambda)$;
$c_2 = -\beta_2 (1 - \lambda)$,

and, with v following a first-order auto-regressive scheme, i.e., $v = \rho_2 v_{-1} + z$, we have

$$\dot{w} = d_0 + d_1 E + d_2 E_{-1} + d_3 E_{-2} + d_4 \dot{p} + d_5 \dot{p}_{-1}$$
$$+ d_6 \dot{w}_{-1} + d_7 \dot{w}_{-2} + z, \qquad (11)$$

where $d_0 = \alpha_2 \lambda (1 - \rho_2)$, $d_4 = \gamma_2 \lambda$,
$d_1 = \beta_2$, $d_5 = -\gamma_2 \lambda \rho_2$,
$d_2 = -\beta_2 (1 - \lambda + \rho_2)$, $d_6 = (1 - \lambda + \rho_2)$,
$d_3 = \beta_2 (1 - \lambda) \rho_2$, $d_7 = -(1 - \lambda) \rho_2$.

These parameters were estimated[16] and the results are set out in Tables 7 and 8. (Asymptotic standard errors are shown in parentheses; and $\hat{\sigma}^2$ is the variance of residuals.)

These results strongly confirm the ordinary least squares estimates reported in Table 6, and add confirmation to the original results on the breaking of the $\dot{w}$-unemployment relation. They also indicate

Table 7   Model 3, $\rho_2 = 0$, equation (10)

	α_2	β_2	γ_2	λ	$\hat{\sigma}^2$
Policy-off	3·609	1·599	0·399	0·613	0·565
	(0·456)	(0·449)	(0·099)	(0·139)	
Policy-on	2·212	−0·975	0·438	0·270	0·791
	(1·711)	(0·517)	(0·432)	(0·087)	
Entire	2·223	−0·011	0·646	0·282	0·815
	(0·751)	(0·346)	(0·170)	(0·076)	

[16] The estimation procedures are the same as those described in note 13, above.

Table 8   Model 4, $\rho_2 \neq 0$, equation (11)

	α_2	β_2	γ_2	λ	ρ_2	$\hat{\sigma}^2$
Policy-off	3·741	1·636	0·364	0·664	0·236	0·554
	(0·542)	(0·508)	(0·119)	(0·234)	(0·259)	
Policy-on	3·098	−0·830	0·230	0·483	0·502	0·711
	(1·905)	(0·583)	(0·488)	(0·896)	(0·943)	
Entire	3·034	0·021	0·436	0·440	0·483	0·701
	(0·885)	(0·380)	(0·203)	(0·204)	(0·230)	

that, whatever has happened to the relation between unemployment and excess demand for labour, some part of the effect of incomes policy arises in the manner indicated in Lipsey-Parkin, i.e., from a breaking of the $\dot{w}$ reaction function.

The effects of incomes policy on the relation between wages and prices (i.e., the coefficient γ) is less clear. Although γ in policy-off periods is not significantly different from its policy-on value, the policy-on γ is so badly determined that its value could be anything between zero and one.

We have established that the relation between $\dot{w}$ and excess demand has shifted in a manner which is consistent with the Lipsey-Parkin findings about shifts in the Phillips curve. This points very strongly to incomes-restraint policies rather than other explanations as the cause of the broken Phillips curve. In order to check this further, we look at the mapping from excess demand to unemployment. This mapping can have shifted for two reasons. First, in some sectors incomes policy may lead to a higher labour turnover rate as people try to avoid the effects of restraints on wage rates. Any such increase in the labour turnover rate should lead to a rightward shift of the mapping. Second, the mapping may shift because of changes in other variables which, in principle, could affect the excess-demand/ unemployment mapping. Examples of likely variables are the rate of unemployment benefits or redundancy payments. It is commonly asserted that there has been such a shift in the relation between excess demand for labour and unemployment in the United Kingdom, after the third quarter of 1966. If the mapping has shifted between policy-off and policy-on, but is independent of changes in redundancy and unemployment benefits, the original Lipsey-Parkin results will be confirmed. If, on the other hand, we find that the mapping shifts in response to changes in unemployment benefit and, in particular, has shifted since 1966(3), then the original results will require modification.

The mapping from excess demand to unemployment which is implied by the simple Phillips relations fitted is equation (8) above. Ordinary least squares estimation of equation (8) is reported in Table 9. (The t values are in square brackets.)

Table 9   Ordinary least squares estimates of equation (8)

	α_3	β_3	R^2	DW
Policy-off	2·771	−1·925	0·943	0·283
	[23·82]	[24·93]		
Policy-on	2·613	−1·671	0·815	0·598
	[12·09]	[13·58]		
Entire	2·505	−1·666	0·834	0·477
	[18·42]	[20·15]		

Casual inspection of these results make the excess-demand/unemployment mapping look remarkably stable. However, there is a strong indication of positive first-order auto-correlation in the residuals. In an attempt to overcome this, we try modification of the hypothesis. We suppose that the relation between excess demand and unemployment will be affected by the terms and conditions on which a person may be unemployed. In particular, we let the weekly wage rate, W, and the weekly level of unemployment benefit, B, affect the mapping. We also employ a shift dummy, D, to search for a change in the relationship at the end of 1966 when earnings-related benefits were introduced. [$D = 0$ to 1966(3) and 1 thereafter.]

The mapping then becomes

$$E = \alpha_3 + \beta_3 U + \gamma_3 W + \delta_3 B + \phi_3 D + \varepsilon. \qquad (12)$$

Estimating this by ordinary least squares yields the results set out in Table 10. (The t values are in square brackets.)

The effects of introducing the additional variables are quite dramatic. First, there is now, apparently, a sizeable shift both in the intercept, α_3, and the unemployment slope, β_3, between policy-off and policy-on. Second, it appears that the mapping between E and U is independent of the weekly wage and unemployment benefit rates in policy-off, but that it depends on those variables in policy-on.

Table 10   Ordinary least squares estimates of equation (12)

	α_3	β_3	γ_3	δ_3	ϕ_3	R^2	DW
Policy-off	3·570	−1·858	−0·010	0·0004	—	0·949	0·274
	[5·29]	[19·47]	[0·94]	[0·09]			
Policy-on	9·680	−1·505	−0·089	0·015	0·245	0·912	0·980
	[7·09]	[13·75]	[4·61]	[2·60]	[2·10]		
Entire	6·266	−1·637	−0·049	0·011	0·240	0·871	0·595
	[6·95]	[17·45]	[3·87]	[2·59]	[2·11]		

It also appears that there was a significant shift in the mapping after 1966(3), indicated by ϕ_3, the parameter on the shift dummy. However, all these results must be viewed with caution in view of the fact that, as indicated by the Durbin-Watson statistic, the residuals are still significantly auto-correlated.

Since we lack a *theory* of the excess-demand/unemployment mapping, we resort to a transformation of the estimating equation to remove the first-order auto-correlation. We assume

$$\varepsilon = \rho_3 \varepsilon_{-1} + z, \tag{13}$$

and obtain

$$E = e_0 + e_1 U + e_2 U_{-1} + e_3 W + e_4 W_{-1} + e_5 B + e_6 B_{-1}$$
$$+ e_7 D + e_8 D_{-1} + e_9 E_{-1} + z. \tag{14}$$

where $e_0 = \alpha_3(1 - \rho_3)$, $e_5 = \delta_3$,
$\quad\quad e_1 = \beta_3$, $e_6 = -\rho_3 \delta_3$,
$\quad\quad e_2 = -\rho_3 \beta_3$, $e_7 = \phi_3$,
$\quad\quad e_3 = \gamma_3$, $e_8 = -\rho_3 \phi_3$,
$\quad\quad e_4 = -\rho_3 \gamma_3$, $e_9 = \rho_3$.

Non-linear estimation of this equation yields the results in Table 11.

Table 11   Non-linear least squares estimation of equation (14)

	α_3	β_3	γ_3	δ_3	ϕ_3	ρ_3	$\hat{\sigma}^2$
Policy-off	2·179	−1·855	0·003	0·002	—	0·873	0·003
	(0·670)	(0·076)	(0·007)	(0·002)	—	(0·058)	
Policy-on	2·925	−1·612	−0·007	0·002	0·062	0·703	0·006
	(0·869)	(0·081)	(0·010)	(0·003)	(0·074)	(0·046)	
Entire	2·329	1·722	0·0002	0·002	0·088	0·758	0·085
	(0·500)	(0·059)	(0·006)	(0·002)	(0·065)	(0·029)	

(Asymptotic standard errors are shown in parentheses; and $\hat{\sigma}^2$ is the variance of residuals.) Notice first that the residuals ε were indeed auto-correlated significantly with a coefficient in the region of 0·8. More important, however, is the effect upon the coefficients on wages, γ_3, unemployment benefit, δ_3, and the shift dummy, ϕ_3, of allowing for the auto-correlation. All these coefficients are very small and none of them is significant at the 5% level. This indicates that, whatever may be the appearance given by inappropriate ordinary least squares estimates, the excess-demand/unemployment mapping is independent of other variables and does not appear to have shifted since 1966(3). It is, however, different for periods with incomes policy and periods without incomes policy.

In view of the non-significance of γ_3, δ_3 and ϕ_3, we re-estimated the mapping function allowing for auto-correlation but without including the additional variables and dummy. That is, we estimated

$$E = f_0 + f_1 U + f_2 U_{-1} + f_3 E_{-1} + z, \tag{15}$$

where $f_0 = (1 - \rho_3)\alpha_3$, $f_1 = \beta_3$, $f_2 = -\beta_3\rho_3$, and $f_3 = \rho_3$.

Non-linear estimation of this equation yielded the results as in Table 12. (Asymptotic standard errors are shown in parentheses, and $\hat{\sigma}^2$ is

Table 12   Non-linear least squares estimation of equation (15)

	α_3	β_3	ρ_3	$\hat{\sigma}^2$
Policy-off	2·607	−1·836	0·860	0·003
	(0·132)	(0·076)	(0·058)	
Policy-on	2·312	−1·565	0·811	0·009
	(0·211)	(0·104)	(0·037)	
Entire	2·590	−1·720	0·822	0·022
	(0·214)	(0·118)	(0·049)	

the variance of residuals.) The policy-off and policy-on equations are significantly different from each other at the 5% level. However, the numerical magnitudes of the differences are trivial compared with the shift in the wage reaction function between the two sub-periods.

As a final check on the behaviour of the $E - U$ mapping for the period since 1966(1), in Figure 2 we plot the residuals from the

Figure 2

Residuals (613–691) from equation
$$E = 2 \cdot 163 - 1 \cdot 671 \text{ U (Policy On)}$$ · · · · ·
Residuals (613–691) from equation
$$E = \alpha(1 - \rho) + \beta U - \beta\rho U_{-1} + E_{-1} + \epsilon$$ ———
where $\alpha = 2 \cdot 312$ $\beta = 1 \cdot 565$ $\rho = 0 \cdot 811$

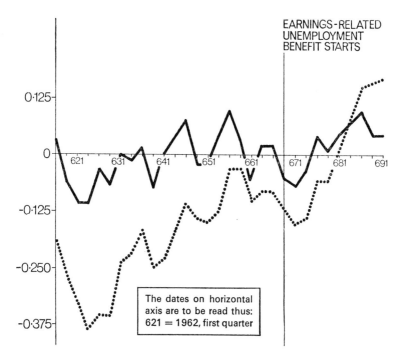

$E - U$ mapping and inspect their behaviour in the last few years. It is clear that, if the auto-correlation is ignored, the residuals have a positive trend from 1962 through to 1969. When, however, the auto-correlation is allowed for, this trend disappears, and there is no apparent tendency for the residuals to be badly behaved. The last seven residuals are all positive; but they are also very small, and could not account for more than the slightest shift in the relation of excess demand and unemployment.

4

The conclusions which emerge from this further study of the determination of wage-rate inflation are clear. The wage-rate reaction function appears to be broken effectively by incomes policy. The excess-demand/unemployment mapping is significantly different between policy-off and policy-on periods, but there is no evidence to suggest that it is anything other than incomes policy itself which shifts the mapping. There is no evidence of a shift in the mapping after the third quarter of 1966 when sizeable changes in the arrangements for unemployment benefit were introduced. Thus the original Lipsey-Parkin finding is sustained: on the average, incomes policy reduces wage inflation at low levels of unemployment and increases wage inflation at high levels of unemployment.

In addition to checking previous results on the effects of incomes policy, the introduction of price-inflation expectations enabled us to test the hypothesis that the trade-off between inflation and employment is only a short-run phenomenon. On the basis of the estimates reported here, it appears that the trade-off is in fact a long-run trade-off, the coefficient on expected price inflation not coming close to unity.

Thus our broad conclusions are: (1) There appears to be a trade-off between inflation and unemployment in both the short run and the long run. (2) The trade-off is effectively broken by incomes policy and replaced by a constant average rate of increase in money wages which is independent of the level of unemployment. (3) Hence, incomes policy reduces inflation at low unemployment levels and increases it at high levels.

Appendix   Definitions of variables and sources of data

P: Index of Retail Prices, MDS, 'all items' index. Quarterly observations obtained by averaging monthly observations.

W: Index of weekly wage rates as found in MDS in 'all industries and services' table and 'male and female' column. Quarterly observations are again obtained by averaging monthly observations.

U: Number of registered labour force wholly unemployed as a percent of total in civil employment as found in the *Ministry of Labour Gazette* (now *Employment and Productivity Gazette*), or MDS. The figures used were seasonally unadjusted, and quarterly figures were obtained as averages of monthly data.

N: Percentage of labour force unionized. Source: *Ministry of Labour Gazette*. Quarterly data obtained by interpolation.

V: Percentage of vacancies to labour force. Source: *Ministry of Labour Gazette*.

E: $V - U$.

B: Index of weekly rate of unemployment benefit, deflated by P. Source: *Annual Abstract of Statistics*.

'MDS' refers to the *Monthly Digest of Statistics* published by the Central Statistical Office.

References

[1] B. Corry and D. E. W. Laidler, 'Some Empirical Tests on the Phillips Relation', mimeographed.
[2] D. Hendry and P. K. Trivedi, 'Experimental Estimates of the Biases in Two Maximum Likelihood Estimators for Single Equation Linear Difference Equations with Autocorrelated Errors', mimeographed, London School of Economics, 1970.
[3] R. G. Lipsey and J. M. Parkin, 'Incomes Policy: A Re-Appraisal', *Economica*, vol. XXXVII (1970), pp. 115–38, and Chapter 4 above.
[4] E. S. Phelps, 'Money-Wage Dynamics and Labor-Market Equilibrium', *Journal of Political Economy*, vol. 76 (1968), pp. 678–711.
[5] D. C. Smith, 'Incomes Policy', in R. E. Caves (ed.), *Britain's Economic Prospects*, 1968, Chapter 3. Abridged as Chapter 3 above.

Kenneth F. Wallis[1]

Chapter 6 Wages, prices and incomes policies: some comments[2]

In a recent paper, Lipsey and Parkin[3] (hereinafter referred to as
L-P) use a two-equation quarterly model of wage and price inflation
in the post-war United Kingdom to examine the effects of the policies
of wage and price restraint which have been applied at various times.
The model is

$$p = a_0 + a_1w + a_2m + a_3q,$$
$$w = b_0 + b_1p + b_2U + b_3n,$$

where p, w, m, n and q are proportionate rates of change of retail
prices, wage rates, import prices lagged one quarter, percentage of
labour force unionized and output per head, respectively, and U is the
unemployment rate. The equations are estimated by ordinary least
squares for the whole sample period 1948(3)–1967(2), and for the
separate 'policy-on' and 'policy-off' periods [these being, policy-on:
1948(3)–1950(3), 1956(1)–1956(4), 1961(3)–1967(2); and policy-off:
1950(4)–1955(4), 1957(1)–1961(2)]. With respect to the wage equation, L-P conclude from the estimates for the policy-on period that
there is then no relation between w and the explanatory variables,
and hence that 'the wage inflation-unemployment trade-off is effectively broken during periods of incomes policy.' These words are
those of Parkin,[4] who confirms this finding in a subsequent study of
the wage equation which takes some account of auto-correlated
errors by introducing a dynamic specification.

This paper is concerned with three aspects of L-P's work. First,

[1] London School of Economics. The author is grateful to Andrew R.
Tremayne for research assistance.
[2] Reprinted from *Economica*, August 1971, by permission of the author and
publisher.
[3] Chapter 4 above [2].
[4] Chapter 5 above [3].

their assessment of the effects of the various policies on the rates of wage and price inflation is re-examined, within the context of their ordinary least-squares estimates. Second, still going along with their assumption that single-equation methods are appropriate, the absence from their work of any treatment of auto-correlation and some implications for the specification of the price equation are noted. Finally, there are some observations on the simultaneous-equations problem.

1 The effects of incomes policies

In order to assess the effectiveness of the various policies of restraint, L-P use their equations, estimated from data for policy-off periods, to predict p and w during policy-on periods. When these predictions $\hat{p}$ and $\hat{w}$ are compared with the actual p and w values during policy-on periods, negative values of the prediction errors $p - \hat{p}$ and $w - \hat{w}$ imply that the policies were successful in holding the inflation rate below what it would otherwise have been. In a statistical test L-P have already rejected the hypothesis that the regression coefficients are equal in the policy-on and policy-off periods, and the present exercise is concerned with the effect of that inequality on the price and wage predictions. Broadly speaking, L-P find that the policies have little effect. However, the appropriate predictors are not the structural equations as specified above but their reduced form. Treating p and w as the jointly dependent variables of the two-equation system, the reduced-form equations express each in turn as a function of all the other variables in the system. This allows for the feedback effect, that is, the fact that a 'rise in wages raises prices and thus will cause a further rise in wages', to quote from a later section of L-P. The equations used by L-P are

$$p = -0{\cdot}140 + 0{\cdot}851w + 0{\cdot}073m - 0{\cdot}092q,$$
$$w = 6{\cdot}672 + 0{\cdot}457p - 2{\cdot}372U + 0{\cdot}136n;$$

and these have the reduced form

$$p = 9{\cdot}289 - 3{\cdot}387U + 0{\cdot}122m - 0{\cdot}154q + 0{\cdot}194n,$$
$$w = 11{\cdot}080 - 3{\cdot}980U + 0{\cdot}058m - 0{\cdot}073q + 0{\cdot}228n.$$

The prediction errors of these equations in policy-on periods are presented in Tables 1 and 2, alongside L-P's results as given in their

Table 1   Estimated effects of incomes policies on the rate of wage inflation

Incomes Policy years	Predictions from structural equation			Predictions from solved reduced form		
	No. of positive prediction errors	No. of negative prediction errors	Mean prediction error, % p.a.	No. of positive prediction errors	No. of negative prediction errors	Mean prediction error, % p.a.
1948(3)–1950(3)	1	8	−1·778	0	9	−2·369
1956(1)–1956(4)	2	2	+0·290	2	2	−1·050
1961(3)–1967(2)	12	12	−0·197	11	13	−0·127
All periods	15	22	−0·529	13	24	−0·772

S.D. of residuals for policy-off equation: 0·774   S.D. of residuals for policy-off periods: 1·058

Table 2   Estimated effects of incomes policies on the rate of price inflation

Incomes Policy years	Predictions from structural equation			Predictions from solved reduced form		
	No. of positive prediction errors	No. of negative prediction errors	Mean prediction error, % p.a.	No. of positive prediction errors	No. of negative prediction errors	Mean prediction error, % p.a.
1948(3)–1950(3)	6	3	+0·745	2	7	−1·229
1956(1)–1956(4)	0	4	−1·922	0	4	−2·815
1961(3)–1967(2)	12	12	+0·255	15	9	+0·147
All periods	18	19	+0·138	17	20	−0·510

S.D. of residuals for policy-off equation: 1·265   S.D. of residuals for policy-off periods: 1·534

Tables 2 and 3.[5] It is seen that once allowance is made for the feed-back between wages and prices, incomes policies appear to have been rather more effective than claimed by L-P. The mean prediction errors are generally negative. L-P compare their mean prediction errors with the standard deviation of the residuals during the policy-off estimation period: this provides a conservative test, for were the residuals independent, a more appropriate comparison would be with the standard deviation divided by the square root of the number of prediction errors entering the particular mean. With the reduced-form prediction errors, whenever the null hypothesis of no effect is rejected, it is rejected in favour of the alternative hypothesis that the various policies have had a genuinely restraining effect.

2   Auto-corelation and the specification of the price equation

In discussing their regression results, L-P observe that the values of the Durbin-Watson statistic indicate 'the presence of significant positive serial correlation in the residuals'. No attempt is made to tackle this problem, although Parkin's later study [3] does attend to first-order auto-correlation in the wage equation. However, the problem is not as simple as that, as I have found when using the price equation as an example in some work on testing for fourth-order auto-correlation in quarterly regression equations (Wallis [5]). The price equation results for the whole period are (with standard errors in parentheses):

$$p_t = 1\cdot374 + 0\cdot562w_t + 0\cdot085m_i - 0\cdot145q_t.$$
$$(0\cdot548) \quad (0\cdot102) \quad\quad (0\cdot019) \quad\quad (0\cdot042)$$
$$R^2 = 0\cdot699 \quad\quad d_1 = 0\cdot945 \quad\quad d_4 = 2\cdot550.$$

Both d_1 and d_4 are significantly different from 2, and on re-estimating the equation subject to an autoregressive error by maximum likelihood methods, the error appears to obey the restricted form

$$u_t = \alpha_1 u_{t-1} + \alpha_4 u_{t-4} - \alpha_1\alpha_4 u_{t-5} + \varepsilon_t,$$
$$\hat{\alpha}_1 = 0\cdot685, \quad\quad \hat{\alpha}_4 = -0\cdot461.$$
$$(0\cdot137) \quad\quad\quad\quad (0\cdot111)$$

[5] All the calculations reported in this paper are based on the 76 observations (or relevant sub-sets of them) used by L-P to estimate their equations. Careful readers of L-P's Table 2 may be surprised to find their mean prediction error for the latest incomes policy period reported in my Table 1 as $-0\cdot197$: their overall positive effect is obtained by including four further quarters 1967(3)–1968(2) which enjoyed substantial wage inflation. There is a misprint in their Table 3: the end-period given as 1968(2) should read 1967(2), as the extra four observations are not included in that table.

10

The possibility always exists that auto-correlation in the errors results from mis-specification of the lags in the original structural equation, and this appears to be the case here. The structural equation modified by introducing one-, four- and five-quarter lagged values of the variables but with an independent error has a substantially lower residual sum of squares than the original structural equation with auto-regressive error as given above. However, it is the addition of one-quarter lagged variables and the removal of α_1 which achieves most of this reduction in residual sum of squares; adding four-quarter lagged values of all variables and dropping α_4 achieves little further reduction. Likelihood ratio tests confirm this conclusion, so the preferred form, after removing most of the non-significant variables, is

$$p_t = 0.220 + 0.567p_{t-1} + 0.364w_{t-1} + 0.070m_t - 0.041q_t,$$
$$\quad\ (0.153)\quad (0.078)\qquad (0.076)\qquad (0.015)\qquad (0.023)$$

$$u_t = -0.459u_{t-4} + \varepsilon_t.$$
$$\quad\ (0.103)$$

There now appears to be an adjustment or expectation mechanism at work. Also the fact that the coefficient of u_{t-4} is approximately -0.5, and that four-period differences of a random series have a fourth-order auto-correlation coefficient of this magnitude, suggests that the auto-correlation in the error term may be due simply to the differencing procedure used by L-P in calculating their rate of change variables. If X_t denotes the level of a variable, then the proportionate rate of change used by L-P is calculated as $x_t = 100(X_{t+2} - X_{t-2})/\frac{1}{2}(X_{t+2} + X_{t-2})$, as a discrete approximation to $d(\log X_t)/dt$. The underlying theory is presented in terms of the levels of the relevant variables, but the estimating equation is presumably expressed in terms of proportionate rates of change because 'virtually all two-equation models of wage and price inflation' have been. One exception is the study by Sargan [4], where the price equation is log-linear in the levels of the variables. Sargan finds that such an equation, containing a trend variable and with a first-order auto-regressive error, is the preferred specification. The trend coefficient of -0.0018 corresponds closely to the constant term of -0.140 in L-P's percentage-difference policy-off price equation, which is not surprising since Sargan's sample period is 1948(1)–1961(4). His first-order auto-regressive parameter is estimated as 0.587 (0.115), which corresponds to my estimate for the whole period of 0·685 (0·137). However, our conclusions regarding the auto-regressive specification differ, and this may reflect the different estimation procedures used. Sargan uses a (consistent) instrumental variable estimator, whereas for the purposes of the present section I have followed L-P in applying single-equation methods. My conclusion is that L-P's differencing procedure introduces noise into the system rather than contributing to its explanatory power, and that henceforth price behaviour equations should seek to explain the *level* of prices.[6]

3   Simultaneous equations problems

L-P's two-equation model is estimated by ordinary least squares, despite the obvious simultaneous nature of the model and the feedback effects noted above. This choice is defended in a paragraph (on page 99 of this volume) which is remarkable for the frequency of mistakes. In order to use two-stage least squares (2SLS) it is *not* necessary to 'treat all the variables in the two equation sub-system, except p and w, as exogenous and as the only exogenous variables in the entire economy', nor it is required 'that we specify the complete macro model'. At the simplest level, what is required is that appropriate pre-determined variables be found to serve as instrumental variables for whatever variables in the two equations are specified as endogenous. That remarkable paragraph has led a number of people to put the L-P model through computer programs for various estimation methods, such as 2SLS, auto-regressive 2SLS, instrumental variables and various maximum likelihood methods. Generally speaking, what happens is that the variables of the L-P model very quickly lose their apparent significance,[7] and thus the model ceases to be identified.

The most stringent test of the model which I have applied is to attempt to estimate the two-equation model for the policy-off period (this being the period in which L-P are most satisfied with the performance of their model) using a program for full-information maximum-likelihood estimation subject to a first-order auto-regressive

---

[6] Taking quasi-fourth differences of a levels equation will produce an error term with moving average as well as autoregressive elements. Pravin Trivedi has observed similar regression coefficients and similar auto-correlation patterns to mine when re-estimating L-P's equation subject to a high-order moving average error.

[7] See, for example, the results obtained by Godfrey [1], with an instrumental variable esimator, treating all variables except m as endogenous.

error. This attempt failed when the 2×2 matrix of coefficients on the 'endogenous' variables was apparently converging to a singular matrix, all other coefficients becoming non-significant. The fact that the method fails with this model, or *vice versa*, is not surprising, since in the least-squares estimates two of the coefficients are already non-significant despite the over-optimistic *t*-ratios caused by auto-correlated errors, and not much more is required before the price equation and the wage equation lose their separate identities and collapse to a simple correlation between p and w. Doubts have been raised above about the specification of the price equation, and that of the wage equation has been revised in Parkin's later study [3]; so, as full-information maximum-likelihood methods are the most sensitive to model specification errors, the program's author (David Hendry) remains unconcerned by the fact that this model produced a singularity for his program.

Presumably, L-P can also say 'we told you so', for they 'think it more reasonable to suppose that p and w, along with U, q and n (but not m) are all jointly determined endogenous variables'. In that situation, it is difficult to see just what is represented by the 'indirect reduced-form' relations between w and U which they use. Such relations, calculated for policy-on and policy-off periods separately, are presented in L-P's Figure 6, and their intersection at an unemployment level of 1.8% is taken to imply that restraint policies are in general successful at levels of unemployment below 1.8%, whereas above this level restraint policies in general fail to reduce the rate of wage inflation. However, given that w and U are both jointly determined endogenous variables, their respective roles might just as well be reversed, and the intersection of the two 'pseudo-reduced forms' at a rate of wage inflation of almost 4% per annum taken to imply that the effect of incomes policy is to reduce unemployment when the rate of wage inflation is above 4% per annum, and to increase unemployment when the rate of wage inflation is below 4%. But I hasten to add that this is an equally inappropriate usage when w and U are jointly dependent. Nevertheless, L-P's attitude to the endogeneity issue through their paper does seem somewhat ambivalent.

As a final comment on this issue, may I suggest that the decision to impose an incomes policy is not independent of the values of the variables in the model, and although treated as exogenous in the L-P study the policy itself must surely also become a jointly dependent endogenous variable. The relationship between the rate of price and wage inflation and the imposition of a policy of restraint is equally a feedback relationship. The division of the sample period into policy-on and policy-off periods is not arbitrary, but is related to actual or expected rates of inflation. Thus, in Figure 6, not only are the two variables of the pseudo-reduced forms endogenous, but the decision as to which function to use is also endogenous. A rather more detailed analysis is required before we can accept L-P's hypothesis that there is a crucial level of unemployment above which restraint policies will on the average fail.

References

[1] L. G. Godfrey, 'The Phillips Curve: Incomes Policy and Trade Union Effects', in H. G. Johnson and A. R. Nobay (eds.), *The Current Inflation*, 1971. Abridged and amended as 'some comments on estimation of the Lipsey-Parkin inflation model,' Chapter 7, below.

[2] R. G. Lipsey and J. M. Parkin, 'Incomes Policy: a Re-appraisal', *Economica*, vol. XXXVII (1970), pp. 115–38, and Chapter 4 above.

[3] J. M. Parkin, 'Incomes Policy: Some Further Results on the Determination of the Rate of Change of Money Wages', *Economica*, vol. XXXVII (1970), pp. 386–401, and Chapter 5 above.

[4] J. D. Sargan, 'Wages and prices in the United Kingdom: a study in econometric methodology', in P. E. Hart *et al.* (eds.), *Econometric Analysis for National Economic Planning*, 1964, pp. 25–54.

[5] K. F. Wallis, 'Testing for Fourth Order Autocorrelation in Quarterly Regression Equations', *Econometrica*, forthcoming.

Leslie G. Godfrey[1]

Chapter 7 Some comments on the estimation of the Lipsey-Parkin inflation model[2]

1 Introduction

In a recent paper Lipsey and Parkin[3] studied the effects of incomes policies in post-war Britain. They estimated a two-equation model and used their point estimates of the structural coefficients and the associated regression residuals to support some arguments which have disturbing implications for policy-makers wishing to reduce inflation. On the basis of their estimated model, Lipsey and Parkin come to the conclusion that not only had wage and price restraints usually been ineffective, but that sometimes they had the perverse effect of increasing the rate of inflation above the value it would otherwise have assumed. If Lipsey and Parkin are correct, then incomes policies must be judged to be rather unsatisfactory tools for the control of wages and prices. However, their conclusions are derived from the estimated equations, and so stand or fall on the acceptability of the model's specification and estimation.

The model specified in [2] was

$$\dot{p} = a_1 + a_2\dot{w}_{-r} + a_3\dot{m}_{-s} + a_4\dot{q}_{-t} \tag{1}$$

$$\dot{w} = a_5 + a_6[f(U)]_{-u} + a_7\dot{p}_{-v} + a_8\dot{N}_{-w} \tag{2}$$

where $\dot{p}$ = the proportionate rate of change of an index of prices;
$\dot{w}$ = the proportionate rate of change of wages;
$\dot{m}$ = the proportionate rate of change of import prices;
$\dot{q}$ = the proportionate rate of change of output per head;

[1] University of York.
[2] Abridged, with amendments, from chapter six of *The Current Inflation*, edited by Harry G. Johnson and A. R. Nobay, Macmillan, 1971. Reprinted by permission of the author and the Money Study Group.
[3] Chapter 4 above [2].

$f(U)$ = some function of the percentage of the labour force unemployed; and

$\dot{N}$ = the change in the percentage of the labour force unionized (see Hines [1]).

r, s, t, u, v and w are lags in quarters. The derivation of the price change equation yielded the restrictions

$$a_1 = 0 \tag{3}$$

$$a_2 + a_4 = 0 \tag{4}$$

This paper uses exactly the same economic specification and data as [2]. However, the equations of the Lipsey-Parkin model contain endogenous regressors and appear to have autocorrelated errors. It follows that the estimation methods and testing procedures used by Lipsey and Parkin are inappropriate.

An alternative method of estimation is, therefore, proposed and some results obtained by re-estimating the model are presented. It should be noted that the statistical methods employed by the author are consistent with the arguments of Lipsey and Parkin in so far as all current dated variables are treated as endogenous. Some comments are made upon the problems of efficient estimation.

2   The estimation of the Lipsey-Parkin model

If the derivation of equation (1) given by Lipsey and Parkin is to be accepted, then it follows that equation (1) should be estimated subject to the restrictions (3) and (4), and that the consistency of these restrictions with the sample information should be tested. Lipsey and Parkin in fact used ordinary least squares (OLS). The cost of using unrestricted OLS, rather than restricted estimation, has at least two aspects: firstly, the opportunity to test the theoretical formulation of the model is lost; secondly, restricted estimation is more efficient, provided that the constraints imposed are valid. But a more obvious cost of the Lipsey-Parkin procedure is that OLS estimators are biased and inconsistent in a simultaneous equation model. The lags present on the variables of the right hand sides of equations (1) and (2) might lead one to believe that OLS would yield consistent estimators, provided the equation errors were serially independent. But it is to be recalled that in the equations actually estimated by Lipsey and Parkin only one of these variables had a non-zero lag and this was the import price variable; so that the regressors of the wage and price equations cannot be regarded as pre-determined and OLS estimators are indeed inconsistent. We therefore have no statistical justification for expecting the resulting point estimates to tell us anything useful about the true values of the parameters of the model.

The authors justified their use of OLS on the grounds that the variables other than $\dot{w}$ and $\dot{p}$ could not be regarded as pre-determined, (with the exception of $\dot{m}$), therefore the usual estimation methods, e.g., two stage least squares, were not feasible. This position is, of course, related to that of Liu [3], and without the specification of the rest of the model containing the wage-price subset, the very identifiability of the equations of this subset must be open to question. In fact, according to the authors, the model of [2] consists of two equations in five endogenous variables, and so at least three more equations will be needed to complete the system. Even if the equations can be estimated at all, OLS estimators have nothing to recommend them statistically. The theory of the classical linear regression model is inapplicable and the test procedures of [2] are invalid. If it is assumed that the Durbin-Watson (DW) statistics calculated from the OLS residuals mean something, then they provide more evidence against the choice of OLS as the estimating technique. The DW statistics reported in [2] often show evidence of strong positive auto-correlation, and so the t-ratios given in the original paper may be extremely misleading and seriously overstate the significance of the estimated coefficients.

3   An alternative method of estimation

The method outlined in this section is designed not only to take account of endogenous regressors and first order auto-regressive errors, but also to incorporate any prior restrictions which may be available. Sargan [4] has considered the case of estimating a structural equation with auto-regressive errors when no restrictions are used. The model is then

$$\mathbf{y} = X\mathbf{b} + \mathbf{u} \tag{5}$$

$$u_t = \rho u_{t-1} + e_t, \qquad |\rho| < 1 \tag{6}$$

$$R\mathbf{b} = r \tag{7}$$

The e_t are assumed to be independently normally distributed with mean zero and variance σ^2, and equation (7) represents the linear between parameter constraints. The number of regressors is p, the number of observations is T, $(T > p)$, and there are m constraints, $(m < p)$. A subscript 1 will be used to denote a lagged value of the relevant matrix or vector, but subscripts on coefficient vectors will denote the relevant iteration value of the corresponding estimate.

Let there be a matrix of instruments Z, so that

$$\text{plim}\,(Z'e/T) = 0 \quad \text{and} \quad \text{plim}\,(Z'X/T) = \bar{M}_{zx},$$

a non-zero matrix of rank p.

The number of instrumental variables, and therefore the rank of Z, is k, $(k > p + 1)$. Define the projection matrix Q by

$$Q = Z(Z'Z)^{-1}Z',$$

so that pre-multiplication by Q projects vectors into the k-dimensional space spanned by the columns of Z. Given a value of ρ, the systematic parts of the auto-regressive transforms of the regressand and the regressors are

$$Q\mathbf{y} - \rho Q\mathbf{y}_1 = \mathbf{y}^*$$

and

$$QX - \rho QX_1 = X^* \quad \text{(say)}.$$

Let Sargan's auto-regressive instrumental variable (AIV) estimator be denoted by $\tilde{\mathbf{b}}$, and the restricted auto-regressive instrumental variable (RAIV) estimator be denoted by $\hat{\mathbf{b}}$. The theory of AIV estimators and computational procedures are to be found in [4]. The RAIV estimators are obtained by minimizing

$$[(\mathbf{y} - \rho \mathbf{y}_1) - (X - \rho X_1)\mathbf{b}]'Q[(\mathbf{y} - \rho \mathbf{y}_1) - (X - \rho X_1)\mathbf{b}]$$

subject to

$$R\mathbf{b} = \mathbf{r}.$$

Define the Lagrangian ϕ by

$$\phi = [(\mathbf{y} - \rho \mathbf{y}_1) - (X - \rho X_1)\mathbf{b}]'Q[(\mathbf{y} - \rho \mathbf{y}_1)$$
$$- (X - \rho X_1)\mathbf{b}] - 2(\mathbf{b}'R' - \mathbf{r}')\lambda \quad (8)$$

where λ is a $m \times 1$ vector of multipliers. We seek to minimize ϕ with respect to $\mathbf{b}$, λ and ρ.

An iterative solution is necessary and an Orcutt-type procedure is sketched which the author has found to work well in practice.

Suppose we take an initial value of ρ, e.g., $\rho_0 = 0$, and determine the associated $\mathbf{y}^*$ and X^* values. The function to be minimized is then

$$\phi = (\mathbf{y}^* - X^*\mathbf{b})'(\mathbf{y}^* - X^*\mathbf{b}) - 2(\mathbf{b}'R' - \mathbf{r}')\lambda$$

For a minimum with respect to $\mathbf{b}$, we have

$$0 = -X^{*\prime}\mathbf{y}^* + (X^{*\prime}X^*)\hat{\mathbf{b}} - R'\hat{\lambda} \tag{9}$$

($\hat{\mathbf{b}}$ in equation (9) is of course the iteration value conditional on ρ_0, and not the final value). Thus,

$$\begin{aligned}
\hat{\mathbf{b}} &= (X^{*\prime}X^*)^{-1}X^{*\prime}\mathbf{y}^* + (X^{*\prime}X^*)^{-1}R'\hat{\lambda} \\
&= \tilde{\mathbf{b}} + (X^{*\prime}X^*)^{-1}R'\hat{\lambda}
\end{aligned} \tag{10}$$

Multiplying both sides of equation (10) by R and applying $R\hat{\mathbf{b}} = \mathbf{r}$, yields

$$\begin{aligned}
\mathbf{r} &= R\tilde{\mathbf{b}} + [R(X^{*\prime}X^*)^{-1}R']\hat{\lambda}, \quad \text{or} \\
\hat{\lambda} &= [R(X^{*\prime}X^*)^{-1}R']^{-1}(\mathbf{r} - R\tilde{\mathbf{b}})
\end{aligned} \tag{11}$$

Combining equations (10) and (11) we obtain

$$\hat{\mathbf{b}} = \tilde{\mathbf{b}} + (X^{*\prime}X^*)^{-1}R'[R(X^{*\prime}X^*)^{-1}R']^{-1}(\mathbf{r} - R\tilde{\mathbf{b}}) \tag{12}$$

So, given ρ_0, equation (12) provides $\hat{\mathbf{b}}_0$ ($\tilde{\mathbf{b}}_0$ also being calculated conditionally upon the ρ_0 value). To continue the iterative method, a new value of ρ is needed, and this derived from the Euler necessary condition for a minimum with respect to ρ. If we define

$$\hat{\mathbf{u}} = \mathbf{y} - X\hat{\mathbf{b}}$$

then

$$\rho = (\hat{\mathbf{u}}_1'Q\hat{\mathbf{u}})/(\hat{\mathbf{u}}_1'Q\hat{\mathbf{u}}_1) \tag{13}$$

Having obtained $\hat{\mathbf{b}}_0$, the next iteration value of ρ, i.e., ρ_1, can be calculated from equation (13), then we find $\tilde{\mathbf{b}}_1$ and subsequently $\hat{\mathbf{b}}_1$ from equation (12). The whole process then continues until convergence is achieved.

We next turn to the asymptotic variance matrix of the RAIV estimators, i.e., $AV(\hat{\mathbf{b}})$. The corresponding matrix for the AIV estimators is to be found in Sargan's paper, ([4], p. 29). We introduce the following notation: $\Delta\hat{\mathbf{b}} = \hat{\mathbf{b}} - \mathbf{b}$; $\Delta\tilde{\mathbf{b}} = \tilde{\mathbf{b}} - \mathbf{b}$;

$$H = (I - (X^{*\prime}X^*)^{-1}R'[R(X^{*\prime}X^*)^{-1}R']^{-1}R);$$

$\bar{H} = \text{plim } H$. A little manipulation yields

$$\Delta \hat{\mathbf{b}} = H \Delta \tilde{\mathbf{b}}$$

so that

$$AV(\hat{\mathbf{b}}) = \bar{H}AV(\tilde{\mathbf{b}})\bar{H}' \qquad (14)$$

The computational costs of the AIV and RAIV methods are not negligible, and so the model specification is well worth testing. Sargan has proposed a test of the specification represented by equations (5) and (6);[4] so a useful first step is to obtain AIV estimates and then to apply this test. If the model passes the test, then we proceed to test the consistency of the *a priori* restrictions of equation (7) with the sample information by calculating

$$(R\tilde{\mathbf{b}} - \mathbf{r})'[RAV(\tilde{\mathbf{b}})R']^{-1}(R\tilde{\mathbf{b}} - \mathbf{r}),$$

which is asymptotically distributed as χ_m^2 on the null hypothesis that the restrictions are correct. If the sample value of the test statistic is less than some pre-set significance level, then the more efficient RAIV estimates should be obtained.

Finally, we show how the Lipsey-Parkin price equation fits into the framework of this section. The restrictions to be imposed upon equation (1) are $a_1 = 0$ and $a_2 = -a_4$, so we have

$$\mathbf{b}' = (a_1 \quad a_2 \quad a_3 \quad a_4)$$

$$R = \begin{bmatrix} 1 & 0 & 0 & 0 \\ 0 & 1 & 0 & 1 \end{bmatrix}$$

and

$$\mathbf{r}' = (0 \quad 0).$$

There only remains the matter of the choice of the instrumental variables. In order to estimate equations (7) and (8) of [2], at least six instruments must be used. The dummy variable $\mathbf{l}$, $\dot{m}_{-1}$ and $\dot{m}_{-2}$ are obvious candidates, and lagged endogenous variables can be included in Z since these are also uncorrelated in the probability limit with the e_t. If one wanted to use some of the pre-determined variables explicitly mentioned by Lipsey and Parkin, e.g., government expenditures and exports, then series could be constructed by interpolation in exactly the same way as they constructed the quarterly series for the Hines trade union variable.

---

[4] The formula for the test statistic is given on p. 29 of [4].

4   The re-estimation of the Lipsey-Parkin model

Two sets of results are reported in this section. The first set of results is intended to demonstrate that estimates obtained by the AIV method, which is designed to take account of auto-regressive errors and endogenous regressors, are quite different from the Lipsey-Parkin estimates obtained by the statistically unsatisfactory OLS method. The second set of results represents an attempt to investigate the influence of incomes policies on the structural coefficients of the model.

Lipsey and Parkin [2], give the following estimated equations as R^2 maximizing for the whole period, i.e., 1948(3)–1968(2), (standard errors are given in parentheses):

$$\dot{p} = 1{\cdot}374 + 0{\cdot}562\dot{w} + 0{\cdot}085\dot{m}_{-1} - 0{\cdot}145\dot{q} \qquad (15)$$
$$\quad\;\; (0{\cdot}548) \quad (0{\cdot}102) \quad\;\; (0{\cdot}019) \qquad\quad (0{\cdot}042)$$
$$R^2 = 0{\cdot}697 \qquad DW = 0{\cdot}946$$

$$\dot{w} = 4{\cdot}147 - 0{\cdot}891U + 0{\cdot}482\dot{p} + 3{\cdot}315\dot{N} \qquad (16)$$
$$\quad\;\; (0{\cdot}973) \quad (0{\cdot}503) \quad (0{\cdot}084) \quad (1{\cdot}590)$$
$$R^2 = 0{\cdot}616 \qquad DW = 0{\cdot}742$$

These equations were re-estimated by the AIV method, and the following results obtained:[5]

$$\dot{p} = 0{\cdot}903 + 0{\cdot}731\dot{w} + 0{\cdot}052\dot{m}_{-1} - 0{\cdot}230\dot{q} \qquad (17)$$
$$\quad\;\; (3{\cdot}070) \quad (0{\cdot}531) \quad\;\; (0{\cdot}048) \qquad\quad (0{\cdot}244)$$
$$\hat{\rho} = 0{\cdot}528 \qquad s^2 = 1{\cdot}444 \qquad \chi^2 = 1{\cdot}438 \text{ (1 d.f.)}$$
$$(0{\cdot}119)$$

$$\dot{w} = 2{\cdot}957 - 0{\cdot}674U + 0{\cdot}728\dot{p} - 1{\cdot}193\dot{N} \qquad (18)$$
$$\quad\;\; (3{\cdot}397) \quad (1{\cdot}556) \quad (0{\cdot}336) \quad (7{\cdot}616)$$
$$\hat{\rho} = 0{\cdot}641 \qquad s^2 = 1{\cdot}044 \qquad \chi^2 = 0{\cdot}137 \text{ (1 d.f.)}$$
$$(0{\cdot}096)$$

The instruments used for the price equation were 1, $\dot{m}_{-1}$, $\dot{m}_{-2}$, $\dot{q}_{-1}$, $\dot{w}_{-1}$ and $\dot{p}_{-1}$, and the instruments for the wage equation were 1, $\dot{m}_{-1}$, $\dot{N}_{-1}$, U_{-1}, $\dot{w}_{-1}$ and $\dot{p}_{-1}$.

The χ^2 statistics act as tests of the consistency of the assumed forms of the structural equations and equation error processes with the sample data. The sample values are insignificant and so the model specification can be accepted.

---

[5] The model was originally estimated with seasonal dummies in each equation in order to test for seasonality. The seasonal dummies were insignificant in every case and so the relationships were re-estimated without them.

The $\hat{\rho}$ values are the estimates of the auto-regressive parameters of the first order schemes, and are both highly significant, suggesting marked serial correlation of the equation errors.

It may be useful to compare the results of the two different methods by considering both the point estimates and the t-ratios.

(a) Price equation: point estimates

Vol.	1	$\dot{w}$	$\dot{m}_{-1}$	$\dot{q}$
OLS	1·374	0·562	0·085	−0·145
AIV	0·903	0·731	0·052	−0·230

(b) Wage equation: point estimates

Vol.	1	U	$\dot{p}$	$\dot{N}$
OLS	4·147	−0·891	0·482	3·315
AIV	2·957	−0·674	0·728	−1·193

(c) Price equation: t-ratios

Vol.	1	$\dot{w}$	$\dot{m}_{-1}$	$\dot{q}$
OLS	2·51	5·53	4·60	3·48
AIV	0·29	1·38	1·08	0·94

(d) Wage equation: t-ratios

Vol.	1	U	$\dot{p}$	$\dot{N}$
OLS	4·26	1·77	5·76	2·09
AIV	0·87	0·43	2·17	0·16

There are clearly substantial differences in the two sets of estimates of the model. It is useful when considering these differences to talk of them in terms of percentage changes in the original Lipsey-Parkin estimates. As far as the economic variables of the price equation are concerned, the coefficient of $\dot{w}$ has increased by 30%, and the co-efficients of $\dot{m}_{-1}$ and $\dot{q}$ have decreased by 39% and 59% respectively. The coefficient of U in the wage equation decreases by 24%, the increase in the coefficient on $\dot{p}$ is about 50% and the $\dot{N}$ coefficient falls by over 100%.[6]

The t-ratios derived from using AIV techniques are all much lower than the corresponding Lipsey-Parkin values, and indeed it is difficult to find a significant variable in the re-estimated price equation. The only significant variable in the wage equation is $\dot{p}$.

The price equation (17) passes the specification test, and so the

[6] These percentage figures should be treated with some caution, given the standard errors on the coefficients.

next step is to apply the test of the acceptability of the *a priori* restrictions that the constant term should be zero and that the coefficient on $\dot{w}$ should be minus the coefficient on $\dot{q}$, (see [2]). The sample value of the test statistic mentioned in section 3 greatly exceeded the 5% value for a χ^2 variate with two degrees of freedom, and so the theoretical constraints on the price equation were rejected in favour of the unrestricted form. RAIV estimates are, therefore, not presented.

In order to test the stability of the model, a dummy variable approach was adopted. Jump variables for the intercept and the slopes were included as additional regressors in the equations. Significant coefficients on the jump variables indicate structural changes due to the influence of incomes policies. This procedure is not entirely satisfactory, since it involves the assumption that each incomes policy has had the same effect on the parameters of the wage-price system. However, this assumption is implicit in the Lipsey-Parkin approach of fitting the equations to the policy-on and policy-off periods separately.

Lipsey and Parkin fitted the price equation to the 'policy-on', 'policy-off' and 'entire' periods, and then applied an F test for the stability of this relationship. The result of their test was that there were significant variations in the regression coefficients. However, it will be recalled that it was strongly argued above that the test procedures used by Lipsey and Parkin were invalid. In fact, no significant jump variable could be found when the augmented price equation was estimated. We present an equation which provides weak evidence that the $\dot{m}_{-1}$ variable has less effect on $\dot{p}$ in policy-on periods. The estimated equation is

$$\dot{p} = 1\cdot519 + 0\cdot624\dot{w} + 0\cdot079\dot{m}_{-1} - 0\cdot117\dot{m}^*_{-1} - 0\cdot241\dot{q} \quad (19)$$
$$(3\cdot856) \quad (0\cdot666) \quad (0\cdot068) \quad (0\cdot085) \quad (0\cdot284)$$
$$\hat{\rho} = 0\cdot560 \qquad s^2 = 1\cdot328 \qquad \chi^2 = 1\cdot316 \,(1 \text{ d.f.})$$
$$(0\cdot125)$$

where

$$\dot{m}^*_{-1} = \dot{m}_{-1} \quad \text{in policy-on periods}$$
$$= 0 \qquad \text{in policy-off periods.}$$

The sum of the coefficients of $\dot{m}_{-1}$ and $\dot{m}^*_{-1}$ is negative, but relatively trivial changes in the coefficients produce a small positive sum. This result would be in line with the findings of Lipsey and Parkin [2]. It should also be noted that both the coefficient and t-ratio on $\dot{w}$ are smaller in the re-specified price equation than in equation (17).

The estimation of the wage equation again gave results very different from those of Lipsey and Parkin who had found 'dramatic changes'. No significant jump variable could be detected, and most of the relevant t-ratios were below one. The following equation was obtained which gave some support to the Lipsey-Parkin argument that incomes policies created a relation between wage increases and union aggressiveness where none previously existed:

$$\dot{w} = 3{\cdot}502 - 0{\cdot}823U + 0{\cdot}677\dot{p} - 2{\cdot}493\dot{N} + 13{\cdot}215\dot{N}^* \quad (20)$$
$$(2{\cdot}213) \quad (0{\cdot}837) \quad (0{\cdot}275) \quad (7{\cdot}548) \quad (22{\cdot}324)$$
$$\hat{\rho} = 0{\cdot}257 \quad s^2 = 1{\cdot}291 \quad \chi^2 = 0{\cdot}470 \ (1 \ \text{d.f.})$$
$$(0{\cdot}818)$$

where

$$\dot{N}^* = \dot{N} \quad \text{in policy-on periods}$$
$$= 0 \quad \text{in policy-off periods.}$$

This effect might be due to unions becoming more aggressive because they feel that incomes policy holds down wages, but allows prices and profits to rise. There are, however, two reasons for not overstating the importance of the implications of equation (20): firstly, the sum of the coefficients of $\dot{N}$ and $\dot{N}^*$ is not significantly different from zero; secondly, the $\dot{N}$ series was constructed by interpolation from annual data and so there are likely to be substantial errors of measurement.

The unemployment variable is insignificant in both of the wage equations estimated in this paper, i.e., equations (18) and (20); so that it is not the case that incomes policies have been successful in breaking the relationship between $\dot{w}$ and U, but simply that no such relation seems to have existed since 1948.

It is important to note that when the model was re-estimated using a method designed to take account of endogenous regressors and auto-regressive errors there was only one significant t-ratio in the whole system, the t-ratio on $\dot{p}$ in the wage equation.[7] If we adopt the criterion of assessing models on the basis of the estimated coefficients being significant, then the Lipsey-Parkin model does not appear to be an adequate representation of the wage-price process.

[7] It is possible that the large standard errors reported in this paper reflect either a high degree of collinearity in the relevant variables, or a lack of identification, rather than the irrelevance of the regressors specified by Lipsey and Parkin.

Two criticisms may be made of the analysis above. The first criticism is that the assumption of only first order auto-regressive errors is restrictive because quarterly data are used and that higher order schemes, in particular a fourth order scheme, may be appropriate. This problem is fairly easy to handle, and all that is needed is a simple generalization of the Sargan AIV estimator.

If L stands for the lag operator, i.e., $L^n x_t = x_{t-n}$, then for the general case of sth order autoregressive errors, we form

$$R(L) = 1 - r_1 L - r_2 L^2 - \cdots - r_s L^s,$$

and minimize

$$\phi^* = [R(L)(\mathbf{y} - X\mathbf{b})]'Z(Z'Z)^{-1}Z'[R(L)(\mathbf{y} - X\mathbf{b})]$$

with respect to the structural and auto-regressive coefficients. The author has re-estimated both equations of the model allowing for up to fifth order processes. The main conclusions were the same for both sets of results: the null hypothesis of serial independence was rejected, only $\hat{r}_1$ was ever significant and it was always significant. The empirical evidence, therefore, supports the assumption of first order auto-regressive errors and the AIV estimator used in section 4 is indeed appropriate.

Secondly, it could be argued that the results obtained by AIV estimation reflect a poor choice of instruments and that the use of an alternative set of instrumental variables might yield much smaller asymptotic standard errors. The usual methods of obtaining efficient estimators require that the model be complete. However, Lipsey and Parkin argue that five variables in their two equation model should be treated as endogenous (see [2]).

In order to proceed with the problem of efficient estimation, it is assumed that productivity changes and the unemployment rate can be treated as pre-determined variables in the wage-price sub-system and $\dot{N}$ is dropped from the wage equation. The Lipsey-Parkin model can now be regarded as including only two endogenous variables and is written as

$$\dot{p} = a_1 + a_2 \dot{w} + a_3 \dot{m}_{-1} + a_4 \dot{q} + u \qquad (21)$$

$$\dot{w} = a_5 + a_6 U + a_7 \dot{p} + v \qquad (22)$$

with the errors u and v being generated by first order auto-regressive schemes.

There is still the problem of whether to use full information or limited information techniques. The use of full information methods is hardly recommended by the results above, since they imply that the matrix of coefficients of endogenous variables is not of full rank. Moreover, full information methods should only be applied when one is satisfied with the specification of each equation of the model and this cannot be said to be the case here. The estimators used in this paper are, therefore, of the limited information class and the assumption is made that the matrix of autoregressive coefficients is diagonal. Although this method is the minimum that can be done to take account of error serial correlation in economic models, it may be greatly superior to methods which ignore auto-correlated errors, or the simultaneous equation problem, or both. Its assumptions do not imply zero cross-auto-covariances between equation errors.

Equations (21) and (22) were estimated by auto-regressive two stage least squares (A2SLS), i.e., AIV with the best set of instruments. A2SLS is, of course, asymptotically equivalent to auto-regressive limited information maximum likelihood and so is efficient in the class of limited information estimators. The results obtained were

$$\dot{p} = -2 \cdot 637 + 1 \cdot 330 \dot{w} + 0 \cdot 011 \dot{m}_{-1} - 0 \cdot 002 \dot{q} \qquad (23)$$
$$(1 \cdot 810) \quad (0 \cdot 357) \quad (0 \cdot 047) \quad (0 \cdot 067)$$
$$\hat{\rho} = 0 \cdot 586 \qquad s^2 = 1 \cdot 779 \qquad \chi^2 = 3 \cdot 778 \text{ (4 d.f.)}$$
$$(0 \cdot 106)$$

$$\dot{w} = 1 \cdot 392 + 0 \cdot 518 U + 0 \cdot 697 \dot{p} \qquad (24)$$
$$(1 \cdot 683) \quad (0 \cdot 837) \quad (0 \cdot 147)$$
$$\hat{\rho} = 0 \cdot 629 \qquad s^2 = 0 \cdot 938 \qquad \chi^2 = 3 \cdot 033 \text{ (5 d.f.)}$$
$$(0 \cdot 093)$$

The asymptotic standard errors are reduced by using A2SLS. However, it is still the case that the estimated model yields only a correlation between $\dot{w}$ and $\dot{p}$. The rate of price inflation is the only variable with a significant t-ratio in the wage equation,[8] and the only significant variable in the price equation is the proportionate rate of change of money wages. The auto-regressive coefficients are very similar in size and significance to those of equations (17) and (18).

To conclude, even when the most efficient AIV estimator is applied to the Lipsey-Parkin model many of the estimated coefficients are insignificant and the model is again underidentified.

[8] It should be noted that the wage equation results are not strictly comparable since equation (18) includes $\dot{N}$ as a determinant of $\dot{w}$.

11

5   Conclusions

This paper considered the recent Lipsey-Parkin article [2] which was concerned with the impact of incomes policy. It was argued that the ordinary least squares estimates calculated by Lipsey and Parkin were of little value, and that the conclusions of their investigation were not well founded. The model was re-estimated using a method designed to take account of the simultaneous equation problem and auto-correlated errors. All current dated variables in the wage-price sub-system were treated as endogenous, but the estimated model collapsed to a correlation between $\dot{w}$ and $\dot{p}$. The findings of the Lipsey-Parkin analysis concerning the existence of significant incomes policy effects on the model's coefficients received no support from our results.

References

[1] A. G. Hines, 'Trade Unions and Wage Inflation in the United Kingdom, 1893–1961', *Review of Economic Studies*, vol. 31 (1964), pp. 221–52.
[2] R. G. Lipsey and J. M. Parkin, 'Incomes Policy: A Re-appraisal', *Economica*, vol. 37 (1970), pp. 115–38, and Chapter 4 above.
[3] T. C. Liu, 'Underidentification, Structural Estimation and Forecasting', *Econometrica*, vol. 28 (1960), pp. 855–65.
[4] J. D. Sargan, 'Wages and Prices in the United Kingdom: A Study in Econometric Methodology', *Colston Papers*, vol. 16 (1964), Butterworths Scientific Publications.

Paul Burrows
and Theodore Hitiris[1]

Chapter 8 Estimating the impact of incomes policy[2]

1 Introduction

Two counter-intuitive results in Lipsey and Parkin's well-known paper[3] on post-war incomes policy provided the initial stimulus for this paper. The first was a failure to identify a significant effect of indirect taxes on the rate of change of prices,[4] a result which conflicted with our own findings for absolute price changes. The second was the curious discovery that both the price and the wage equations collapse (in the sense that the regression coefficients for the explanatory variables become insignificant) for the periods in which policy was operating, implying that incomes policy destroys the explanations of the rate of change of prices ($\dot{p}$) and wages ($\dot{w}$). This result is central to the authors' interpretation of the impact of incomes policy, and one of the aims of this paper is to test whether it could be attributed to the effectiveness of incomes policy between 1948 and 1950. In the early post-war years the attitudes of the unions and the employers were perhaps influenced by their experiences of the 1930's, and the unions were willing to co-operate with a policy of voluntary wage restraint from 1948 to 1950. In contrast, incomes policy since the mid-1950's has operated in the context of unions' and employers' expectations of continuing high employment and inflation. Having learnt that severe deflation is no longer a threat to strengthen the resolve of employers and the government, the willingness of unions to co-operate has declined. In an attempt to estimate the impact of

[1] University of York.
[2] This paper is a by-product of a study of the incidence of indirect taxes being undertaken with support from the Social Science Research Council. We wish to thank Professor R. Crossley, Keith Hartley and Charles Rowley for a number of helpful comments. Reprinted from the *Bulletin of Economic Research*, May 1972, by permission of the authors and publisher.
[3] Chapter 4 above, [2]. Referred to henceforth as L-P.
[4] See L-P, Chapter 4 above, note 6. Solow [4] p. 9 achieved a similar result.

recent incomes policy a series of $\dot{p}$ and $\dot{w}$ equations is presented in section 3 for the years 1955 to 1967, a period which excludes the years 1948 to 1954 included in L-P's sample.[5] In addition to providing evidence on incomes policy these estimates have a broader purpose: to test whether the now conventional explanations of $\dot{p}$ and $\dot{w}$ are appropriate for the economy with expectations of high employment and inflation prevailing.[6]

In essence our tests for the shorter period provide a check on the possibility, which is consistent with the above arguments about expectations, that there has been a shift in the parameters of the price and wage equations between the 1948 to 1954 and 1955 to 1967 periods. Such a shift would be reflected in contrasting results in this paper and the L-P study. It is assumed in this paper, however, that the parameters have not changed *within* the period we are using.

One feature of the L-P paper which we found worrying was the absence of any indication of the robustness (i.e., stability over different equation forms) of the coefficients of the $\dot{p}$ and $\dot{w}$ equations. It is necessary, if we are to evaluate the implications for policy of the empirical results, to have some evidence on the sensitivity of the estimates to equation specification. We return to this point in section 3.

2 Methods

The definitions of variables and data sources are those used by L-P, except where alternatives offer clear advantages. Where such changes are made they will be noted and explained. Since this paper is concerned mainly with the economics of estimating the impact of incomes policy we have not examined the suggestion, discussed by Parkin [3], that simultaneous estimation methods are appropriate. We have used ordinary least squares.

Although we have followed suit to preserve comparability of results, the use of four-quarter rates of change for the dependent variables and some explanatory variables does raise problems. The introduction of a three-quarter overlap for each observation, while it perhaps rescues our hypothesis ($\dot{p}$ and $\dot{w}$ equations estimated using

---

[5] There are additional reasons for excluding the earlier part of L-P's period, such as the lingering effect of rationing and data advantages for 1955 onwards such as the availability of a more comprehensive labour-cost variable.

[6] Hines [1], p. 66, for example, has argued that during such periods other factors, such as the degree of union pressure, become the dominant influence on $\dot{w}$.

quarter-to-quarter changes yielded no significant explanations!) creates problems of serial correlation.

It is assumed for our tests that the impact of incomes policy will be reflected in changes in the slope coefficients or the constant term in either the $\dot{p}$ or $\dot{w}$ equations between policy-off and policy-on periods. There are some possible effects of incomes policy which might elude the tests for shift and slope changes[7] but these are not considered here. There are two alternative methods of testing for changes in the constant term and/or slope coefficients between periods. L-P estimate separate equations for 'policy-off' and 'policy-on' periods whereas we introduce dummy variables to represent these effects. The use of dummy variables is more flexible in that it is possible to test for individual slope changes without allowing the whole equation to vary between periods. Hence, the coefficients which do not vary between the periods are estimated using the whole sample, the 'policy-on' and 'policy-off' periods combined. For equations in which some of the coefficients change and some remain constant this method provides more efficient estimates than can be achieved by estimating separate equations for the two sub-periods.

3   The equations estimated and their interpretation

Price equations

Initially the $\dot{p}$ equation was fitted to the whole period with no account taken of incomes policy effects. The model is

$$\dot{p}_t = a + b_1\dot{T}_t + b_2\dot{C}_t + b_3\dot{m}_{t-3}$$

where $\dot{p}_t$ = rate of change of market prices

$\dot{T}_t$ = rate of change of effective indirect tax rate[8]

$\dot{C}_t$ = rate of change of labour cost per unit of output

$\dot{m}_{t-3}$ = rate of change of import prices

The price and import variables are as in L-P except that a three-quarter lag for $\dot{m}$ was found to be more significant than a one-quarter lag.[9] The labour cost variable, $\dot{C}_t$, the sum of wages, salaries

---

[7] L-P point this out (Chapter 4, above) though their interpretation of results substantially concentrates on the shift and slope change effects of incomes policy. It is to be noted, however, that the dummy variables used in this paper could identify only 'policy effects' which are systematically related to variables included in the equations.

[8] $T = \dfrac{\text{Yield of indirect taxes minus subsidies}}{\text{Consumers' expenditure}}$, which is a weighted average of nominal tax rates.

[9] For sources of data see the Appendix.

and employers' national insurance contributions per unit of output, is preferred to the $\dot{w}_t$ in L-P's equations on the grounds that the standard wage rate is likely to be a poor indicator of labour cost.[10] Since it is the labour cost per unit of output there is no need to include a separate productivity variable.

The estimated equation is the first in Table 1 [equation (1.1)]. As L-P found, the labour and import cost variables are highly significant but in contrast to their unreported results the indirect tax variable is also an important determinant of $\dot{p}$.[11] The problem of serial correlation, not tackled in this paper except for the introduction later of the lagged dependent variable, remains. In general our success in explaining $\dot{p}$ seems to be about the same for the shorter period, when inflation had come to be accepted as the norm, as for the post-war period as a whole.

Equation (1.2) tests for a shift from policy-on to policy-off periods and for changes in the slope coefficients. The variable D is the change in the constant term and TS, CS and MS are the changes in the respective slopes.[12] The constant and the coefficients for $\dot{T}$, $\dot{C}$ and $\dot{m}$ are for policy-on periods since the dummies represent the change *from* 'on' *to* 'off' periods. Equation (1.4) drops the tax and import slope-change dummies but retains CS; equation (1.6) leaves out the shift dummy and equation (1.8) all of the slope change dummies. [The equivalent equations for policy-off are (1.3), (1.5) and (1.7).]

The general conclusion from these estimates is that the $\dot{p}$ equation does *not* collapse in the policy-on periods. In fact, there is no evidence from them that there is even a significant *change* in the constant or the slopes as a result of incomes policy. Each of the slope dummies is insignificant (a finding which applied to a number of equations, not reported, which tested other combinations of variables). The tax and labour cost variables remain significant

---

[10] The use of $\dot{w}_t$ in place of $\dot{C}_t$ would be advantageous if the reduced form Phillips curve were to be derived from the $\dot{p}$ and $\dot{w}$ equations; but this is not required here, as is explained below.

[11] Little emphasis is placed here on a comparison of the sizes of the coefficients; see the comments below on the stability of the coefficients and the derivation of reduced forms.

[12] $D = 1$ in policy-off periods, 0 in policy-on periods. A slope change variable is the product of D and the particular variable whose slope change it represents. Thus, the hypothesis $Y_t = a + (b_1 + b_2 W)x_t$, (where $W = 1$ in 'off' periods, 0 in 'on' periods) is tested by re-arranging as follows. Let $Z = Wx_t$, the product mentioned above, then $Y_t = a + b_1 x_t + b_2 Z$, where b_2 is the change in slope whose size and significance is available from the regression equation.

Table 1   Dependent variable $\dot{p}_t$

Equation Number	Constant	D	$\dot{T}$ Policy-on	$\dot{T}$ Policy-off	TS	$\dot{C}$ Policy-on	$\dot{C}$ Policy-off	CS	$\dot{m}_{t-3}$ Policy-on	$\dot{m}_{t-3}$ Policy-off	MS	$\dot{p}_{t-1}$	R^2	D.W.
1.1	1·323			0·151 (5·21)			0·219 (3·51)			0·127 (3·16)			0·650	0·912
1.2	1·634	-0·213 (0·33)	0·125 (3·03)		0·096 (1·04)	0·206 (2·43)		-0·055 (0·31)	0·069 (0·76)		0·096 (0·82)		0·670	0·983
1.3	1·421	0·213 (0·33)		0·220 (2·65)	-0·096 (1·04)		0·151 (0·98)	-0·055 (0·31)		0·165 (2·27)	-0·096 (0·82)		0·670	0·983
1.4	1·529	-0·483 (0·79)	0·136 (3·95)			0·208 (2·63)		-0·064 (0·45)	0·105 (2·10)				0·658	0·901
1.5	1·046	0·483 (0·79)	0·136 (3·95)				0·272 (2·34)	-0·064 (0·45)	0·105 (2·10)				0·658	0·901
1.6	1·337		0·145 (4·45)			0·234 (3·26)		-0·033 (0·44)	0·128 (3·15)				0·652	0·912
1.7	1·337		0·145 (4·45)				0·201 (2·71)	0·033 (0·44)	0·128 (3·15)				0·652	0·912
1.8	1·444	-0·251 (0·80)	0·137 (4·02)			0·229 (3·58)			0·116 (2·74)				0·656	0·904
1.9	0·491		0·074 (2·87)			0·121 (2·40)			0·096 (3·09)			0·532 (5·58)	0·803	1·680
1.10	0·508	-0·327 (0·65)	0·080 (2·44)		-0·031 (0·41)	0·077 (1·10)		0·131 (0·93)	0·080 (1·13)		-0·013 (1·41)	0·561 (5·11)	0·809	1·664
1.11	0·435	0·089 (3·56)	0·078 (2·77)			0·116 (2·19)			0·099 (3·03)			0·541 (5·43)	0·804	1·703

Notes

1. The numbers in brackets are t values. R^2 are corrected for degrees of freedom.
2. Symbols in Table 1:

    D: change in constant from policy-on to policy-off [equations (1.2), (1.4), (1.8), (1.10) and (1.11)] or for policy-off to policy-on equations (1.3) and (1.4).

    $\dot{T}, \dot{C}, \dot{m}$: as defined in the text. In these columns a single number is the value for the whole period [e.g., 0·151 for T in equations (1.1)] where a slope dummy is included the coefficient is placed under either the policy-on sub-column [for policy-on equations (1.2), (1.4), (1 6) and (1.10)] or the policy-off sub-column [for policy-off equations (1.3), (1.5) and (1.7)].

    TS, CS, MS: slope dummy variables for $\dot{T}, \dot{C}$, and $\dot{m}$.

    $\dot{p}_{t-1}$: lagged dependent variable.

[except for $\dot{C}$ in equation (1.3)] in the presence of their slope dummy
variables but the inclusion of MS makes $\dot{m}_{t-3}$ insignificant during
policy-on. However, since MS is never significant it can be excluded
and $\dot{m}$ is again significant.

Our failure, in contrast to L-P, to find any significant effect on the
price equation does not, of course, deny an impact of incomes policy
on $\dot{p}$ since policy may affect the values of one or more of the explanatory variables. But this evidence *is* inconsistent with the view that
recent (prices and) incomes policy has controlled $\dot{p}$ independently of
the values of $\dot{T}$, $\dot{C}$ and $\dot{m}$. It seems probable therefore that the effects
of incomes policy postulated by L-P derive solely from the immediate
post-war period, a view which corresponds with their own findings
when analyzing the prediction errors of policy-off equations for
policy-on periods (Chapter 4, pp. 103–4).

To test the hypothesis that the rate of change of prices is a function
of the *expected* rate of change of prices we introduce the lagged
dependent variable. The conventional theoretical justification[13] is
to postulate that

$$\dot{p} = f(x) + \dot{p}^*$$

where $\dot{p}^*$ is the expected rate of inflation, x the real variables, ($\dot{T}$, $\dot{C}$
and $\dot{m}$) in the economy which influence $\dot{p}$. Assume that

$$\dot{p}^* = \gamma\dot{p}_{t-1}$$

that is, that expectations are passively formed on the basis of the
most recent experience of $\dot{p}$, then

$$\dot{p} = f(x) + \gamma\dot{p}_{t-1}$$

Equations (1.9), (1.10) and (1.11) are respectively equations (1.1),
(1.2) and (1.8) with $\dot{p}_{t-1}$ added. The effect is to eliminate the serial
correlation and to raise R^2 by about 0·15, at the cost of weakening
the tax and cost variables (though $\dot{T}$ remains significant throughout
and $\dot{C}$ and $\dot{m}$ are significant except when their slope dummy variables
are also included). Since the inclusion of $\dot{p}_{t-1}$ adds little to our understanding of the determinants of $\dot{p}$ it may be doubted whether we are
much better off. However, again, no slope change is indicated but in
one equation (1.11) the shift dummy becomes significant, though

[13] See, for example, Solow [4], p. 3. Parkin [3] (Chapter 5, above) tried a more
sophisticated approach, for wage equations, the introduction of the lagged
dependent variable and one or more of the explanatory variables in lagged as
well as current form. Given collinearity between the current and lagged values
of variables with trends we prefer the simple approach.

small, its positive sign suggesting that in policy-on periods $\dot{p}$ is slightly lower, for given values of $\dot{T}$, $\dot{C}$ and $\dot{m}$, than during policy-off periods. This must remain a highly uncertain, though beneficial, effect of incomes policy.

Overall, we cannot conclude with any confidence that the structure of the $\dot{p}$ equation has been affected by incomes policy. We need, therefore, to test for an influence on prices via labour cost, in particular through $\dot{w}$.

Wage equations

In many respects the estimation of $\dot{w}$ equations proved more difficult and less conclusive. Since L-P's conclusions about incomes policy hinge on their $\dot{w}$ equations, our difficulties raise serious questions as to their relevance to incomes policy in the period we are dealing with.

The basic model tested by L-P was

$$\dot{w}_t = a_0 + a_1 U'_t + a_2 \dot{p}_t + a_3 \dot{N}_t$$

where $\dot{w}$ = the rate of change of money wage rates
$\quad U'$ = the percentage level of unemployment (see below)
$\quad \dot{N}$ = the rate of change of percentage of labour force unionized.

In this model the unemployment variable enters the wage equation in a linear form. While this hypothesis conflicts with much of the theory and evidence published before the L-P paper we have adopted the same specification to maintain comparability with their results. The relative significance of the linear and non-linear forms is not, therefore, tested in this paper.

To tackle one problem at the beginning, the definition of U adopted by L-P, $U'_t = (U_t + U_{t-1} + U_{t-2})/3$, while having the advantage (from a Phillips curve point of view) of increasing the significance of U'_t and raising R^2 compared with U_t in equations without slope dummies, increased the collinearity between U and $\dot{p}$ sufficiently to weaken $\dot{p}$ as an explanatory variable.[14] This effect can be seen by comparing equations (2.1) and (2.2) in Table 2. Given the possibility that U' picks up some of the weight of $\dot{p}$ and the absence of any convincing theoretical reason for using U' we chose to define U as U_t.[15]

[14] This was true of overall equations and equations where shift and slope dummies were included; the only exception was an equation with D but not slope dummies.
[15] An added reason for using U_t was that its size and significance proved less sensitive to variations in equations specification.

Table 2   Dependent variable: $\dot{w}_t$

Equation Number	Constant	D	U		US	U'	$\dot{p}_t$		PS	$\dot{N}$		NS	$\dot{p}_{ott}$	N_{on}	$\dot{w}_{t-1}$	R^2	D.W.
			Policy on	Policy off			Policy on	Policy off		Policy on	Policy off						
(2.1)	3·702		−0·459 (0·99)				0·422 (2·65)			0·864 (3·00)						0·314	0·679
(2.2)	5·913					−1·460 (2·80)	0·257 (1·72)			1·173 (4·00)						0·406	0·745
(2.3)	6·403	−0·718 (1·50)	−1·070 (2·00)		−0·408 (0·47)		−0·068 (0·30)		0·314 (0·93)	1·069 (3·51)		−1·404 (1·90)				0·496	0·722
(2.4)	5·692	0·547 (0·09)		−1·522 (2·01)	0·463 (0·60)			0·248 (0·83)	−0·318 (0·99)		−0·312 (0·47)	1·386 (1·88)				0·498	0·766
(2.5)	5·934	−0·736 (1·49)	−0·328 (1·55)		−0·409 (0·45)		−0·051 (0·22)		0·657 (2·23)	0·812 (2·88)						0·449	0·840
(2.6)	4·815	−0·095 (0·21)		−1·329 (1·72)	0·522 (0·65)			0·596 (2·45)	−0·647 (2·35)		0·821 (2·92)					0·452	0·830
(2.7)	4·482	1·634 (3·50)	−1·024 (2·97)										0·423 (2·27)	1·095 (3·81)		0·489	0·973
(2.8)	5·353	1·468 (2·75)		−1·425 (2·04)	0·498 (0·66)								0·355 (1·66)	1·086 (3·75)		0·494	0·775
(2.9)	0·983	−0·058 (0·18)					0·091 (0·76)			0·415 (1·99)					0·716 (6·98)	0·682	1·463
(2.10)	1·702	0·514 (1·28)		−0·342 (1·20)									0·038 (0·25)	0·598 (2·57)	0·632 (5·77)	0·718	1·407

Symbols in Table 2:

D: change in constant from policy-on to policy-off [equations (2.3) and (2.5)] or from policy-off to policy-on to policy-on [equations (2.4), (2.6), (2.7), (2.8) and (2.10)].

U, $\dot{p}$, $\dot{N}$: as defined in the text. Interpretation similar to $\dot{T}$, $\dot{C}$ and $\dot{m}$.

US, PS, NS: slope dummy variables for U, $\dot{p}$ and $\dot{N}$.

$\dot{p}_{ott}$: $\dot{p}$ restricted to policy-off periods.

N_{on}: $\dot{N}$ restricted to policy-on periods.

$\dot{w}_{t-1}$: lagged dependent variable.

The full equation with all slope dummies included for policy-on periods is (2.3) [the equivalent for policy-off is equation (2.4)].[16] The general conclusions from these estimates [confirmed by the equation for the whole period (2.1)] are that the conventional form of the $\dot{w}$ equation explains a lower proportion of the variation in $\dot{w}$ than L-P achieved for the whole post-war period,[17] and that serial correlation is present as with the $\dot{p}$ equations. But the degree of explanation is similar for policy-on and -off periods, so that L-P's finding that the $\dot{w}$ equation collapses in policy-on periods is not supported by our evidence for the shorter period. Of the individual explanatory variables only U is significant in both policy-on and policy-off periods; N is significant only in policy-on periods; the $\dot{p}$ variable appears to be insignificant in both periods. The slope dummies for U and $\dot{p}$ (US and PS respectively) are insignificant but the slope for $\dot{N}$ increases significantly from zero when policy takes effect. However, collinearity between US, PS and NS suggested that it might be profitable to test further the significance of US and PS. This is done by dropping NS and estimating equations (2.5) and (2.6), the effect being to suggest that $\dot{p}$ is significant in policy-off periods but not in policy-on periods. The change in the slope of U however does not appear to be significant.[18] L-P found that $\dot{p}$ was significant in policy-off periods only and $\dot{N}$ (nearly) significant in policy-on periods only. This formulation is estimated [equation (2.7)] by setting $\dot{p} = 0$ and $\dot{N} = \dot{N}$ for policy-on quarters and setting $\dot{N} = 0$ and $\dot{p} = \dot{p}$ for policy-off periods. The results confirm the influence of $\dot{N}$ when policy is operating and $\dot{p}$ when it is not, ($\dot{p}_{off}$ and $\dot{N}_{on}$ are significant).[19] The addition of the dummy variables for the change in the slope of U [equation (2.8)] obscures the influence of $\dot{p}$ but again the hypothesis that the slope of U is unaffected by incomes policy is not rejected.[20]

To test the hypothesis that the rate of change of wages is a function

[16] With the dummies now taking the value of zero for the policy-off periods.
[17] And *a fortiori* a much poorer explanation than similar equations for earlier periods. See for example Hines [1].
[18] This was true also when PS was omitted and when L-P's unemployment variable U' was substituted for U.
[19] A reversed test confirmed that $\dot{p}$ was insignificant during policy-on and N insignificant during policy-off.
[20] The influence of incomes policy on the constant term is not clear, the size and significance of the shift dummy being very vulnerable to changes in the form of the equations. However, its significance with a positive sign in equation (2.7) is some confirmation of L-P's findings that incomes policy tends, perversely, to increase the constant term.

of the *expected* rate of change of wages we adopt an analogous theoretical formulation to that used for the price equation (page 156). This implies the addition of the lagged dependent variable [as in equations (2.9) and (2.10)], and this proves to have a drastic effect on the wage equations. Although the R^2 is raised and the $D.W.$ statistic pushed into the lower inconclusive region,[21] so much of the weight of explanation is taken by $\dot{w}_{t-1}$, that U_t and $\dot{p}_t$ become insignificant. Certainly there is no indication that introducing this variable adds any confirmation to L-P's results.

These tests of the $\dot{w}$ equation for 1955–67 provide sufficient evidence on which to base some conclusions relevant to the debate on the existence of $\dot{w} - U$ trade-offs and the effects of incomes policy.[22]

The conventional formulation of $\dot{w}$ equations performs worse for the high-employment-norm economy, regardless of whether incomes policy is in operation, than it did for the early post-war, pre-war and earlier periods. Perhaps it can tentatively be argued, however, that the $\dot{w} - U$ trade-off does hold, whether or not incomes policy is operating. L-P's suggestion that the trade-off is broken[23] by incomes policy is not substantiated by our estimates for recent experience. But incomes policy may cut the feedback from $\dot{p}$ to $\dot{w}$, though the consequent dampening effect on the inflation spiral may be offset by a compensating increase in union influence. In addition to the doubts about firm conclusions expressed below, the interpretation of $\dot{N}$ as the influence of trade union pressure seems to us to be optimistic,[24] particularly in view of the substantial influences not included in the equations. Experimentation with alternative measures of union strength (e.g., the proportion of working days lost through strike action?) is needed to provide a cross-check on the influence of union pressure, but this has not been attempted for this paper.

Linked to the problem of the poor fit, there is another major deficiency of the $\dot{w}$ equations. This is the sensitivity of the size of the constant and slope coefficients to changes in equation form. The estimate of the slope for U, for example, is -0.459 in equation (2.1) and -1.425 in equation (2.8). And the estimate proved extremely

[21] Though the statistic is now biased against indicating the presence of serial correlation.

[22] An extra source of uncertainty connected with evaluation of policy, the danger of attributing the effects of one measure to another, is ignored here.

[23] Lipsey and Parkin [2]; see also Parkin [3].

[24] The rate of unionization fell between 39·76% and 40·57% over the whole period. It is difficult to believe that such trivial variations in membership provide a good indicator of changes in union pressure.

volatile when further slight variations were tried (but not reported here for the sake of brevity). Similar instability was found for several of the other coefficients.[25] Consequently, the calculation of a reduced form Phillips curve from the $\dot{p}$ and $\dot{w}$ equations would lead to very uncertain conclusions; the effect of incomes policy on the reduced form (in the case of our estimates, this effect could arise through the constant term or the $\dot{p}$ slope but not the U slope) would vary widely for different equations.

4   Conclusions

To summarize, we have reached the following conclusions:

(1) Changes in indirect taxes do influence the rate of change of prices.

(2) The conventional theory of the determinants of the rate of change of wage rates provides a poorer explanation for the 1955–67 period as a whole than for earlier periods. The theory is essentially a free market explanation and fails to emphasize the significance of the expectations and bargaining power of the institutions operating in the labour market. Perhaps this provides some rationale for the weakening of the degree of explanation of wage inflation, in the context of the development in recent years of the firm expectation of continuing high employment. Should not the theory now shift towards attempting to explain the relative bargaining strengths of the institutions involved in the wage determination process?

(3) Our tests do not support Lipsey and Parkin's contention that the price equations collapse when incomes policy is operating, nor their finding that the slope of the unemployment variable in the wage equations is altered by incomes policy.

(4) The regression coefficients in the wage equations are very sensitive to equation specification so that we cannot conclude, as Lipsey and Parkin did, that incomes policy has pivoted the Phillips curve.

(5) The overall effect of recent incomes policy on the rate of change of prices and wages has been small. However, the tests are capable of identifying only differences on the average between periods when incomes policy is operating and periods when it is not. It remains possible that incomes policy causes changes in the time

[25] The coefficients of the $\dot{p}$ equations, on the other hand, were rather more stable perhaps reflecting the better fit.

162   Paul Burrows and Theodore Hitiris

profile of price and wage rate increases *within* the policy-on and policy-off periods.

Appendix   Sources of data

The sources are those used by Lipsey and Parkin except for:
T: index of the effective rate of indirect tax (minus subsidies). Annual figures on tax yield available at current prices in the Blue Book, 1967. The annual figures were allocated to quarters by the following method. Assuming that tax rates do not change within the fiscal year taxes are proportional to consumers' expenditure. Therefore, a plausible hypothesis is that tax yields follow the quarterly pattern of expenditure. Dividing the tax yield by consumers' expenditure at 1958 prices we derive the tax per unit of output (consumed). The series was then transformed to an index.
C: labour cost per unit of output; labour cost was defined as the sum of wage, salary and national insurance payments by employers. Labour cost at current prices divided by G.D.P. at 1958 factor cost provided a measure of labour cost per unit of output. Source: *Economic Trends*, October 1968.

References

[1] A. G. Hines, 'Unemployment and the Rate of Change of Money Wage Rates in the United Kingdom 1862–1963: A Reappraisal', *Review of Economics and Statistics*, February 1968.
[2] R. G. Lipsey and J. M. Parkin, 'Incomes Policy: A Reappraisal', *Economica*, May 1970, and Chapter 4, above.
[3] J. M. Parkin, 'Incomes Policy: Some Further Results on the Determination of the Rate of Change of Money Wages', *Economica*, November 1970, and Chapter 5, above.
[4] R. M. Solow, *Price Expectations and the Behaviour of the Price Level*, Manchester University Press, 1969.

Michael T. Sumner[1]

Chapter 9 Aggregate demand, price expectations and the Phillips curve

In a recent contribution to the empirical literature on inflation, Lipsey and Parkin [14] (Chapter 4, above) concluded that the effect of incomes policy has been to pivot the reduced-form Phillips curve at an unemployment rate of about 1·8%. This conclusion was based on a comparison of the wage and price equations in policy-on and policy-off periods; by implication, the policy-off period, at least,[2] was regarded by them as homogeneous. It is the contention of this paper that their dichotomy between policy-on and policy-off is an over-simplification which conceals important problems and may result in erroneous policy recommendations. In order to justify this assertion in the present state of uncertainty as to the effects of incomes policy, attention is confined to the policy-off period, 1950(4)–1955(4) and (1957(1)–1961(2).

Further tests of structural stability

It is instructive to begin by applying the Chow test to the Lipsey-Parkin policy-off equation, which relates the rate of change of money wages ($\dot{W}$) to the level of unemployment (U) and the rate of change of prices ($\dot{P}$).[3] The division of the period which this test requires is largely arbitrary, but a natural procedure is to split the policy-off period in 1956, a policy-on interlude. The resulting estimates are shown in Table 1. For the entire policy-off period, the results seem quite acceptable: all the coefficients are correctly signed

[1] University of Manchester. I am grateful to Michael Parkin for making his data available to me, and for valuable comments on an earlier draft.
[2] The low value of the Durbin-Watson statistic in the policy-on wage equation suggested that 'there is some systematic variability in policy-on wage changes which is not caught by the...model.'
[3] The precise derivation and sources of the variables will be found in [14]. The irrelevant unionization variable is omitted throughout; this omission has very little effect on the other parameters.

Table 1

Period	Intercept	U	$\dot{P}$	$\bar{R}^2$	d
Policy-off	6·68	−2·38 [3·77]	0·48 [7·35]	0·848	1·23
1950(4)–1955(4)	7·80	−2·85 [4·72]	0·44 [10·40]	0·930	2·20
1957(1)–1961(2)	8·12	−2·85 [2·47]	0·004 [0·02]	0·509	1·27

[ ] = 't' statistic

and appear to be well-determined, and the overall 'fit' is satisfactory. However, the Durbin-Watson test indicates the presence of positive serial correlation in the residuals, and this suggestion of instability is amply confirmed by the sub-period estimates. The equation for the first half of the 1950's requires little comment; in the second sub-period, however, the basic model fitted very badly, and in particular the coefficient on $\dot{P}$ lost all significance. The computed value of the F statistic is 9·37, and the critical value with (3, 33) degrees of freedom is 4·44 at the 1% significance level; thus the null hypothesis that the vectors of regression coefficients are the same in the two sub-periods is strongly rejected.[4] The effects of the structural shift are illustrated in Table 2; for the purposes of comparison, the mean prediction

Table 2 Errors in predictions of $\dot{W}$ beyond the sample period, using equation for 1950(4)–1955(4)

Period	Number of positive prediction errors	Number of negative prediction errors	Mean predictions error, % p.a.
1957(1)–1959(1)	2	7	−0·69
1959(2)–1961(2)	2	7	−0·631
1957(1)–1961(2)	4	14	−0·663

Standard deviation of residuals within sample period: 0·480

[4] The results of this test are qualified by the uncertain value of d in the second sub-period. Some further experiments, not worth reporting in detail, indicate that this result is not in any way attributable to the particular division of the policy-off period adopted above.

error in using the Lipsey-Parkin policy-off wage equation to predict $\dot{W}$ in policy-on was -0.174% p.a., and the standard deviation of residuals from their policy-off wage equation was 0.882 (c.f. their Table 2).

A necessary condition for acceptance of the Lipsey-Parkin thesis concerning incomes policy is that the Phillips curve should be relatively stable within the policy-off period. As their estimated wage equation manifestly does not satisfy that condition, the remainder of this paper is addressed to the task of reformulating the equation in an attempt, albeit unsuccessful, to provide the basis for estimation of incomes policy effects.

Within the confines of received doctrine two approaches are feasible. Firstly, the macro Phillips curve is derived from the wage-change/unemployment relations in individual labour markets; in general, therefore, the shape and position of the function relating the average rate of wage change to the national level of unemployment will depend on the distribution of unemployment across the micro-labour markets (see Archibald [1]). Detailed consideration of the aggregation problem is not undertaken here, but it is worth pointing out that in some preliminary trials, the addition of the variance of industrial unemployment rates to the Lipsey-Parkin wage equation did not improve the results; on the contrary, the variance term appeared with the wrong sign and never attained statistical significance.[5]

The second approach arises from the fact that both the arguments of the Lipsey-Parkin wage equation are proxies for the 'true' independent variables. The unemployment term is required to serve as a measure of demand pressure; it has recently been suggested [3] that an alternative proxy, *viz.* unfilled vacancies, is preferable on both *a priori* and empirical grounds. The relevance of this contention to wage behaviour in the 1950's is examined in the next section. The role of the price-change variable was succinctly explained by Lipsey and Parkin [14] in terms which emphasize the independent significance only of *expected* price changes: '*Unanticipated* changes in prices affect wages through excess demand. . . . *Anticipated* changes in prices lead to an increase in wages independently of excess demand for labour. Hence, in common with previous studies, we enter the

---

[5] I am indebted to G. C. Archibald for making his data available to me. His results suggested that regional variance was marginally more powerful than the industrial measure used here; but cf. Thirlwall [21].

rate of change of prices in the wage equation as a proxy for the *anticipated* rate of change of prices.' In a subsequent section experiments will be made with alternative proxies for the expected rate of change of prices, in an attempt to discover whether there was a shift in the side relation between actual and anticipated price changes, rather than in the relation between wage changes and price expectations. Such an approach is of wider interest than might be inferred from the present context, for it has been argued, notably by Friedman [7] and Phelps [17], that the Phillips relation exists only in the short run: if sufficient time is allowed for expectations to adjust to any stable rate of increase of actual prices, then $\dot{W}$ will itself rise above its constant-price value by the magnitude of $\dot{P}$, so that the choice facing policy-makers is not between higher employment and a lower rate of inflation, but between present and future unemployment, since a steadily increasing rate of inflation ultimately becomes unacceptable. The Friedman-Phelps reformulation of the Phillips hypothesis is clearly of considerable significance for policy purposes; however, while both theorists deny the validity of the trade-off between inflation and employment, the models they employ are different, as explained below.

The measurement of excess demand

Bowers *et al.* [3] have recently argued that for the 1960's, vacancies (V) are superior to unemployment as a proxy for excess demand. A further possibility is to use the (algebraic) difference between vacancies and unemployment (E) as a simplified variant of the series constructed by Dow and Dicks-Mireaux [6]. Since all three approximations to the 'true', unobservable variable are highly collinear, it is not surprizing that the results recorded in Table 3 differ little from those in Table 1.

In particular, the null hypothesis that the two sub-periods are homogeneous is rejected,[6] and the coefficient of determination in the second sub-period remains very low in each case. Whatever may be true of subsequent periods, therefore, there is no case for replacing unemployment by vacancies or 'excess demand' in the wage equation.

A Friedman model

This section examines the hypothesis that the instability reported above stems from the defects of actual price changes as a proxy

---

[6] The F statistics are 3·62 (V) and 6·36 (E); the 5% critical value is 2·89.

Table 3

Period	Intercept	V	E	$\dot{P}$	$\bar{R}^2$	d
Policy-off	−1·26	3·55 [4·68]		0·33 [4·08]	0·868	1·23
		3·62	1·61 [4·52]	0·39 [5·37]	0·865	1·25
1950(4)–1955(4)	−0·42	3·18 [3·57]		0·33 [4·41]	0·909	1·90
		3·93	1·55 [4·27]	0·38 [7·04]	0·923	2·07
1957(1)–1961(2)	0·15	2·33 [1·79]		0·22 [1·22]	0·430	1·18
		4·06	1·60 [2·43]	0·04 [0·22]	0·504	1·21

for the corresponding anticipated magnitude. A second question concerns the size of the coefficient on the expected price change series: provided the latter is proxied suitably, Friedman predicts that the coefficient will not differ significantly from unity.

An assumption commonly made in the construction of a proxy measure of expectations is that they are formed adaptively: in obvious notation,

$$\dot{P}^E = \lambda\dot{P} + (1 - \lambda)\dot{P}^E_{-1} \qquad (1)$$

The wage equation is now specified as

$$\dot{W} = \alpha + \beta U + \gamma\dot{P}^E + \varepsilon \qquad (2)$$

where ε is an error term, the properties of which will be considered below. Combining equations (1) and (2), and applying the Koyck transformation yields the estimating equation

$$\dot{W} = \alpha + \beta U - \beta(1 - \lambda)U_{-1} + \gamma\lambda\dot{P} + (1 - \lambda)\dot{W}_{-1} + Z \qquad (3)$$

where $Z = \varepsilon - (1 - \lambda)\varepsilon_{-1}$

The Lipsey-Parkin wage equation may be regarded as a special case of equation (3) with $\lambda = 1$.

As equation (3) is overidentified, the ordinary least squares estimation procedure will not in general provide unique estimates of the structural parameters; fortunately, a non-linear estimation technique is available and has been applied to the wage equation in some further work by Parkin [15] (Chapter 5, above). A more serious problem concerns the properties of the error term in equation (3), for if the classical assumptions are made about ε, *viz.*

$$E[\varepsilon] = 0$$
$$E[\varepsilon_i \varepsilon_j] = I\sigma_\varepsilon^2$$

then to a first approximation the composite error term in equation (3) will be first-order auto-correlated; moreover, the Durbin-Watson statistic will generally fail to indicate the presence of serial correlation when the lagged value of the dependent variable appears among the regressors (see Griliches [9]). A convenient, but usually untested, assumption is to attribute the classical properties to the composite error term, Z. This implies that the disturbance term in equation (2) follows the first-order Markov scheme

$$\varepsilon = (1 - \lambda)\varepsilon_{-1} + e$$

where $E[e] = 0$
$\qquad E[e_i e_j] = I\sigma_\varepsilon^2.$

Since the data used are four-quarter overlapping changes this assumption is at least as plausible as the alternative specified above, and it appears to be justified by some additional results obtained by Parkin, who reported that the auto-correlation parameter in a further transformation of equation (3) was numerically small and statistically insignificant.

Equation (3) was fitted to the policy-off data in an attempt to test whether the poor results described above are a consequence of mis-specifying $\lambda = 1$, but it is immediately apparent from the estimates presented in Table 4 that this more general wage equation does nothing to resolve the instability problem.[7] The one new result is the intuitively appealing inference from the sub-period point estimates of λ that price expectations are based on more recent experience the more rapidly prices are rising,[8] but the significance of this result is dubious: in the second section of the policy-off period λ lies well

---

[7] Applying the Chow test, the computed F statistic is 4·15; the critical value with (4,31) degrees of freedom is 4·00 at the 1% significance level.
[8] Cf. Cagan [4].

Table 4 Non-linear constrained least-squares estimates of equation (3)

Period	α	β	$\gamma(\geq 0)$	$\lambda(\leq 1)$	σ_z^2
Policy-off	7·03	−2·57	0·47	0·55	0·602
	(1·59)	(0·87)	(0·10)	(0·14)	
1950(4)–1955(4)	7·80	−2·85	0·44	1·00	0·284
	(0·98)	(0·62)	(0·04)	—	
1957(1)–1961(2)	7·93	−2·71	0	0·69	0·634
	(1·53)	(0·90)	—	(0·24)	

σ_z^2 = variance of residuals
( ) = asymptotic standard errors

within two standard errors from unity, while in the first section the point estimate of λ was (marginally) above unity in the absence of the restriction noted at the head of the column. In the light of these results some suspicion must be attached to the estimated value of λ for the entire policy-off period. None of the estimates of γ offers any encouragement to the members of the 'strict' expectations school: in the second sub-period the unrestricted estimate of γ was *negative*, and neither of the other estimates is consistent with Friedman's prediction that in the long run the Phillips curve becomes a vertical straight line.

Rejection of Friedman's hypothesis is, however, contingent on acceptance of the adaptive expectations mechanism expressed in equation (1). The latter has been criticized as being unduly rigid, and indeed some slight support for this view may be derived from the variations in the estimates of λ in Table 4. A conceptually more satisfying approach to the measurement of the expected rate of price increase is to utilize Fisher's famous distinction between the 'real' rate (Re) and the money rate (Rb) of interest: in equilibrium, for the marginal investor,

$$\dot{P}^E = Rb - Re \qquad (4)$$

To employ equation (4) as a means of calculating $\dot{P}^E$, proxies for the (expected) rates of return on 'real' and 'money' assets are required. In most previous applications of Fisher's distinction (see, for example, Cagan [5], Appendix B and Friedman and Schwartz [8], pp. 584n., 599) the rate of interest on bonds has been used as a measure of the 'money' rate and the earnings—or dividend—price ratio on equities as an index of the 'real' rate. Hence a three-quarter moving average of the difference between debenture yields and equity dividend yields was substituted in the wage equation (2), which was then fitted to data for the entire policy-off period and the two sub-periods used above. However, the coefficient on the new proxy for $\dot{P}^E$ was incorrectly signed in all cases. (Table 5)

Table 5

Period	Intercept	U	$(Rb - Re)$	$\bar{R}^2$	d
Policy-off	12·17	−4·93 [6·88]	−0·51 [2·49]	0·677	0·52
1950(4)–1955(4)	16·13	−9·57 [6·99]	−2·76 [3·51]	0·711	0·86
1957(1)–1961(2)	8·16	−2·86 [4·31]	−0·02 [0·08]	0·509	1·27

The failure of so crude an attempt to apply Fisher's distinction is hardly surprising. Differences of opinion are necessarily ignored in applying equation (4). The dividend yield would approximate the rate of return on equities only if the expected growth rate of dividends were zero.[9] It is not obvious *a priori* that price expectations in labour markets will coincide exactly with price expectations in financial markets; and conventional wisdom asserts that the latter adjust more rapidly to changes in economic conditions. Given the period in question, perhaps the most important factor in accounting for these absurd results is that equation (4) relates to the pure rates on real and money assets, while their empirical counterparts incorporate a risk premium. Equation (4) can be re-written as

$$\dot{P}^E = (r_b - S_b) - (r_e - S_e),$$

[9] Gupta [10] defines *Re* as 'the ratio of the expected real earnings, net of depreciation and corporate income tax, to the real market price of an equity'; in turn, expected real earnings per share are measured by a weighted average of current and past real earnings per share. However, he does not employ a growth factor in the calculation, so that, at least for the post-war period, his method is no better than the simpler technique used above. It is notable that the worst results of his attempt to include price expectations explicitly in a money demand function relate to the years 1941–60.

where r_b and r_b represent the observed rates of return on bonds and equities respectively, and S_b and S_e are the corresponding risk premia. In the absence of additional information, it is convenient to assume that the differential risk premium on equities $(S_e - S_b)$ remains constant at least over short periods, but such an assumption may well be unwarranted in this case, for as the Radcliffe Committee explained ([23], para. 574), '...the shift of investors...from bonds to equities...is partly due, no doubt, to fears of inflation, but partly also to the development of institutional facilities for investing with reasonable safety in equities, [and] to the influence of financial journalism.' Hence, in the absence of additional information on variations in the differential risk premium, further speculation on this topic would not be fruitful. In the next section the adaptive expectations hypothesis is invoked again without further search for more satisfactory alternatives.

A Phelps model

Whereas Friedman amends the Phillips relation by including the expected rate of price increase as an additional argument, Phelps [17] substitutes for the latter the expected rate of wage increase, on the grounds that:

...the expectation of price increases affects money wages only through its effects on expected vacancy rates and the expected unemployment rate. *Given the latter*, a rise of the expected rate of inflation will have little or no effect upon the wage increase which a firm grants if it expects other firms to hold the line on the money wage rates they pay; in particular, the threat of an employee expecting a rise of the cost of living to quit in search of another job will be empty if it is not expected that other firms' wages will rise with the cost of living.

Hence, although both models deny the long-run validity of the Phillips trade-off, they differ markedly in terms of specification.

One way of making Phelp's model:

$$\dot{W} = \alpha + \beta U + \delta \dot{W}^E \tag{5}$$

operational is as follows. Assume the expected wage is equal to the expected value of the marginal product of labour:

$$W^E = M^E \tag{6}$$

and define

$$M^E = N^E . P^E \tag{7}$$

where P^E is the expected price level and N^E is the expected marginal physical product of labour. Assume, further that the latter is proportional to the expected average physical product of labour (Q^E),

$$N^E = \theta Q^E. \tag{8}$$

Substitute equations (7) and (8) in equation (6), rewrite in natural logarithms, and differentiate with respect to time to obtain:

$$\dot{W}^E = \dot{P}^E + \dot{Q}^E. \tag{9}$$

Equation (9) is substituted in the wage equation (5) without constraining the coefficients on $\dot{P}^E$ and $\dot{Q}^E$ to be equal; thus,

$$\dot{W} = \alpha + \beta U + \eta \dot{P}^E + \theta \dot{Q}^E. \tag{10}$$

Finally, augment the adaptive price expectations hypothesis (1) with a similar assumption regarding labour productivity,

$$\dot{Q}^E = \mu Q + (1 - \mu)\dot{Q}^E_{-1}. \tag{11}$$

Substitution of equations (1) and (11) in equation (10) yields, after repeated application of the Koyck transformation, the estimating equation

$$\dot{W} = \alpha\lambda\mu + \beta U - \beta(2 - \lambda - \mu)U_{-1} + \beta(1 - \lambda)(1 - \mu)U_{-2} + \eta\lambda\dot{P}$$
$$- \eta\lambda(1 - \mu)\dot{P}_{-1} + \theta\mu\dot{Q} - \theta\mu(1 - \lambda)\dot{Q}_{-1} + (2 - \lambda - \mu)\dot{W}_{-1}$$
$$- (1 - \lambda)(1 - \mu)\dot{W}_{-2} + e. \tag{12}$$

The stochastic term, e has been inserted in an *ad hoc* manner; it is assumed to possess the usual properties.

This version of the Phelps model was estimated with the results shown in Table 6. The addition of the rate of productivity growth does not improve the results obtained from the Friedman model. The sub-period estimates continue to reveal differences in the response of wage-change to its supposed determinants, and the expectation $\eta = \theta = 1$ is not fulfilled. The additional refinement of re-estimating equation (12) subject to the *a priori* constraints on the parameters was not undertaken in this case as comparison of the free and constrained estimates of equation (3) suggested that the parameters which satisfied the constraints initially would be affected only slightly.

The objection to the adaptive expectations assumption in the specification of the Friedman model applies equally, of course, to the Phelps version of the expectations thesis; but the model expressed in equation (12) is subject to additional reservations. The restriction,

Table 6   Non-linear constrained least-squares estimates of equation (12)

Period	α	β	η	θ	λ	μ	σ_e^2
Policy-off	7·37 (1·88)	−2·74 (1·10)	0·43 (0·13)	0·01 (0·06)	0·61 (0·21)	0·74 (0·24)	0·599
1950(4)–1955(4)	7·73 (0·92)	−2·90 (0·61)	0·46 (0·07)	0·02 (0·06)	0·98 (0·17)	1·18 (0·35)	0·316
1957(1)–1961(2)	5·82 (3·72)	−1·31 (2·17)	0·02 (0·26)	−0·06 (0·09)	0·82 (0·84)	0·70 (0·80)	0·687

implicit in the assumption of proportionality between the average and marginal products of labour, that the aggregate production function is Cobb-Douglas, would be regarded as unacceptable by many economists. In defence of the formulation used above, it is worth pointing out that this specification provides an explicit rationale for introducing the rate of change of labour productivity into the Phillips relation, whereas other models which have employed this variable as an argument in the wage equation[10] have been constructed on a purely *ad hoc* basis. A more practical problem concerns the choice of price index, for the retail price index is clearly unsuitable in the present context and the obvious alternative, the G.D.P. deflator, is not available on a quarterly basis for the whole policy-off period.

Both the additional problems can be circumvented by combining equation (5) with the assumption that expected wage-changes themselves are formed adaptively,

$$\dot{W}^e = \rho \dot{W} + (1 - \rho)\dot{W}^e_{-1} \tag{13}$$

to yield the simpler estimating equation

$$\dot{W} = \frac{\alpha\rho}{(1 - \delta\rho)} + \frac{\beta}{(1 - \delta\rho)} U - \frac{\beta(1 - \rho)}{(1 - \delta\rho)} U_{-1} + \frac{(1 - \rho)}{(1 - \delta\rho)} \dot{W}_{-1} + v \tag{14}$$

The OLS estimates of this reduced form for the two policy-off sub-periods are presented in Table 7. Standard errors and the Durbin-Watson statistic are dubious in view of the presence of the lagged

[10] E.g., Argy [2], Kuh [12].

dependent variable. The failure of the model in the second sub-period is evident in the negative coefficient on the lagged unemployment term; less obviously, the implied value of δ in the first period is *negative*. Hence, both sets of results are inconsistent with this modified Phelps model. Auto-regressive transformations of the equation using the estimated value of r from the relation

$$v = rv_{-1} + e$$

yielded a positive though small value of $\delta (< 0.3)$ in the first period, but the coefficient of lagged unemployment continued to exhibit a perverse sign in the second sub-period. Thus, this version of the Phelps model, like the preceding formulation, is inconsistent with the strict expectations thesis, and also fails in the more modest task of reconciling the apparent difference in the determination of wage-changes between the two parts of the policy-off period.

Table 7

Period	Intercept	U	U_{-1}	W_{-1}	$\bar{R}^2$	d
1950(4)–1955(4)	2·39	−5·68	4·75	0·81	0·808	1·296
		[3·30]	[2·15]	[5·28]		
1957(1)–1961(2)	5·20	−1·36	−0·48	0·36	0·557	1·397
		[0·89]	[0·35]	[1·47]		

A Phillips model

It is sometimes forgotten that the rate of change of prices appeared as an independent variable in the wage equation long before Friedman and Phelps spelt out the role of expectations. The original interpretation of $\dot{P}$, as 'a measure of the "cost-push" element in wage adjustments' [Phillips (18)] is inconsistent with the competitive model which is usually hypothesized, but there is no reason why the earlier studies should not be re-interpreted as using the actual rate of price change as a proxy for the expected rate. It is particularly interesting to recall Phillip's hypothesis that price increases operate with a threshold effect, influencing the wage bargain only when real wages would otherwise fall: when the rate of money wage increase predicted from the nominal Phillips curve is less than the expected rate of price increase, workers attempt at least to maintain a constant real wage.[11]

The threshold hypothesis has recently been invoked by Rees [19] in his defence of the Phillips curve against the charge that the trade-off which it appears to offer can persist only in a world characterized by money illusion. This term has acquired a special historical significance; as Tobin [22] puts it: 'The current debate strikes me as the Keynes-classics debate of the 1930's, removed thirty years and one time derivative'. However, Phillips' model suggests a flaw in Tobin's parallel. The debate of the 1930's concerned the levels of real and money wages in a short-run static model; the current debate rages in an environment which permits a persistent if variable rise in real wages. Failure to react fully to price increases is, to the trained economist, synonymous with money illusion whether money wages are increasing at a faster or slower rate, but Phillips' intuition, or perhaps his elementary mistake, may nevertheless throw some light on human behaviour. Economists may have relied too much on the *ceteris paribus* assumption: casual observation suggests that what would otherwise have happened is not the usual standard of reference adopted by the rest of the community.

In the present context, the threshold hypothesis provides more than an explanation for the existence of a long-run trade-off between unemployment and inflation. Its principal virtue is that it supplies a rationale for the insignificance of any form of price-change variable in the second part of the policy-off period. The actual rate of price change exceeded the rate of change of wages predicted by the (effectively) nominal Phillips curve of Table 1 in only two quarters of the period 1957(1)–1961(2), and then by less than 0·15 percentage points in each case. Given the behaviour of prices in the post-Korean years and the smoothing effect of the expectation-generating mechanism usually adopted, it follows *a fortiori* that expected real wages were rising continuously during this period; hence on the modified Phillips hypothesis a price-change variable has no place in the wage equation.

---

[11] The re-interpretation of Phillips' $\dot{P}$ in terms of *expected* price changes provides a cheap answer to Lipsey's refutation of the threshold hypothesis [13]: it seems plausible to assume that in the latter part of the nineteenth century $\dot{P}^E$ was zero or negative for the most part, so that the fifteen years in which actual real wages fell, and which Lipsey used for his test of Phillips' hypothesis, may well have been years in which real wages were expected to remain constant or even to increase.

To determine whether the threshold hypothesis was also relevant to wage behaviour in the earlier sub-period, an equation of the form

$$\dot{W} = \alpha + \beta U + \Pi\sigma\dot{P} + e \qquad \sigma = 1 \quad \text{for } \hat{W} < \dot{P}$$
$$\sigma = 0 \quad \text{for } \hat{W} > \dot{P}$$

was fitted to data for 1950(4)–1955(4). Recursive estimation was used to achieve consistency. The resulting regression equation was

$$\dot{W} = 12\cdot09 - 4\cdot90U + 0\cdot26\sigma\dot{P}$$
$$\qquad\qquad [7\cdot28] \qquad [7\cdot61]$$
$$\bar{R}^2 = 0\cdot885 \qquad d = 1\cdot324$$

The estimate of Π is surprisingly low, and confidence in the general applicability of the threshold hypothesis is weakened by the observation that the statistical properties of this regression are inferior to those of the corresponding equation in Table 1. The impression that Phillips' formulation is inferior to the model used by Lipsey and Parkin was confirmed when 'Phillips-irrelevant' price increases were included as an additional variable; the augmented equation was

$$\dot{W} = 8\cdot16 - 3\cdot01U + 0\cdot43\sigma\dot{P} + 0\cdot40(1 - \sigma)\dot{P}$$
$$\qquad\quad [3\cdot91] \qquad [7\cdot53] \qquad\quad [3\cdot39]$$
$$\bar{R}^2 = 0\cdot927 \qquad d = 2\cdot15$$

Hence the insertion of price increases previously found to be irrelevant on the threshold hypothesis affects all the regression coefficients and raises the coefficient of determination; the coefficient of the irrelevant price series is not only significantly different from zero, but there is no significant difference between the two price parameters. It follows that Phillips' hypothesis is not capable of explaining the difference in wage behaviour between the two policy-off sub-periods.

Non-linearity in the influence of price-changes

The final hypothesis considered is that the influence of price-expectations operates non-linearly on wage bargaining, but in a simpler manner than that suggested by Phillips: the threshold below which $\dot{W}$ is independent of $\dot{P}$ is specified without regard to the sign of $\hat{W} - \dot{P}$. The suggestion is simply that the participants in the labour market become more sensitive to price changes as the rate of inflation rises. This hypothesis has been considered recently by, *inter alios*,

Solow [20] and Hamermesh [11]. The former employed a quadratic transform of the price-change data; the latter specified a 2% rate of inflation as an arbitrary cut-off point below which wage negotiations were held to be insensitive to price changes.

The approach adopted here is similar to (though independent of) the method used by Hamermesh. Additional series, $\dot{P}_T$, were defined such that

$$\dot{P}_T = \dot{P}, \qquad \dot{P} > Z\%$$
$$\dot{P}_T = 0, \qquad \dot{P} < Z\%$$

Z was assigned the values 1, 2 and 3 successively, and $Z = 2$ was chosen on the grounds that for the total policy-off period it gave the highest coefficient of determination in the regression of $\dot{W}$ on U and $\dot{P}_T$. The results of applying this hypothesis to the policy-off sub-periods are shown in Table 8. In every case, this formulation gives a better fit than the Lipsey-Parkin equation (cf. Table 1). Again, the Friedman-Phelps prediction is clearly refuted; indeed, in the equations for the entire policy-off period and the first sub-period, the coefficients on the price-change variable decline slightly. The point estimate of the price term in the second sub-period is no longer derisory, and its t-ratio begins to approach a respectable value, but a puzzling difference between the two sections of the period remains, for the F test still indicates a structural shift.[12] Moreover, there is a change in the character of the shift: the unemployment variable is insignificant in the second sub-period, and the Phillips relation pivots around an unemployment level of about 2% (for $\dot{P} \leq 2\%$). This

Table 8

Period	Intercept	U	$\dot{P}_T$	$\bar{R}^2$	d
Policy-off	6·45	−2·10 [3·46]	0·46 [8·10]	0·87	1·25
1950(4)–1955(4)	7·68	−2·62 [4·50]	0·42 [11·04]	0·94	2·22
1957(1)–1961(2)	6·08	−1·83 [1·74]	0·20 [1·22]	0·55	1·45

[12] $F = 8·88$.

phenomenon is particularly interesting in view of the results obtained by Lipsey and Parkin in their comparison of policy-on and policy-off. The temptation to draw strong conclusions is, however, reduced when price increases below the threshold are introduced as a separate variable, in Table 9. These price increases do indeed appear irrelevant in the regressions for the whole period and the first sub-period: the coefficient on the additional variable is indistinguishable from zero

Table 9

Period	Intercept	U	$\dot{P}_T$	$(\dot{P}-P_T)$	t	$\bar{R}^2$	d
Policy-off	6·46	−2·10	0·46	−0·02	2·13	0·862	1·25
		[3·41]	[7·42]	[0·07]			
1950(4)–1955(4)	7·68	−2·62	0·42	−0·01	1·36	0·934	2·22
		[4·28]	[9·67]	[0·02]			
1957(1)–1961(2)	7·38	−2·35	0·05	−0·36	1·75	0·568	1·59
		[2·10]	[0·26]	[1·24]			

and its inclusion does not affect any of the other coefficients. According to the t-ratio listed in the pre-penultimate column, the null hypothesis of no significant difference between the two price coefficients is rejected at the 10% level in the first sub-period—the apparently stronger result for the whole period is dubious on account of the low Durbin-Watson statistic. In the second sub-period, the apparent change in the partial relation between $\dot{W}$ and U, noted above, is eliminated, and the two price coefficients exhibit the same algebraic difference as previously, but the magnitudes of the separate coefficients defy interpretation. Thus $\dot{P}$ again appears as the source of instability in the determination of wage changes.

An attempt was made to determine whether a finer grouping of price changes improved the results, but no additional information was obtained. The results for the second sub-period remained uniformly poor, and markedly different from those of the first period in respect of the role of $\dot{P}$. Rather surprisingly, in view of the relatively large variance of $\dot{P}$ during 1950(4)–1955(4), none of the groupings applied to the first sub-period was as successful as the simple dichotomy used above. In particular, the expectation of a positive relation between the average level of $\dot{P}$ and the magnitude of its coefficient was not fulfilled.

Conclusions

The only positive finding to emerge from the present investigation is that price increases below 2% do not appear to have any effect on the rate of change of wage rates. Whether failure to react to 'small' price increases reflects adjustment costs or a trade-off between product quality and price is an interesting subject for speculation, but beyond the scope of this paper.

The main conclusion, demonstrated by consideration of a variety of models, is that the policy-off period was far from a homogeneous interlude; it follows that the comparison of policy-on and policy-off periods is a dangerous procedure, in that the policy-off results do not provide a sufficiently firm foundation for predicting what would have happened in the absence of incomes policy. This inference, however, requires further discussion, for it must be admitted that the partial effect of unemployment on wage increases appears to have been highly stable, both between the sub-periods and across models (see, for example, Tables 1, 4 and 9, supra). As an additional precaution, tests for non-linearity in the $\dot{W} - U$ relation were conducted by ranking the residuals from the several policy-off regressions according to the magnitude of the dependent variable; in no case was the Durbin-Watson statistic constructed from the ranked residuals indicative of positive serial correlation, as would have been the case if the 'true' relation were strongly non-linear. The stability of the coefficient on unemployment within the policy-off period strengthens the Lipsey-Parkin conclusion that attempts to restrain $\dot{W}$ resulted in a twist of the $\dot{W} - U$ relation. But the coefficient on $\dot{P}$ does not exhibit such stability, and predictions based upon it are subject to a correspondingly large margin of error. If the wage equation for the second policy-off sub-period were used to predict subsequent values of $\dot{W}$, incomes policy would appear in a much less favourable light than even Lipsey and Parkin suggest; conversely, their conclusion might well be reversed if allowance could be made for a learning process. The latter appears as a *deus ex machina*, but the policy-off data do not permit it to be anything else; in particular, the observation that no evidence of learning, but rather the reverse, emerges from a comparison of the two policy-off sub-periods, is largely irrelevant because of the predominance of price increases below the 2% threshold after 1956.

The possibility of a learning process seems a more significant qualification to the rejection, above, of the strict expectations thesis than the excuse offered by Phelps [16]: '...impeccable statistical rejection at the one per cent significance level is not really possible; the data are too shaky, and the statistical methods employed too crude for that.' What the ultimate result of a learning process would be is not obvious given the existence of two expectational models which emphasize the supply and demand sides of the labour market respectively. While each model in isolation denies the existence of a long-run trade-off between unemployment and inflation, their combined result involves an element of indeterminacy.

Although the policy-off data to 1961(2) do not permit a satisfactory test of the hypothesis that eventually wage-earners become accustomed to persistent inflation, even at variable rates, recent developments provide some relevant information. The date of the termination of incomes policy is uncertain, but it seems reasonable to regard the publication of the final White Paper in December 1969 as no more than a belated epitaph. While formal calculations are impossible, given the shortness of the intervening period and the requirements of first central differences as a method of measuring rates of change, casual empiricism suggests that the recent behaviour of $\dot{W}$ is consistent with the policy-off relationship between $\dot{W}$ and U, and equality of actual and expected rates of price increase. Naturally, this is not the only explanation which fits the facts, but at least it has the merit of not requiring a structural change in the labour market sufficiently powerful to have shifted the (partial) Phillips curve further in ten years than in the previous century.

If the suggestion of a learning process is substantiated, it will be necessary to consider the contribution of incomes policy to delaying the disappearance, or at least the steepening, of the long-run trade-off between unemployment and inflation. In the meantime, the participants in the various debates over the Phillips curve must wait with baited breath until the system generates more data.

References

[1] G. C. Archibald, 'The Phillips Curve and the Distribution of Unemployment', *A.E.R. Papers and Proceedings*, 1969.
[2] V. Argy, 'International Comparisons of Rates of Change in Earnings', *Oxford Economic Papers*, 1968.
[3] J. K. Bowers, P. C. Cheshire and A. E. Webb, 'The Change in the Relationship between Unemployment and Earnings Increases', *National Institute Economic Review*, 1970.
[4] P. Cagan, 'The Monetary Dynamics of Hyperinflation', in M. Friedman (ed.) *Studies in the Quantity Theory of Money*, University of Chicago Press, 1956.

[5] P. Cagan, *Determinants and Effects of Changes in the Stock of Money*, N.B.E.R., 1965.
[6] J. C. R. Dow and L. A. Dicks-Mireaux, 'The Excess Demand for Labour', *Oxford Economic Papers*, 1958.
[7] M. Friedman, 'The Role of Monetary Policy', *A.E.R.*, 1968.
[8] M. Friedman and A. J. Schwartz, 'A Monetary History of the United States 1867–1960', *N.B.E.R.*, 1963.
[9] Z. Griliches, 'Distributed Lags: A Survey', *Econometrica*, 1967.
[10] S. B. Gupta, 'The Portfolio Balance Theory of the Rate of Change of Prices', *Review of Economic Studies*, 1970.
[11] D. S. Hamermesh, 'Wage Bargains, Threshold Effects and the Phillips Curve', *Quarterly Journal of Economics*, 1970.
[12] E. Kuh, 'A Productivity Theory of Wage Levels', *Review of Economic Studies*, 1967.
[13] R. G. Lipsey, 'The Relation between Unemployment and the Rate of Change of Money Wage Rates in the United Kingdom, 1862–1957: A Further Analysis', *Economica*, 1960.
[14] R. G. Lipsey and J. M. Parkin, 'Incomes Policy: A Re-appraisal', *Economica*, 1970, and Chapter 4, above.
[15] J. M. Parkin, 'Incomes Policy: Some Further Results on the Determination of the Rate of Change of Money Wages', *Economica*, 1970, and Chapter 5, above.
[16] E. Phelps, 'Reply' (to a comment by J. Williamson), *Economica*, 1968.
[17] E. Phelps, 'Money-Wage Dynamics and Labour-Market Equilibrium', *J.P.E.*, 1968.
[18] A. W. Phillips, 'The Relation between Unemployment and the Rate of Change of Money Wage Rates in the United Kingdom, 1861–1957', *Economica*, 1958.
[19] A. Rees, 'The Phillips Curve as a Menu for Policy Choice', *Economica*, 1970.
[20] R. M. Solow, *Price Expectations and the Behaviour of the Price Level*, Manchester University Press, 1969.
[21] A. P. Thirlwall, 'Demand Disequilibrium in the Labour Market and Wage Rate Inflation in the United Kingdom', *Yorkshire Bulletin*, 1969.
[22] J. Tobin, 'Comment' (on P. Cagan's contribution), in S. Rousseas (ed.) Proceedings of a *Symposium on Inflation: Its Causes, Consequences and Control*, The Calvin K. Kazanjian Economics Foundation Inc., 1969.
[23] Report of the Committee on the Working of the Monetary System, Cmnd. 827, 1959.

13

Jim Taylor[1]

Chapter 10 Incomes policy, the structure of unemployment and the Phillips curve: the United Kingdom experience, 1953–70

It is the contention of this paper that the search for a trade-off between wage inflation and excess supply in the labour market (*viz.* the Phillips curve) has been severely hampered by the use of poor data. It has been common practice in the work on United Kingdom wage inflation to use the basic weekly wage rate index as a measure of the price of labour, and to use the recorded unemployment rate as a measure of the excess supply of labour. Unfortunately, neither of these empirical variables appears to be an efficient proxy for the theoretical variables which they purport to represent, as this paper will attempt to demonstrate. One of the major consequences of using poor data in the work on United Kingdom wage inflation has been the apparent disappearance of the Phillips curve during the second half of the 1960's. Furthermore, appraisals of the effectiveness of incomes policy in the United Kingdom have been severely hampered by the use of inadequate data.

The three main findings of this paper are, first, that registered unemployment is not an adequate indicator of excess supply in the labour market; second, that the Lipsey-Parkin conclusion (that incomes restraint policies have been effective at low rates of registered unemployment but not at high rates) fails to hold when more efficient proxy variables are used to measure wage inflation and excess supply in the labour market; and third, that the Phillips curve has not

[1] University of Lancaster. I would like to thank Professor Parkin for his advice and encouragement, and for making the data used in the Lipsey-Parkin study readily available to me. I am also grateful for helpful advice from Dr. Corina, Dr. El-Mokadem, Professors Finegan and Hamermesh, Tin Nguyen, Michael Artis and Leslie Godfrey. I am indebted to the Nuffield Foundation for providing the funds (under the Social Sciences Small Grants Scheme) which made the research for this paper possible. I alone am responsible for the errors.

'disappeared' since 1966. Indeed, there is firm evidence that a strong short-run trade-off between wage inflation and excess supply in the labour market continued to exist throughout the period 1966–70.[2]

The paper is in four sections. Section 1 argues that the excess labour supply model of wage change requires reformulating to take the structure of unemployment explicitly into account (following Taylor [24] and Perry [21]). The second section examines the case for using alternative proxy variables in analyses of wage change. Section 3 examines the effectiveness of incomes policy in the United Kingdom, the primary aim of this section being to see how far the conclusions of Lipsey and Parkin [14][3] are disturbed when suitable alternative data are used for measuring wage inflation and unemployment. Finally, section 4 investigates the proposition that the Phillips curve 'disappeared' during the second half of the 1960's.

1   A modification to the excess labour supply model of wage change
The foundation stone of wage change analysis is the excess supply of labour. Unfortunately, the excess supply of labour is not directly observable and the empirical model has to be formulated to accommodate a proxy for excess labour supply. The proxy usually adopted, in empirical work on wage change, is the rate of registered unemployment (following Phillips [22] and Lipsey [13]):

$$\frac{D_L - S_L}{S_L} = f\left(\frac{R}{N + R}\right)$$

where D_L is the demand for labour, S_L is the supply of labour, R is registered unemployment, and N is the number employed.

The use of registered unemployment as a measure of excess labour supply has long been challenged.[4] To measure excess labour supply

---

[2] It was not possible to extend the analysis to 1971 since appropriate data on wage changes was not available at the time this paper was written.
[3] Chapter 4 of the present volume.
[4] See Long's 1942 article [15]. Klein and Ball [12], in the first major econometric study of post-war wage and price movements in the United Kingdom, used an hours worked index to measure tightness in the labour market. Other researchers have attempted to estimate the excess supply of labour more directly by measuring hidden unemployment (Simler and Tella [23]) and labour hoarding (Armstrong [1], Fair [6] and Taylor [24]). The present study uses a weighted average of labour hoarding calculated for sixteen major United Kingdom industry groups (under the Nuffield Small Grant project mentioned in footnote 1).

efficiently, labour hoarding (D) and hidden unemployment (H) must be incorporated into the proxy variable:

$$\frac{D_L - S_L}{S_L} = g\left(\frac{R + D + H}{N + R + H}\right)$$

This is the unemployment gap, which has a corresponding relationship to Okun's [19] output gap. The labour hoarding and hidden unemployment components require further explanation.

Labour hoarding is the under-utilization of employed labour. It occurs because of the lagged adjustment of inputs of labour to fluctuations in output (Brechling [3]), and is reflected by pro-cyclical movements in the output/employee ratio. The main causes of hoarding have been described elsewhere (Oi [18], Okun [19]), and only a summary is required here. Labour is a quasi-fixed factor of production for five main reasons: First, contractual agreements guarantee a minimum term of employment. Second, indivisibilities in the processes of production (e.g., fixed man-machine ratios irrespective of output levels) mean that it is easier to adjust the length of the work week than to adjust the number of employees on the books. In this case, labour is hoarded in the sense that there is a temporary reduction in the productivity of labour, as measured by the output/employee ratio. Third, the existence of hiring and firing costs will encourage employers to minimize labour turnover. Fourth, employers will hold on to skilled and experienced labour if reductions in demand are expected to be temporary. Finally, labour attaches some importance to the security aspect of employment, and this will encourage employers to hoard labour temporarily in order not to disturb the morale of their workers.

Hidden unemployment[5] arises because secondary workers (mainly married women and retired men) withdraw from the recorded work force during recessions in business activity. Unlike primary workers, who are permanently attached to the recorded work force, secondary workers drop out of the recorded work force when the job market is slack. They see no point in actively searching for a job when the probability of success is very low. The fact that secondary workers are ineligible for unemployment benefit is an added incentive not to

---

[5] See Mincer [17] for a critical appraisal of the concept and measurement of hidden unemployment.

register as unemployed, even though they will re-join the work force when the job market recovers.

The formulation of the excess labour supply proxy given above is restrictive, however, since it implies that the three components have an equal proportionate influence within the wage bargaining mechanism. But there are sound reasons why the various components of the unemployment gap are likely to have a differential impact upon aggregate wage setting. Specifically, labour hoarding will have a more significant role to play than either registered unemployment or hidden unemployment in wage determination.

Let us examine the reasons for this. First, there are likely to be marked differences in the skill structure between labour hoarding, registered unemployment and hidden unemployment. Labour hoarding occurs over a wide spectrum of skills and occupations, and will probably be more biased towards highly skilled workers than the registered unemployment component. At the other extreme, the average skill level will be low for the hidden unemployment component since the hidden unemployed consist mainly of married women seeking part-time work. The difference in the average skill level of these three components of unemployment means that they are non-additive as they stand, and should be weighted in the construction of an aggregate index of unemployment.[6] The second main reason for the differential influence of the three components of unemployment on wage determination is that labour hoarding appears on the shop floor, within the factory, and will therefore have a direct personal impact on the wage bargaining mechanism, unlike the registered and the hidden unemployed. Furthermore, the intensity of inter-firm competition for scarce labour is likely to be closely related to current and expected levels of labour hoarding.

2 Alternative proxy variables

Excess labour supply
This study assumes that the excess supply of labour can be adequately measured by adding labour hoarding to registered unemployment. Hidden unemployment has been ignored despite the existence of acceptable methods of measuring it. This exclusion appears reasonable in view of the results obtained by Taylor [24] and Perry [21]

---

[6] Perry [21] suggests that average hourly earnings would be an appropriate weight for each component of excess labour supply.

for the United States, where hidden unemployment was found to be empirically insignificant in the determination of aggregate wages. Consequently, we have restricted our measure of excess labour supply to include only registered unemployment and labour hoarding, and we have used this modified proxy variable in the analysis of wage inflation that follows (in sections 3 and 4).

The method used to calculate labour hoarding has been described elsewhere (Taylor [24]), and only the formula is given here. For each industry, the percentage of employed labour which is hoarded (U_d) is calculated as follows:

$$U_d = \left(1 - \frac{Q/N}{(Q/N)^*}\right) \times 100$$

where Q/N is output per employee, and $(Q/N)^*$ is the full employment output/employee ratio. $(Q/N)^*$ was calculated by fitting linear segments to selected full employment peaks in the quarterly, seasonally adjusted time series of the Q/N ratio.[7] Of course, if labour hoarding and registered unemployment moved in proportion, the unemployment rate would be just as efficient a proxy variable as one which also included labour hoarding. Unfortunately, registered unemployment and labour hoarding have not moved together systematically over recent business cycles in the United Kingdom, with the result that registered unemployment alone is a completely unreliable measure of the excess supply of labour. This fact can be demonstrated most easily by examining the post-1966 changes in the United Kingdom labour market.

Up until the 1967–8 recovery, registered unemployment followed the fluctuations in labour hoarding, the lag being longer on the downswing in business activity than on the upswing. A cursory examination of the turning points in the labour hoarding and the registered unemployment time series (1954–71) plotted in Figure 1, suggests that registered unemployment lags labour hoarding by about six quarters at the onset of a recession, whereas the lag is down to about two quarters at the onset of a sustained expansion. In other words, registered unemployment has been historically a lazy indicator of changes in labour market pressures in the United Kingdom, particularly when the economy has been moving into a recession. During the 1967–8 recovery in business activity, however, the rela-

---

[7] This formula implicitly assumes constant short-run returns to labour, and zero substitution between labour and other inputs in the short-run.

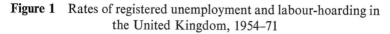

Figure 1 Rates of registered unemployment and labour-hoarding in the United Kingdom, 1954–71

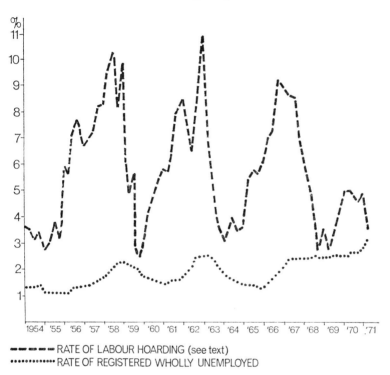

tionship between labour hoarding and registered unemployment apparently disappeared. The sharp fall in labour hoarding during 1967–8 was not followed by a corresponding fall in registered unemployment as earlier experience suggests ought to have happened. Registered unemployment simply levelled off. Apparently, the relationship between labour hoarding and registered unemployment was beginning to crumble. The subsequent rise in registered unemployment during 1970–1 to its highest post-war levels confirms this suggestion.

In an extension of the Lipsey-Parkin work, Parkin [20][8] tests the assertion that there was a shift in the mapping from excess labour

---

[8] Chapter 5 of the present volume.

demand (defined as unfilled vacancies minus registered unemployment) to unemployment towards the end of the study period. He concludes, from a detailed statistical analysis of the relationship between registered unemployment and vacancies, that a shift did not occur. More recent research by Bowers, Cheshire and Webb [2] suggests otherwise. This latter study has tried to explain why registered unemployment shifted upwards, relative to excess labour demand, towards the end of 1966. The story, however, does not end here. It is just as pertinent to ask why registered unemployment did not move downwards during 1967 and 1968 as the economy's output expanded. During 1967 and 1968, the GDP was increasing at an annual rate of 2·9% (compared to a rate of 1·7% during 1966), but this output growth did not lead to a reduction in registered unemployment. The recovery of output growth during 1967–8 was achieved without a corresponding reduction in the level of registered unemployment. The sharp fall in labour hoarding between 1966(4) and 1968(4) suggests that the extra input of labour required to raise output was extracted from already employed labour. This contrasts sharply with labour market behaviour in earlier periods, when a reduction of labour hoarding was followed by a fall in registered unemployment. It is clear from this analysis that labour hoarding must be included in the measurement of the excess supply of labour.

Since employers expanded their input of labour during the 1967–8 upturn by extracting more labour services from already employed labour, and not by employing more workers, this implies that a behavioural change occurred in the labour market. The reasons for the failure of registered unemployment to follow the decrease in labour hoarding during the 1967–8 recovery are not yet clear,[9] but three tentative explanations can be suggested: First, if employers' expectations of future product demand were relatively pessimistic during 1967–8, despite the rising output levels experienced, it is probable that they would be unwilling to engage additional workers. If only a temporary upturn in output growth was expected, employers would be reluctant to incur the extra hiring and training costs that arise when new workers are hired. Instead, they would aim to squeeze more output from existing labour. Second, the redundancy payments scheme (December 1965) would raise the overhead element in labour costs and would consequently shift the optimum combination

[9] See Bowers, Cheshire and Webb [2] for a detailed discussion of the reasons for the upward shift in registered unemployment.

of workers and hours worked per worker in favour of the latter. The rise in the index of average weekly hours worked per worker from 93·8 at the end of 1966 to 94·9 at the end of 1968 (in spite of a dominant downward trend) supports this explanation. Furthermore, overtime working was on the increase: in June 1967, 33·0% of all operatives were working overtime, but this proportion had risen to 36·5% by June 1969. These data, however, may simply reflect an increasing urge on the part of employers to rid themselves of under-employed labour in view of their pessimistic outlook of Britain's economic prospects. Third, the introduction of the redundancy payments scheme and earnings related unemployment benefit (1966) may have caused an increase in voluntary unemployment. The registered unemployed may now be spending more time in their search for a suitable job because of a reduction in the dis-utility of unemployment caused by the two schemes.

The price of labour
Two measures of the price of labour have been commonly used in wage change analysis: the index of weekly wage rates is one, and the index of average hourly earnings is the other. The decision as to which of these two variables to use as the proxy for the true price of labour cannot be made until the structure of the wage change model has been fully specified. Some studies are explicitly concerned with organized labour markets (e.g., Hamermesh [10]), and intend only to explain movements in the base wage rate. But the base wage rate is only one of a number of components which constitute the price of labour. Consequently, numerous studies of wage change have adopted the rate of change in average hourly earnings as the variable to be explained.

Let us briefly examine the difference between the base wage rate and average hourly earnings.[10] The base wage rate is determined through negotiations between labour unions and employers in organized markets, the outcome of these negotiations being the wage contract. Rates are set for large configurations of the working population. Hourly earnings, however, can display more flexibility for a number of reasons. First, the hourly earnings index will change when the base rate changes. Second, it will change if piece rates are adjusted, or if bonus schemes are altered. Third, an arbitrary

[10] See Lydall [16], Eckstein and Wilson [5] and Hamermesh [10] for discussions about the appropriate measure of wage change.

190   Jim Taylor

Figure 2   Wage inflation in the United Kingdom, 1953-70

■■■■ RATE OF CHANGE IN AVERAGE HOURLY EARNINGS, CORRECTED FOR OVERTIME
•••••• RATE OF CHANGE IN WEEKLY WAGE RATE INDEX

regrading of workers can cause a change in hourly earnings. Fourth, hourly earnings will change when the utilization rate of employed labour changes, though the extent of the change will depend upon the relative significance of the piece rate system. To take an example, an increase in labour productivity will cause an increase in average hourly earnings to the extent that earnings are related to output. Fifth, hourly earnings will be affected by the amount of overtime worked because of higher rates of pay for overtime.

It is evident from this comparison of the base wage rate and average hourly earnings that neither of these two variables is an adequate proxy for the price of labour as it is usually defined in studies of aggregate wage inflation. The base wage rate represents too little, whilst average hourly earnings represents too much. Fortunately, the hourly earnings index can be corrected for overtime working because data on normal and overtime hours is available. In this study, the average hourly earnings index has been corrected by assuming time-and-a-half for overtime work.[11]

Before proceeding to the analysis of wage inflation in the United

[11] This is described in more detail in the Appendix.

Figure 3   Deviations of policy-on observations from values predicted by using policy-off equation (9)

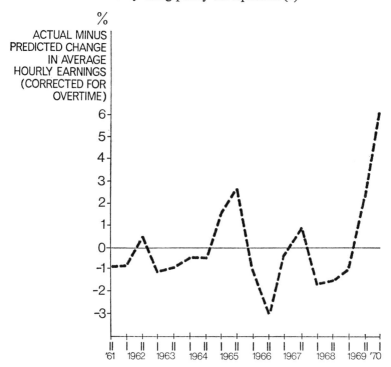

Kingdom, it will be useful to compare the time path of these two measures of changes in the price of labour. The pattern of wage inflation in the United Kingdom between 1953 and 1970 varies, in fact, according to whether the wage rate index or the corrected average hourly earnings index is used to measure wage changes. From Figure 2, it is clear that the percentage change in the wage rate index ($\dot{W}$) and the percentage change in the average hourly earnings index ($\dot{E}$) have moved together between 1953 and 1970 with the marked exception of the period 1961–5. $\dot{W}$ strangely became cyclically insensitive during these years, and then once again followed the $\dot{E}$ series closely from mid-1966 onwards. A different picture of wage inflation in the United Kingdom is therefore obtained depending upon which index of the price of labour we adopt as the relevant proxy.

3   The effectiveness of incomes restraint policies: some results

This section examines the effectiveness of incomes policy in the United Kingdom. In sections 1 and 2 of this paper, the case was argued for using a measure of excess labour supply which included both registered unemployment and labour hoarding in empirical work on wage change. We also suggested that aggregate wage inflation would be more accurately measured by the average hourly earnings index than by the basic weekly wage rate index. Consequently the empirical work of Lipsey and Parkin [14], on the effectiveness of incomes policy in the United Kingdom, has been re-examined with these two modifications incorporated into the analysis. In addition, an alternative variable was adopted to measure trade union pushfulness in view of Godfrey's work [8,9]. Godfrey has suggested that the number of stoppages may be a more efficient index of union pushfulness than is the rate of change in unionization.

The analysis of the effectiveness of incomes policy in the United Kingdom divides conveniently into four parts. First, the Lipsey-Parkin equations for the policy-off and policy-on periods are re-estimated, but with $U_r + U_d$ (registered unemployment plus labour hoarding) as the proxy for excess labour supply instead of U_r alone. Second, the rate of change in the basic weekly wage rate ($\dot{W}$) is replaced by the rate of change in the corrected average hourly earnings index ($\dot{E}$) as the measure of wage inflation. Third, a trade-union pushfulness variable is then introduced into the analysis. Finally, an alternative method of measuring the effectiveness of incomes policy (i.e., an alternative to the policy-off/policy-on approach) is suggested.

Our first task was to re-estimate the Lipsey-Parkin equations, but with three changes: $U_r + U_d$ was substituted for U_r, the trade union pushfulness variable used by Lipsey and Parkin was omitted (following Parkin [20]), and a shorter time period was used because the labour hoarding estimates were only available from 1953 onwards. The results of this first stage of our investigation are given in Table 1, which also includes the original Lipsey-Parkin equations. The substitution of the 'corrected' index of unemployment for the rate of registered unemployment in the Lipsey-Parkin equations yielded disappointing results. The only significant feature of these results is the considerable fall in the coefficient of determination for the policy-off equation when the 1948–53 period is excluded from the analysis [compare equations (1) and (3)].

Table 1 The original Lipsey-Parkin equations and some modified
Lipsey-Parkin type equations: a quarterly analysis

(*t*-ratios in parentheses)

Eq. No.	Description of equation	Constant	U_r	$U_r + U_d$	$\dot{P}$	$\dot{N}$	$\bar{R}^2$	D.W.
The original Lipsey-Parkin equations								
(1)	Policy-off $\dot{W} =$	6·67 (5·79)	−2·37 (3·64)		0·48 (6·25)	0·14 (0·07)	0·86	1·23
(2)	Policy-on $\dot{W} =$	3·92 (2·27)	−0·40 (0·56)		0·23 (0·93)	3·76 (1·61)	0·14	0·72
Modified Lipsey-Parkin equations								
(3)	Policy-off $\dot{W} =$	8·22 (6·99)	−2·87 (4·52)		0·19 (1·95)		0·64	1·01
(4)	Policy-on $\dot{W} =$	4·24 (3·03)	−0·38 (0·74)		0·31 (1·68)		0·13	0·56
(5)	Policy-off $\dot{W} =$	4·69 (5·95)		−0·22 (2·30)	0·37 (3·70)		0·46	1·13
(6)	Policy-on $\dot{W} =$	5·09 (3·03)		−0·16 (1·14)	0·18 (0·78)		0·15	0·54

Notes:
1. In the original Lipsey-Parkin equations, the policy-off period was 1950(4)–1961(2) excluding 1956(1)–1956(4). The policy-on period consisted of three sub-periods as follows: 1948(3)–1950(3), 1956(1)–1956(4), 1961(3)–1967(2).
2. In the modified Lipsey-Parkin equations, the policy-off period was 1953(3)–1961(2) excluding 1956(1)–1956(4). The policy-on period consisted of two sub-periods as follows: 1956(1)–1956(4), 1961(3)–1968(2). The omission of 1948(3)–1953(2) was necessary because data on labour hoarding was not available for pre-1953(3).
3. Definition of variables (see Appendix).
$\dot{W}$ = annual rate of change in index of basic weekly wage rates.
U_r = rate of registered unemployment.
U_d = rate of labour hoarding.
$\dot{P}$ = percent change in index of retail prices (at annual rates).
$\dot{N}$ = percent change in union membership (at annual rates).

The results given in Table 2 are much more interesting. $\dot{E}$ has now replaced $\dot{W}$ as the measure of wage inflation. In both the policy-off and the policy-on equations, the coefficient on U_r is not significant [compare equations (7) and (8)]. Nothing can be deduced about the effectiveness of incomes policy from these two equations. The corrected unemployment index, however, performs much better (in equations (9) and (10)] and yields the interesting conclusion that the Lipsey-Parkin results are, if anything, reversed. The Phillips curve appears to be steeper during the policy-on period than the policy-off period. Incomes policy has apparently been more effective at high rates of unemployment than at low rates of unemployment. However, when a Chow *F*-test [4] was used to test for the stability of the coefficients between the two sample periods, it was discovered that the regression coefficients in the policy-on equation do not differ significantly from the regression coefficients in the policy-on equation.

Table 2   Policy-off/Policy-on equations with the rate of change in average hourly earnings (adjusted for overtime) as the dependent variable, a bi-annual analysis

(*t*-ratios in parentheses)

Eq. No.	Description of equation	Constant	U_r	$U_r + U_d$	$\dot{P}$	D_i	D_s	$\bar{R}^2$ D.W.
(7)	Policy-off $\dot{E} =$	6·51 (1·69)	−1·32 (0·71)		0·52 (1·25)			0·34 1·92
(8)	Policy-on $\dot{E} =$	4·76 (1·84)	−1·07 (0·95)		0·99 (2·77)			0·30 1·80
(9)	Policy-off $\dot{E} =$	7·98 (5·57)		−0·46 (3·18)	0·47 (2·19)			0·61 2·96
(10)	Policy-on $\dot{E} =$	10·01 (3·32)		−0·67 (2·63)	0·14 (0·32)			0·51 1·55
(11)	Whole period $\dot{E} =$	6·96 (4·40)		−0·37 (2·15)	0·57 (2·52)	0·36 (0·22)	−0·12 (0·50)	0·53 2·03

Notes:
1. The policy-off/policy-on periods are defined as follows:
Policy-off: 1953(11)–1961(1).
Policy-on: 1961(11)–1969(1).
2. Definition of variables (see Appendix):
$\dot{E}$ = rate of change in the index of average hourly earnings, adjusted for overtime.
U_r, $U_r + U_d$ and $\dot{P}$ are as in table 1.
D_i = dummy variable on the intercept: $D_i = 0$ for policy-off and $D_i = 1$ for policy-on.
D_s = dummy variable on $U_r + U_d$: $D_s = 0$ for policy-off and $D_s = U_r + U_d$ for policy-on.

This result is supported by equation (11), which includes a dummy variable on the intercept and a dummy variable on $U_r + U_d$ (see notes to Table 2). Since neither of the coefficients on the two dummies was significant, this implies that a structural change in the extended Phillips curve did not occur between the two sample periods.

Union militancy must now be incorporated into the analysis. In its simplest form, the Phillips curve postulates that money wages are determined through competitive elements in the labour market. The widespread existence of bilateral monopoly in the labour market, however, suggests that money wages can be pushed upwards through autonomous union militancy. A model that purports to explain the setting of money wages in a market system which includes large elements of bilateral monopoly ought to allow explicitly for the influence of these extra-market forces. Although the rate of change in unionization has been extensively used as a proxy for militancy (Hines [11], Lipsey and Parkin [14]), recent work by Godfrey [8,9] suggests that stoppages due to industrial disputes may be a more relevant proxy variable. The main effect of including stoppages (S) in the wage change analysis is to induce a stable trade-off between $\dot{E}$ and $U_r + U_d$. The coefficient on U_r is $-0\cdot68$ in both the policy-off and policy-on equations [compare equations (12) and (13) in Table 3].

An alternative and simpler method of assessing the impact of wage restraint policies is to use the policy-off wage equation as a bench mark for the purpose of comparison. For the policy-on period, actual values of $U_r + U_d$ and the price change variable can be fed directly into the policy-off equation in order to generate a series for $\dot{E}$. These estimated values of $\dot{E}$ are those that would have been expected in the absence of an incomes policy during 1961(11)–1969(1). The estimated values of $\dot{E}$ for the policy-on period are then subtracted from the actual values. Positive differences indicate that incomes policy has been ineffective.

Table 3 Policy-off/policy-on equations with a union militancy variable added, a bi-annual analysis

(*t*-ratios in parentheses)

Eq. No.	Description of equation	Constant	$U_r + U_d$	$\dot{P}$	S	$\bar{R}^2$	$D.W.$
(12)	Policy-off $\dot{E} =$	3·48 (1·43)	−0·68 (4·17)	0·36 (1·85)	5·00 (2·16)	0·70	2·61
(13)	Policy-on $\dot{E} =$	9·13 (2·57)	−0·69 (2·59)	0·03 (0·06)	1·20 (0·52)	0·48	1·57

Notes:
 1. Policy-off: 1953(11)–1961(1). Policy-on: 1961(11)–1969(1).
 2. $\dot{E}$, $U_r + U_d$ and $\dot{P}$ are as in Table 2.
 S = number of stoppages in thousands due to industrial disputes.

Negative differences indicate the reverse. The results of this exercise are summarized in Figure 3, which clearly suggests that incomes policy was quite ineffective during the early 1960's. Only during 1966, 1968 and the first half of 1969 did incomes policy have any really significant effect upon wage inflation. This, of course, is the period during which incomes policy was at its most severe. The figure also shows that periods of successful wage restraint have been quickly followed by periods during which the reverse was true.

4 The disappearance of the Phillips curve

The wage equations so far estimated cover only the period 1953(11) to 1969(1). Ending the analysis at 1969(1), however, begs an important

Table 4   Wage equations for the 'extended' period (1953(11)–1970(1)), a bi-annual analysis

(*t*-ratios in parentheses)

Eq. No.	Dependent variable	Constant	U_r	$U_r + U_d$	$\dot{P}$	S	$\bar{R}^2$	D.W.
(14)	$\dot{E} =$	−0·11 (0·07)	−0·23 (0·35)		0·95 (4·77)	3·09 (2·54)	0·58	1·54
(15)	$\dot{E} =$	3·78 (2·48)			−0·57 (4·04)	0·37 (1·74)	4·22 (4·21)	0·73	1·97

Definition of variables (see Appendix):
$\dot{E}$, U_r, $U_r + U_d$, $\dot{P}$ and S are as in Tables 2 and 3.

question by excluding a year (1969(11)–1970(1)) during which wage inflation was running at a level of between 10% and 15%, and at the same time, registered unemployment reached its highest post-war level and was on a rising trend. This phenomenon of simultaneously high levels of wage inflation and registered unemployment is clearly seen in the upper part of Figure 4, which strongly suggests that the Phillips curve has collapsed. Of course, only a partial picture of the wage change/unemployment trade-off can be obtained from a simple scatter diagram. Even so, a comparison of the upper and lower parts of Figure 4 is suggestive, since the collapse of the Phillips curve is not so apparent when $\dot{E}$ is plotted against $U_r + U_d$ instead of against U_r alone.

A more comprehensive analysis of the wage change/unemployment trade-off over the extended period (1953(11)–1970(1)) is clearly required. Consequently, wage equations were estimated for the extended period, two of which are reported in Table 4. Equation (14) attempts to explain wage inflation in terms of registered unemployment, price changes and stoppages. The fact that the coefficient on the unemployment variable is not significant indicates that a trade-off between wage inflation and registered unemployment does not exist. Equation (13) yields much more encouraging results for the Phillips curve. A firm trade-off is established between wage change and the excess supply of labour, for the extended period, when $U_r + U_d$ is used as the proxy for excess labour supply. In addition, equation 15 suggests that union militancy has a strong effect on wage changes. Stoppages (measured in thousands) varied from a minimum of 0·75 in the wage freeze period of 1966(11) to a maximum of 2·36 in 1970(1), when wage inflation was at its highest level during the period. This suggests that incomes policy has tended to operate through the suppression of union militancy. One final point must be made

Figure 4   Wage inflation and unemployment in the United
Kingdom, 1954–70

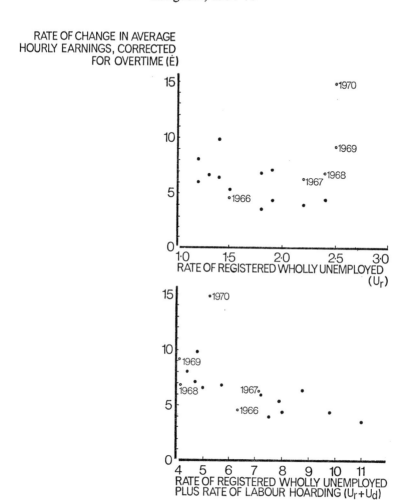

about equation (15). In view of the plausibility of the expectations hypothesis (Friedman [7]), the low coefficient on $\dot{P}$ is disturbing. Perhaps this can be explained by the fact that $\dot{P}$ enters into the determination of S (Godfrey [9]). More sophisticated estimation techniques than those used here are required if such problems are to be solved.

Conclusion

The three main findings of this paper are as follows. First, the structure of unemployment in the United Kingdom has changed remarkably since 1966. The rate of registered unemployment has commonly been used as an indicator of labour market pressures. But since 1966, there has been a sharp reduction of labour hoarding in the United Kingdom relative to registered unemployment. Since labour hoarding is an important component of the excess supply of labour, this has meant that registered unemployment is no longer an appropriate indicator of labour market pressures. At the heart of this paper is the proposition that labour hoarding must be added to registered unemployment in order to measure the tightness of the labour market efficiently.

Second, the Lipsey-Parkin conclusion that incomes policy has been more successful at low rates of unemployment than at high rates was found not to hold when alternative (and, we believe, more efficient) proxy variables were used. The policy-off and policy-on equations were found not to differ significantly. When an alternative method of measuring the effectiveness of incomes policy on restraining wage inflation was used, incomes policy appears to have had only temporary success. Hard won gains have been quickly lost when the brakes have been released.

Finally the Phillips curve did not 'disappear' at the end of the 1960's. In an empirical analysis of United Kingdom wage inflation, from mid-1953 to mid-1970, a consistent trade-off between wage change and unemployment could be detected when three conditions were met: the average hourly earnings index, corrected for overtime, was used as the proxy for the price of labour; labour hoarding was added to the recorded unemployment rate to measure the tightness of the labour market; and stoppages at work due to industrial disputes was used as a measure of union militancy.

Appendix 1:   Definition of variables used in wage equations

$\dot{W}$ = rate of change in the quarterly index of basic weekly wage rates (W). The rate of change in W was calculated as follows:

$$\dot{W} = \frac{W_{+2} - W_{-2}}{\frac{1}{2}(W_{+2} + W_{-2})} \times 100$$

$\dot{E}$ = rate of change in the bi-annual index of average hourly earnings, adjusted for overtime. The adjustment for overtime was made as follows:

$$E = \frac{A}{h_1 + \frac{3}{2}h_2}$$

where A is average weekly earnings, h_1 is normal hours and h_2 is overtime hours. The rate of change in E was calculated as follows:

$$\dot{E} = \frac{E_{+1} - E_{-1}}{E} \times 100$$

U_r = rate of registered wholly unemployed.
U_d = rate of labour hoarding. Estimates of labour hoarding were made for sixteen major industry groups in the United Kingdom (including all the index of production industries), from which an aggregate figure was calculated by using industry employment levels as weights. The aggregate figure was then assumed to approximate labour hoarding in the economy at large. Ideally, U_d should have been scaled so as to be consistent with U_r. The error, however, will be very small. The employment data was kindly made available to me by the Department of Employment.
$\dot{P}$ = rate of change in the index of retail prices (all items), and was calculated in the same way as $\dot{W}$ above.
$\dot{N}$ = rate of change in unionization. See Lipsey and Parkin [14].
S = number of stoppages in thousands 'due to disputes connected with the terms and conditions of employment'. See the Department of Employment *Gazette*, January 1971, footnote to Table 133.
 The source of all data was the *Monthly Digest of Statistics* unless otherwise stated.

Appendix 2:   A further result

In view of the discussion (in part I) about the possibility of a differential impact of labour hoarding and recorded unemployment on aggregate wage change, an additional equation covering the period 1953(11)–1970(1) is belatedly added to this paper. U_r and U_d are included as separate determinants in order to distinguish their comparative impact on wage change:

Eq. (16) $\dot{E} = 4.20 - 0.34\ U_r - 0.58\ U_d + 0.37\ \dot{P} + 3.52\ S$
  $\qquad$ (2.18) (0.60) $\quad$ (3.35) $\qquad$ (1.51) $\quad$ (3.34)

$$\bar{R}^2 = 0.69 \qquad D.W. = 1.89$$

The estimated coefficients on both U_r and U_d carry the expected sign, though the one on U_r is not significantly different from zero. This result supports the assertion that hoarded labour has a greater impact than the registered unemployed on wage adjustments.

References

[1] A. G. Armstrong, 'Output and Employment 1961–63', London and Cambridge Bulletin No. 48, *Times Review of Industry and Technology*, December 1963.

200   Jim Taylor

[2] J. K. Bowers, P. C. Cheshire and A. E. Webb, 'The Change in the Relationship between Unemployment and Earnings Increases: A Review of Some Possible Explanations', *N.I.E.R.* No. 54, November 1970.
[3] F. Brechling, 'The Relationship between Output and Employment in British Manufacturing Industries', *Review of Economic Studies*, July 1965.
[4] G. C. Chow, 'Tests of Equality between Sets of Coefficients in Two Linear Regressions', *Econometrica*, July 1960.
[5] O. Eckstein and T. A. Wilson, 'The Determination of Money Wages in American Industry', *Quarterly Journal of Economics*, 1962.
[6] R. C. Fair, 'The Short-Run Demand for Workers and Hours', *Contributions to Economic Analysis*, No. 59, North Holland (1969).
[7] M. Friedman, 'The Role of Monetary Policy', Presidential Address, American Economic Association, December 1967.
[8] L. G. Godfrey, 'The Phillips Curve: Incomes Policy and Trade Union Effects', in *The Current Inflation*, edited by H. G. Johnson and A. R. Nobay, 1971. Abridged and amended as Chapter 7, above.
[9] L. G. Godfrey, 'A Study of the Relationship between Strikes, Wage Rate Changes and the Rate of Inflation' (mimeo).
[10] D. Hamermesh, 'Wage Bargains, Threshold Effects and the Phillips Curve', *Quarterly Journal of Economics*, August 1970.
[11] A. G. Hines, 'The Determinants of the Rate of Change of Money Wage Rates and the Effectiveness of Incomes Policy', in *The Current Inflation*, edited by H. G. Johnson and A. R. Nobay, 1971.
[12] L. R. Klein and R. J. Ball, 'Some Econometrics of the Determination of Absolute Prices and Wages', *Economic Journal*, September 1959.
[13] R. G. Lipsey, 'The Relation between Unemployment and the Rate of Change of Money Wage Rates in the United Kingdom, 1862–1957: A Further Analysis', *Economica*, February 1960.
[14] R. G. Lipsey and J. M. Parkin, 'Incomes Policy: A Reappraisal', *Economica*, May 1970 and Chapter 4 above.
[15] C. D. Long, 'The Concept of Unemployment', *Quarterly Journal of Economics*, November 1942.
[16] H. Lydall, 'Inflation and the Earnings Gap', *Bulletin of the Oxford Institute of Statistics*, Vol. 20, 1958.
[17] J. Mincer, 'Labor-Force Participation and Unemployment: A Review of Recent Evidence; in *Prosperity and Unemployment*, edited by R. A. and M. S. Gordon, 1966.
[18] W. Oi, 'Labor as a Quasi-Fixed Factor', *Journal of Political Economy*, December 1962.
[19] A. Okun, 'Potential GNP: Its Measurement and Significance', Proceedings of the Business and Economic Statistics Section of the American Statistical Association, 1962.
[20] J. M. Parkin, 'Incomes Policy: Some Further Results on the Determination of the Rate of Change of Money Wages', *Economica*, November 1970, and Chapter 5 above.
[21] G. L. Perry, 'Changing Labor Markets and Inflation', Papers of the Brookings Institute, 1971.
[22] A. W. Phillips, 'The Relation between Unemployment and the Rate of Change of Money Wage Rates in the United Kingdom, 1861–1957', *Economica*, May 1958.
[23] N. J. Simler and A. Tella, 'Labour Reserves and the Phillips Curve', *Review of Economics and Statistics*, February 1968.
[24] J. Taylor, 'Hidden Unemployment, Hoarded Labor and the Phillips Curve', *Southern Economic Journal*, July 1970.
[25] J. Taylor, 'The Behaviour of Unemployment and Unfilled Vacancies: Great Britain, 1958–71. An Alternative View', *Economic Journal*, December 1972.

R. L. Thomas
and P. J. M. Stoney[1]

Chapter 11 Unemployment dispersion as a determinant of wage inflation in the United Kingdom, 1925–66[2]

1 Introduction

This paper examines the influence of varying unemployment rates in different areas of the labour market on the aggregate rate of wage inflation. Since the publication in 1958 of A. W. Phillips' article on the relationship between the level of unemployment and the rate of wage change [10], much empirical work has been done on the determination of wage rates in the United Kingdom. These studies have generally been aggregate in nature and, with the exception of a paper by G. C. Archibald [1], little attention has been paid to the existence of varying unemployment rates in different areas of the labour market.

A dispersion in unemployment rates of this kind can influence aggregate wage inflation in two distinct ways. Firstly non-linearity in the relationship between the rate of wage change and the level of unemployment at the individual market level, implies an aggregate wage adjustment equation which lies above the individual market equation. Moreover the greater the dispersion in market unemployment rates, the more marked is the upward shift in the aggregate equation.

Secondly, since an important factor in trade union bargaining for higher wage rates is the existence of recent wage increases for comparable employees in different labour markets, there may be a 'transfer mechanism' at work whereby wage increases in markets with low unemployment rates spill over into other labour markets. Again, the greater the dispersion in market unemployment rates, the greater is the resulting upward pressure on the aggregate rate of wage change.

[1] University of Manchester Institute of Science and Technology, and University of Liverpool.
[2] Reprinted from *The Manchester School*, June 1971, by permission of the authors and editor.

From the economic policy point of view, it is clearly important to determine whether these dispersion effects are quantitatively important in their influence on the rate of wage inflation. If dispersion effects are small an aggregate approach to the problem of wage inflation would seem appropriate. If not then some attention must be given to such disaggregate factors as regional and industrial imbalances in labour demand and unemployment rates. The main purpose of this paper is the development of an aggregate wage equation, suitable for estimation purposes, which allows for the possible influence of unemployment dispersion and moreover enables an attempt to be made to assess its quantitative importance in determining the rate of wage inflation.

The aggregate estimating equation is developed in parts 2, 3 and 4 of the paper. The remainder of the paper consists of a testing of the dispersion hypothesis using regional unemployment data for both post-war and pre-war periods. The results suggest that unemployment dispersion is both a statistically significant and quantitatively important factor in the determination of wage inflation. For both periods variations in the rate of wage change can be adequately explained by a combination of price-change, unemployment level and unemployment dispersion variables. Furthermore, we believe that this is the first satisfactory explanation of pre-war variations in the rate of wage change which relies on price and unemployment variables alone.

Finally, it is possible to derive from the estimted aggregate wage equation, the form of the individual market wage equation. The pre- and post-war results are consistent in the sense that they imply a market wage equation in the post-war period that is very similar to that for the pre-war period.

2   Dispersion effects resulting from non-linear Phillips curves

We consider first a situation where no 'wage transfer mechanism' is operative and wage increases in any given labour market are completely independent of wage increases elsewhere. In such a situation any influence of unemployment dispersion on aggregate wage inflation is the result solely of non-linearity in the wage adjustment equation at the market level, i.e., in the so-called market Phillips curve.

As Lipsey [6] first pointed out, if the market Phillips curve is non-linear, unequal unemployment rates in different labour markets will

Figure 1

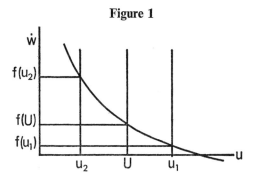

result in an aggregate Phillips curve which lies above the individual market curve. Furthermore, the greater is the unemployment dispersion, the more pronounced is the upward shift in the aggregate curve.

This can easily be seen by examining a simple model with just 2 sectors—a high unemployment sector and a low unemployment sector, with unemployment rates u_1 and u_2 respectively. Let the two sectors have equal weights, i.e., $u_1 - U = U - u_2$ where U is the overall aggregate unemployment rate. Suppose the wage adjustment relationship $\dot{w} = f(u)$ is identical in both sectors and is of the non-liner Phillips type as shown in Figure 1.

Since $f(u_2) - f(U) > f(U) - f(u_1)$ it follows that the aggregate wage change is given by:

$$\dot{W} = \frac{f(u_1) + f(u_2)}{2} > f(U) \qquad (2.1)$$

In other words $\dot{W}$ is greater than it would have been if the aggregate unemployment rate had been unchanged at U, but there had been no unemployment dispersion.

A recent analysis of the non-linearity effect of unemployment dispersion on aggregate rates of wage change is that of Archibald [1]. Archibald fits non-linear Phillips curve relationships to post-war data for both the United Kingdom and the United States but also includes a measure of unemployment dispersion as an additional variable. In the absence of data which coincides with 'true' labour markets, the dispersion measures are calculated from available regional and industrial data. The measure of dispersion used is the weighted variance of market unemployment rates, $s^2 = \sum \alpha_i (u_i - U)^2$ where U is the overall unemployment rate and u_i is the unemployment rate and α_i the proportion of the labour employed in the ith region or industry.

Archibald's conclusions are clouded by a high positive correlation between U and s^2, but his findings suggest that unemployment dispersion does have a positive effect on the aggregate rate of change of wages. However there is some evidence of serial correlation in the residuals of Archibald's final equations which suggests that there may be an additional factor influencing the rate of change of wage rates which has not been allowed for.

The main purpose of this section is to develop an aggregate wage adjustment equation which takes account of the non-linearity effects of unemployment dispersion. In other words we wish to determine, firstly, whether Archibald's measure of unemployment dispersion is the correct measure to include in the aggregate equation and secondly if it is the correct measure, in what manner should it be included.

We now derive the aggregate wage adjustment equation for the case where dispersion effects are due solely to non-linearity in the Phillips curve.

Suppose there are n distinct labour markets in the economy with unemployments rates, $u_1, u_2, \ldots, u_n$.

Let U be the overall aggregate unemployment rate. Then if α_i is the proportion of the total labour force employed in the ith labour market, we have

$$\sum_{i=1}^{n} \alpha_i = 1 \qquad (2.2)$$

and

$$\sum_{i=1}^{n} \alpha_i u_i = U \qquad (2.3)$$

Let us assume that all the individual labour markets have wage adjustment equations of the form

$$\dot{w}_i = k\dot{P} + f(u_1) \qquad (2.4)$$

where $\dot{w}_i$ is the rate of wage change in the ith market and $\dot{P}$ is the aggregate rate of price change. We are in other words assuming that wage changes at the market level are dependent on both local labour market conditions and on anticipated price changes, but that anticipated price changes are the same in all markets and may be represented by changes in the aggregate price level.

We further assume that, given the rate of price change, the wage adjustment equation is of the form shown in Figure 2, with the properties that $f'(u_i) < 0$ and $f''(u_i) \geq 0$.

Figure 2

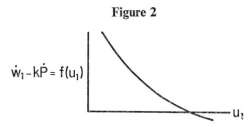

The aggregate wage change over all sectors is given by

$$\dot{W} = \sum \alpha_i \dot{w}_i$$
$$= \sum \alpha_i[(k\dot{P} + f(u_i)] = k\dot{P} + \sum \alpha_i f(u_i) \qquad (2.5)$$

Taking a truncated Taylor series expansion of $f(u_i)$ about the aggregate unemployment rate U

$$f(u_i) = f(U) + (u_i - U)f'(U) + \frac{(u_i - U)^2}{2}f''(U)$$

Hence

$$\sum \alpha_i f(u_i) = \sum \alpha_i f(U) + \sum \alpha_i(u_i - U)f'(U) + \frac{\sum \alpha_i(u_i - U)^2}{2}f''(U)$$
$$= f(U) + \tfrac{1}{2}s^2 f''(U)$$

using equations (2.2) and (2.3) and where $s^2 = \sum \alpha_i(u_i - U)^2$, the weighted variance of the market unemployment rates.

Substituting in equation (2.5) yields for the aggregate rate of wage change

$$\boxed{\dot{W} = k\dot{P} + f(U) + \tfrac{1}{2}s^2 f''(U)} \qquad (2.6)$$

Equation (2.6) is similar to the estimating equation used by Archibald in that it involves the weighted variance of unemployment rates s^2. However if we let $f(U) = a + (b/U)$, $b > 0$, Archibald's formulation, then we have $f''(U) = 2b/U^3$ and the aggregate wage equation becomes:

$$\dot{W} = a + k\dot{P} + \frac{b}{U} + b\left(\frac{s^2}{U^3}\right) \qquad (2.7)$$

This contrasts with Archibald's estimating equation

$$\dot{W} = a + k\dot{P} + \frac{b}{U} + cs^2 \qquad (2.8)$$

Two points are to be noted here. Firstly if unemployment dispersion is to be allowed for, it is not sufficient merely to include the variance of unemployment rates, s^2, in the wage equation. For example if the formulation $f(U) = a + b/U$ is used the correct dispersion variable to employ is s^2/U^3. Moreover if equation (2.7) is employed, we have an *a priori* restriction on the form of the wage equation in that the coefficients on the unemployment and dispersion variables must be equal.

Secondly, Archibald's form for the aggregate wage equation, (2.8), combined with his observed high correlation between U and s^2, implies that the separate influences of U and s^2 on the rate of wage change tend to offset one another. In other words, any damping effect on $\dot{W}$ caused by increases in U tends to be countered by the upward push given to $\dot{W}$ by the simultaneous increases in s^2. In equation (2.7), however, the dispersion measure s^2 is deflated by U^3, so that the positive correlation between dispersion of unemployment and aggregate unemployment is masked and indeed a negative correlation is to be expected between U and s^2/U^3. It follows that when U varies in equation (2.7) the effects of the unemployment variable and of the dispersion variable, s^2/U^3 tend to reinforce one another, rather than offset one another as they do in Archibald's formulation.

3 Dispersion effects resulting from the wage transfer mechanism

An important factor in trade union bargaining for higher wages, is the existence of recent wage increases for comparable employees in different labour markets. There may therefore be a transfer mechanism at work, whereby wage increases obtained in one bargaining area, which we may call a 'leading' market and in which there is a heavy demand for labour, are passed on, by this principle of comparability to other 'non-leading' markets where the pressure in the labour market is much less severe. Obviously the greater the dispersion of unemployment rates, the stronger will be the transfer mechanism and the greater the upward pressure on the aggregate wage rate.

There are a number of alternative possible formulations of the transfer mechanism. The chief problems arise in identifying the leading markets and determining whether a market which qualifies as 'leading' in any one particular year is necessarily leading in other years. The versions of the transfer mechanism proposed in this paper are of the following general form.

For all leading markets, i.e., for what we may term the 'leading sector', wage rates are regarded as being determined by a normal Phillips curve relationship.

$$\dot{w}_i = f(u_i) \tag{3.1}$$

For all non-leading markets, i.e., for the 'non-leading' sector, however we have

$$\dot{w}_i = f(u_i) + h_i[\dot{w}^* - f(u_i)] \tag{3.2}$$

Thus wage changes in the non-leading sector may be separated into a wage change resulting from labour market conditions in that sector and an additional wage change which is proportional to the difference between some rate of wage change w^*, and the wage changes which would have occurred in the non-leading sector in the absence of any transfer mechanism. w^* may be termed the 'leading rate of wage change' for the non-leading sector and is representative in some sense of wage changes which occur in the leading sector. For example, w^* might in practice be either the maximum or the average rate of wage change among the markets in the leading sector.

What we are assuming, then, is that employees in the non-leading labour markets, are able to eliminate some, if not all, of the difference which would exist, in the absence of any transfer mechanism, between the rates of wage increase in their own markets and those in the leading sector. Normally it is to be expected that employees in non-leading markets will not be able to eliminate all of this discrepancy and that h_i will lie between zero and unity.

We shall concentrate, in this section, on the special case where the market Phillips curve has a linear form, i.e., $f(u_i) = a + bu_i$ with $b < 0$. We shall therefore derive aggregate wage adjustment equations for the case where *any dispersion effects are the result solely of the operation of wage transfer mechanisms—non-linearity effects are assumed absent.*

We turn now to a discussion of the possible forms for the transfer mechanism which is to be introduced in the model. The simplest possible case is where the leading sector contains just one labour market and this single given market comprises the leading sector throughout the period under consideration. For this situation to exist, it is necessary that there should be one labour market in which, throughout the period, labour demand pressures are invariably greatest, i.e., the rate of unemployment is invariably the lowest, and in which the rate of wage change is always the highest. This single, 'lowest-unemployment market' then comprises the leading sector, while the non-leading sector consists of all other labour markets. The leading rate of wage change, w^*, for the non-leading sector is the rate of wage change in the single leading market.

A more likely possibility in practice is that there is no single labour market which invariably has the lowest unemployment rate, but that there are a number of low unemployment markets and that the distinction of being the lowest unemployment market passes from one to another of these markets over time. The transfer mechanisms might then take one of two forms which we may call Model I and Model II.

Model I

The leading sector still consists of a single labour market, but the identity of this single leading market varies from time period to time period. In any given time period the leading market will be whichever market has, during that period, the lowest unemployment rate and largest rate of wage change.

Suppose the leading market is market j (j varying over time), then using the formulation of equations (3.1) and (3.2) and introducing price changes into the model, we have, for the linear case:

$$\dot{w}_i = a + k\dot{P} + bu_i \qquad\qquad i = j \quad (3.3)$$
$$\dot{w}_i = a + k\dot{P} + bu_i + h_i(\dot{w}^* - a - k\dot{P} - bu_i) \qquad i \neq j \quad (3.4)$$

where the leading rate of wage change for the non-leading sector, $\dot{w}^*$ is the rate of wage change in market j.

$$\dot{w}^* = a + k\dot{P} + bu_j \qquad\qquad (3.5)$$

Using equations (3.3), (3.4) and (3.5), the aggregate rate of wage change is given by

$$\dot{W} = \sum_{i=1}^{n} \alpha_i \dot{w}_i$$

$$= a + k\dot{P} + bU + \sum_{\substack{i=1 \\ i \neq j}}^{n} \alpha_i h_i (bu_j - bu_i)$$

$$= a + k\dot{P} + bU + \sum_{i=1}^{n} \alpha_i h_i (bu_j - bu_i) \text{ since } \alpha_j h_j (bu_j - bu_j) = 0$$

If we now make the simplifying assumption that $h_i = h = $ const, or in other words that the transfer mechanism operates with equal strength in all non-leading markets, we have

$$\dot{W} = a + k\dot{P} + bU + bh \sum_{i=1}^{n} \alpha_i (u_j - u_i)$$

or using equation (2.3)

$$\boxed{\dot{W} = a + k\dot{P} + bU + bh(u_j - U)} \qquad (3.6)$$

The last term on the right-hand side of equation (3.6) represents the upward shift in the aggregate wage adjustment equation caused by the operation of the transfer mechanism. In the special case $h_i = h = 1$, that is when employees in the non-leading markets are able to eliminate all the differences between wage changes in their markets and the wage change in the leading market, equation (3.6) becomes

$$\dot{W} = a + k\dot{P} + bu_j \qquad (3.7)$$

Thus, in this special case, aggregate wage change is dependent only on the rate of price change and on the level of unemployment in the leading labour market.

Equation (3.6) is the aggregate wage equation for the case where there is one leading market only—market j, and where j varies over time. If j is fixed over time, e.g., $j = $ const $= 1$, then we are back in the simplest situation of all, discussed above, where the single leading market remains unchanged from period to period. This is a special case of Model I and may be referred to as Model IA. For Model IA, the aggregate wage change is given by

$$\dot{W} = a + k\dot{P} + bU + bh(u_1 - U) \qquad (3.8)$$

Model II

The assumptions of Model I imply two related and possibly unrealistic processes. Firstly, in Model I, it is possible for any given labour market to be in the non-leading sector during one time period, to be the leading market in the next period, to be back in the non-leading sector in the next, etc., etc. Secondly since the identity of the leading market changes over time, Model I implies that markets in the non-leading sector take as the leading rate of wage change, the rate of wage change, first in one market, then in another, etc., etc.

Model I therefore implies that the process by which rates of wage change are determined at the disaggregated level can change rapidly over time. It may be more reasonable to assume that a given labour market remains either constantly in the leading sector or constantly in the non-leading sector. If this is a more reasonable assumption, the transfer mechanism is better formulated as follows.

In Model II, the leading sector consists of more than one labour market. Suppose in fact there are m leading markets in the leading sector. These m markets are those with the m lowest unemployment rates and in the absence of any transfer mechanism would have the m highest rates of wage change. They must include all markets which at one time or other have been the lowest unemployment market. (Otherwise a situation may arise, where the market with the greatest rate of wage change is outside the leading sector.) They may or may not include other labour markets. The number of leading markets m may or may not be constant over time. We assume for the moment that m is in fact constant and that the identity of these m markers remains unchanged over time.

Two possibilities now arise:

(a) Wage changes in any market within the leading sector are influenced not only by labour market conditions in that particular market, but also by market conditions elsewhere in the leading sector. That is, there is a transfer mechanism at work within the leading sector itself. This situation is most likely to occur when there is a considerable disparity in unemployment rates within the leading sector and hence a considerable disparity in rates of wage change.

(b) Wage changes in any market within the leading sector may be regarded as being determined independently of labour market conditions outside that market, i.e., no transfer mechanism is at work within the leading sector itself. This situation is likely to occur when there is little disparity between unemployment rates within the leading sector, so that either there is insufficient disparity in rates of wage change, for a transfer mechanism to become operative, or if a transfer mechanism is operating its effects are sufficiently small to be ignored.

Possibility (a) is most easily dealt with. If a transfer mechanism operates within the leading sector, then the leading rate of wage change for markets in this sector may be assumed to be the highest rate of wage change within it, i.e., that in the lowest unemployment market. The leading sector thus operates as does Model I. For the non-leading sector, the leading rate of wage change might be either the average rate of wage change, or the highest rate of wage change in the leading sector. Since there is a clear disparity in unemployment levels in the leading sector, the latter must exceed the former by a noticeable margin and it seems reasonable to assume that the latter is the leading wage rate for the non-leading sector. Under possibility (a) then, all markets have a leading rate of wage change—that in the lowest unemployment market and the situation reduces to Model I, where there is a single leading market, the identity of which varies over time. Under these assumptions then, we are back in the situation where the process by which wage changes are determined may change rapidly and continuously over time.

If possibility (b) hold then this process becomes more stable. No transfer mechanism now operates within the leading sector, so that if this sector consists of markets 1, 2, ..., m, then the rate of wage change within these markets is given by

$$\dot{w}_i = a + k\dot{P} + bu_i \qquad i = 1, 2, \dots, m \qquad (3.9)$$

For markets in the non-leading sector we then have

$$\dot{w}_i = a + k\dot{P} + bu_i + h_i(\dot{w}^* - k\dot{P} - a - bu_i)$$
$$i = m + 1, m + 2, \dots, n \qquad (3.10)$$

Since we are now assuming that there is little disparity in unemployment rates within the leading sector and hence that there is no rate of wage change which noticeably exceeds the average rate of wage change in that sector, a reasonable assumption is that $\dot{w}^*$ may in this case be regarded as the average rate of wage change in the leading sector, i.e., since we are dealing with linear functions:

$$\dot{w}^* = a + k\dot{P} + b\hat{u} \qquad (3.11)$$

where $\hat{u}$ is the overall aggregate unemployment rate in the leading sector.

Assuming again that $h_i = h = \text{const}$, by a similar derivation to that for equation (3.6), we obtain for the aggregate rate of wage change:

$$\dot{W} = a + k\dot{P} + bU + bh(\hat{u} - U) \qquad (3.12)$$

which in the special case $h_i = h = 1$ becomes

$$\dot{W} = a + k\dot{P} + b\hat{u} \qquad (3.13)$$

This implies that if employees in the non-leading sector are able to eliminate all the difference between rates of wage change in this sector, and the average rate of wage change in the leading sector, then aggregate wage change depends only on price changes and unemployment levels in the leading sector.

We have so far assumed that the number of labour markets m, in the leading sector is constant over time and that the identity of these leading markets is unchanged over time. If these assumptions hold then the process by which rates of wage change are determined is 'stable' over time, in the sense that any given labour market is either always inside or always outside the leading sector. If we relax either of these assumptions, equations (3.12) and (3.13) still hold, but the process of wage determination is then less 'stable', in the sense that some labour markets may shift in and out of the leading sector. However, the 'instability' in this process is less than in Model I, since any market which has ever been the lowest unemployment market remains constantly within the leading sector.

We shall refer to the case where no restrictions are placed on the number or identity of the leading markets as Model II. When m is constant and the identity of the leading markets is unchanged over time, we have a special case of Model II, which we may call Model IIA.

4   The dispersion model with non-linear Phillips curves and wage transfer mechanisms

We now combine the ideas of sections 2 and 3 and examine the general case where dispersion effects are the result both of non-linearity in the market Phillips curve and of the operation of a wage transfer mechanism.

Model I

Consider first Model I, where there is a single leading market—market j, with j varying over time. We now have the following expressions for the market rates of wage change.

$$\dot{w}_i = k\dot{P} + f(u_i) \qquad\qquad i = j \qquad (4.1)$$

$$\dot{w}_i = k\dot{P} + f(u_i) + h_i[\dot{w}^* - k\dot{P} - f(u_i)] \qquad i \neq j \qquad (4.2)$$

where $f(u_i)$ is now a non-linear function of u_i and $\dot{w}^*$ is, again, the rate of wage change in market j, the leading market.

$$\dot{w}^* = k\dot{P} + f(u_j) \qquad (4.3)$$

By a similar derivation to that for equation (3.6), again assuming $h_i = h = $ const, we obtain for the aggregate rate of wage change in Model I

$$\dot{W} = k\dot{P} + \sum_{i=1}^{n} \alpha_i f(u_i) + h\left[f(u_j) - \sum_{i=1}^{n} \alpha_i f(u_i) \right]$$

or using equation (2.6)

$$\boxed{\dot{W} = k\dot{P} + f(U) + \tfrac{1}{2}s^2 f''(U) + h[f(u_j) - f(U) - \tfrac{1}{2}s^2 f''(U)]}$$

$$(4.4)$$

The last term on the right-hand side of equation (4.4) represents the upward shift in the aggregate wage adjustment caused by the operation of the transfer mechanism, while the third term represents the upward shift resulting from the non-linearity in the market Phillips curve.

In the special case $h = h_i = 1$, equation (4.4) reduces to

$$\dot{W} = k\dot{P} + f(u_j) \qquad (4.5)$$

Thus as in the linear case, under these circumstances aggregate wage change is dependent only on the rate of price change and the level of unemployment in the leading market.

For Model IA, where the identity of the leading market is unchanged over time, e.g., $j = $ const $= 1$, equation (4.4) becomes:

$$\dot{W} = k\dot{P} + f(U) + \tfrac{1}{2}s^2 f''(U) + h[f(u_1) - f(U) - \tfrac{1}{2}s^2 f''(U)]$$

$$(4.6)$$

15

Model II

For Model II where the leading sector consists of markets 1, 2, 3, ..., m, we have for the market rates of wage change:

$$\dot{w}_i = k\dot{P} + f(u_i) \qquad\qquad\qquad i = 1, 2, \ldots, m \qquad (4.7)$$

$$\dot{w}_i = k\dot{P} + f(u_.) + h_i[\dot{w}^* - k\dot{P} - f(u_i)] \qquad i = m + 1, m + 2, \ldots, n \qquad (4.8)$$

where the leading rate of wage change, $\dot{w}^*$, is again the average rate of wage change in the leading sector, i.e., using (2.6)

$$\dot{w}^* = k\dot{P} + f(\hat{u}) + \tfrac{1}{2}\hat{s}^2 f''(\hat{u}) \qquad (4.9)$$

where $\hat{u}$ is again the overall unemployment rate in the leading sector and $\hat{s}^2$ is the weighted variance of unemployment rates in the leading sector.

Again assuming $h_i = h = $ const, we obtain by a similar derivation to that for equation (4.4) the aggregate rate of wage change for Model II.

$$\dot{W} = k\dot{P} + f(U) + \tfrac{1}{2}s^2 f''(U) + h[f(\hat{u}) - f(U) + \tfrac{1}{2}\hat{s}^2 f''(\hat{u}) - \tfrac{1}{2}s^2 f''(U)]$$

$$(4.10)$$

As for equation (4.4) the third and fourth terms on the right-hand side of equation (4.10), represent the upward shift in the aggregate wage equation caused by non-linearity and by the wage transfer mechanism.

Finally, since there is little disparity in unemployment rates within the leading sector, $\hat{s}^2$ will be small compared with s^2, so that equation (4.10) may be written

$$\dot{W} = k\dot{P} + f(U) + \tfrac{1}{2}s^2 f''(U) + h[f(\hat{u}) - f(U) - \tfrac{1}{2}s^2 f''(U)] \qquad (4.11)$$

which in the special case $h = h_i = 1$ becomes

$$\dot{W} = k\dot{P} + f(\hat{u}) \qquad (4.12)$$

Thus, under these assumptions aggregate wage change again depends only on price changes and unemployment rates in the leading sector.

We have developed in this section an aggregate wage adjustment equation which allows for both the non-linearity effects and the wage transfer effects of unemployment dispersion. The remainder of the paper consists of an attempt to assess the statistical significance and quantitative importance of these effects. In the empirical sections that follow we experimented initially with three non-linear functional forms for $f(u)$.

(a) $$f(u) = a + b \log u \qquad b < 0 \qquad (4.13)$$

Using equations (4.4) and (4.10), and the fact that $f''(u) = -(b/u^2)$, yields aggregate wage adjustment equations of the form

$$\dot{W} = a + k\dot{P} + b \log U - b \frac{s^2}{2U^2} - bh\left[\log U - \log u_j - \frac{s^2}{2U^2}\right] \qquad (4.14)$$

for Model I, and

$$\dot{W} = a + k\dot{P} + b \log U - b \frac{s^2}{2U^2} - bh\left[\log U - \log \hat{u} + \frac{\hat{s}^2}{2\hat{u}^2} - \frac{s^2}{2U^2}\right] \qquad (4.15)$$

for Model IIA.

We may re-write equations (4.14) and (4.15) as

$$\boxed{\dot{W} = a + k\dot{P} + bg_1(U) - bS_1 - bhA_1} \qquad (4.16)$$

where $g_1(U) = \log U$,

$$S_1 = s^2/2U^2$$

and $\quad A_1 = \log U - \log u_j - (s^2/2U^2)$ for Model I

and $\quad A_1 = \log U - \log \hat{u} + (\hat{s}^2/2\hat{u}^2) - (s^2/2U^2)$ for Model IIA.

We have an *a priori* restriction on the form of the wage equation, in that the coefficients on the unemployment variable $g_1(U)$ and the non-linearity dispersion variable S_1 are constrained to be equal in size but opposite in sign. Alternative estimating equations are therefore given by

$$\boxed{\dot{W} = a + k\dot{P} + bS_1^* - bhA_1} \qquad (4.17)$$

where $S_1^* = g_1(U) - S_1$.

(b) $$f(u) = a + \frac{b}{u} \qquad b > 0 \qquad (4.18)$$

We now have $f''(u) = 2b/u^3$ and aggregate wage adjustment equations may be written

$$\dot{W} = a + k\dot{P} + bg_2(U) + bS_2 + bhA_2 \qquad (4.19)$$

where $g_2(U) = 1/U$,

$$S_2 = s^2/U^3$$

and $\qquad A_2 = (1/u_j) - (1/U) - (s^2/U^3)$ for Model I

and $\qquad A_2 = \dfrac{1}{\hat{u}} - \dfrac{1}{U} + \dfrac{\hat{s}^2}{\hat{u}^3} - \dfrac{s^2}{U^3}$ for Model IIA.

The constrained estimating equations now have the form

$$\dot{W} = a + k\dot{P} + bS_2^* + bhA_2 \qquad (4.20)$$

where $S_2^* = g_2(U) + S_2$.

(c) $\qquad\qquad\qquad f(u) = a + b\sqrt{u} \qquad b < 0 \qquad (4.21)$

We now have $f''(u) = (-b/4u^{3/2})$ and wage adjustment equations of the form

$$\dot{W} = a + k\dot{P} + bg_3(U) - bS_3 - bhA_3 \qquad (4.22)$$

where $g_3(U) = \sqrt{U}$,

$$S_3 = s^2/8U^{3/2}$$

and $\qquad A_3 = \sqrt{U} - \sqrt{u_j} - (s^2/8U^{3/2})$ for Model I

and $\qquad A_3 = \sqrt{U} - \sqrt{\hat{u}} + (\hat{s}^2/8\hat{u}^{3/2}) - (s^2/8U^{3/2})$ for Model IIA.

The constrained estimating equations now are

$$\dot{W} = a + k\dot{P} + bS_3^* - bhA_3 \qquad (4.23)$$

where $S_3^* = g_3(U) - S_3$.

Two points are to be noted about the above estimating equations. Firstly from equations (4.17), (4.20) and (4.23), it is in each case possible to obtain an estimate of the parameter h, and of the strength of the transfer mechanism, from the ratios of the estimated coefficients of the relevant composite variables S_i^* ($i = 1, 2, 3$) and the relevant transfer dispersion variables A_i ($i = 1, 2, 3$).

Secondly, in empirical wage adjustment equations it has become customary to introduce the unemployment variable in a non-linear manner. The *a priori* restrictions imposed in equations (4.17), (4.20) and (4.23), suggest that not only should this variable be introduced non-linearly, but *also that it should be adjusted by an appropriate measure of unemployment dispersion, that measure being dependent on the exact form of the non-linearity introduced.*

5   Empirical results for the post-war period

In attempting to obtain empirical estimates of wage adjustment functions of the type represented by equations (2.5), (4.4) and (4.10), the problem one is immediately confronted with is that of finding suitable data. Until comprehensive data by individual labour market becomes available, it is not possible to perform a rigorous test of the dispersion hypothesis.

In the United Kingdom context, unemployment data is available by industry, as defined in the Standard Industrial Classification and by geographical region based on Ministry of Labour classifications. A preliminary and tentative testing of the dispersion hypothesis is possible using this data. Initial examination of both sets of data suggested that dispersion measures calculated from regional data are likely to be more successful in the statistical explanation of changes in wage rates than measures calculated from the industrial data. Archibald [1] has suggested one reason why this should be so. Industrial unemployment data refers to the industry of previous employment and so may not as required, reflect differences in the availability of labour between industries. This defect does not however apply to the regional data. Since the ideal classification of a labour market cuts across both the regional and industrial classifications, and there is no other reason for preferring one set of data to the other, it was decided to concentrate on the regional data in the hope that dispersion resources calculated from this data would provide adequate proxies for the required dispersion measures. However until more suitable data becomes available any conclusions reached in the following empirical study must be treated with caution.

Details of the weights and unemployment rates used in the regional analysis may be found in the Appendix. Examination of these series for the post-war period, reveals that there is no single geographical region which can be identified as a minimum unemployment region. There are in fact three regions—London and South-East, Midlands, and Yorkshire and Lincolnshire, which at sometime during the post-war period qualify for this distinction. It is not possible, then, to use the regional data to estimate a model of type IA, but models of type I may be employed with a leading sector consisting of one region only—this region being London and South East during the years 1958–63, and in 1966, Midlands during the years 1964–5 and either Midlands, or Yorkshire and Lincolnshire during 1950–7. (These regions have virtually equal unemployment rates for this period.)

The regions mentioned above are also, throughout the post-war period, the regions possessing the three lowest unemployment rates. Moreover unemployment dispersion within these regions is small with an average $\hat{s}_2^2 = 0\cdot02$ compared with an overall unemployment dispersion of average $s^2 = 1\cdot3$. An alternative then is to regard these three regions as comprising a leading sector, within which no transfer mechanism operates, and to adopt a formulation corresponding to Model II. Since the number of regions in the leading sector is constant $(m = 3)$, and the identity of these regions is unchanged over time, we have in fact, the special case of Model II, i.e., Model IIA.

In the empirical study that follows we use the regional data to estimate models of type I—implying a wage determination process changing over time, and of type IIA, implying a wage determination process which is stable over time in the sense that any region is either constantly within or constantly outside the leading sector. For the post-war years we used the three non-linear forms for $f(u)$ and their corresponding estimating equations outlined in section 4.

For the post-war period, ordinary least squares estimates of equations (4.17), (4.20) and (4.23) were obtained for the years 1950–66. Earlier years were omitted in order to avoid the distorting effect of the apparently successful period of wage restraint in the late 1940's and later years to avoid the complications caused by the more recent enforcement of incomes policy. The results are given in Table 1.

For purposes of comparison, the wage equations were first estimated without the inclusion of any dispersion variables. (See first section of Table 1.) The results were as expected. Both the price variable and the non-linear unemployment variables are significant in

Table 1

Formulation	const	$\dot{P}$	$g_i(U)$	S_i	S_i^*	A_i (Model IIA)	A_i (Model I)	$\bar{R}^2$	d
$i = 1$, $g_1(U) = \log U$	4·74 (0·51)	0·495 (0·062)	−2·27 (0·61)					0·895	1·92
$i = 2$, $g_2(U) = 1/U$	1·06 (0·56)	0·490 (0·060)	4·12 (1·04)					0·901	1·87
$i = 3$, $g_3(U) = \sqrt{U}$	7·95 (1·38)	0·497 (0·063)	−3·38 (0·94)					0·892	1·93
$i = 1$, $g_1(U) = \log U$	2·52 (0·86)	0·429 (0·049)	−2·20 (0·66)	4·36 (2·55)		6·31 (2·03)		0·943	1·72
$i = 2$, $g_2(U) = 1/U$	1·31 (0·59)	0·417 (0·047)	1·15 (1·60)	4·55 (1·71)		7·62 (2·16)		0·951	1·81
$i = 3$, $g_3(U) = \sqrt{U}$	7·78 (1·48)	0·439 (0·051)	−5·15 (1·10)	7·01 (9·02)		11·51 (4·06)		0·935	1·77
$i = 1$, $g_1(U) = \log U$	3·02 (1·08)	0·441 (0·068)	−1·54 (0·79)		5·11 (3·24)		1·22 (1·12)	0·908	1·84
$i = 2$, $g_2(U) = 1/U$	1·83 (0·77)	0·456 (0·072)	1·50 (2·17)		3·01 (2·30)		0·67 (1·00)	0·905	1·82
$i = 3$, $g_3(U) = \sqrt{U}$	6·65 (1·67)	0·438 (0·067)	−3·59 (1·03)		14·88 (10·70)		3·08 (2·37)	0·905	1·90
$i = 1$, $g_1(U) = \log U$	3·04 (0·44)	0·431 (0·048)			−2·57 (0·41)	6·56 (1·95)		0·946	1·97
$i = 2$, $g_2(U) = 1/U$	0·83 (0·39)	0·419 (0·047)			2·79 (0·42)	7·26 (2·15)		0·950	2·08
$i = 3$, $g_3(U) = \sqrt{U}$	8·04 (0·95)	0·436 (0·049)			−5·32 (0·88)	12·06 (3·56)		0·941	1·80

Notes:
1. Dependent variable in all cases is $\dot{W}$.
2. Figures in brackets are standard errors.
3. For definitions of variables see section 4 and Appendix.

all formulations (logarithmic, $i = 1$, reciprocal, $i = 2$ and square root, $i = 3$). The coefficient of multiple determination $\bar{R}^2$ adjusted for degrees of freedom is in the region of 0·90.

When the non-linearity dispersion variables, S_i, and the transfer dispersion variables, A_i, are introduced into the equation, it becomes clear that Model IIA (second section of Table 1) provides a better explanation of post-war data than does Model I (third section of Table 1). A_i (Model I) is statistically insignificant in all three formulations, while for Model IIA the inclusion of the dispersion variables improves the fit in all three cases, $\bar{R}^2$ rising to the range 0·93 to 0·95. The results for Model IIA confirm that during the post-war period, the upward pressure resulting from unemployment dispersion has been a statistically significant factor in determining aggregate wage change. The discussion from here on is restricted to Model IIA.

For Model IIA, all the unemployment and dispersion variables have the correct sign, but contrary to *a priori* expectations, the absolute magnitude of the coefficients on the S_i variables is in all cases greater than those on the unemployment variables. This is not altogether surprising considering the inadequacy of the data and moreover the order of magnitude is the same in all three formulations. It is possible to perform a t-test on the hypothesis that either the sum of the coefficients on the unemployment and non-linearity dispersion variables is zero (logarithmic and square root cases, $i = 1, 3$) or that their difference is zero (reciprocal case $i = 2$). In no formulation is the relevant t-value anywhere near being sufficiently large to warrant rejection of the *a priori* hypothesis. (The t-values are 0·72, 1·05 and 0·15 respectively. With 12 degrees of freedom the 0·05 critical value of t is 2·18.)

There is evidence of fairly strong correlation between the unemployment variable and both the dispersion variables and this is reflected in the size of their standard errors especially in the reciprocal and square root formulations. The nature of this correlation is however the reverse of that found by Archibald. As noted above, given the observed positive correlation between unemployment dispersion and the aggregate unemployment rate, Archibald's final wage equation implies that the separate influences on the aggregate rate of wage change of these variables tend to offset one another. However the non-linearity dispersion variables used in this paper $s^2/2U^2$, s^2/U^3 and $s^2/8U^{3/2}$ are all negatively correlated with aggregate unemployment, so that the wage equations presented in Table 1 all imply that the effects of the unemployment and dispersion variables will reinforce rather than offset one another as far as their influence on aggregate wage change is concerned.

The statistical problems caused by this collinearity can be avoided by replacing the unemployment variables, $g_i(U)$, and the non-linearity dispersion variables, S_i, by the composite variables, S_i^*. (The S_i^* variables are the sum of the former variables in the reciprocal case and the difference in the logarithmic and square-root formulations.) This is done, for Model IIA, in the fourth section of Table 1.

The imposition of these *a priori* restrictions, results in an increase in $\bar{R}^2$ for the logarithmic and square-root cases ($i = 1, 3$) and a very slight fall in the reciprocal formulation ($i = 2$). All variables now become significant with the correct sign.

A comparison of the coefficients of the variables S_i^* and A_i enables estimates of the parameter h, and hence the strength of the transfer mechanism to be obtained. Again using Model IIA, the estimates of h are 2·55 for the logarithmic function, 2·60 for the reciprocal formulation and 2·27 for the square root function. The estimates are higher than anticipated in that, on *a priori* grounds, the value of h is to be expected to lie between zero and unity. However it is possible that the discrepancy is merely a reflection of data inadequacies. While dispersion series calculated from regional data may adequately reflect relative variations over time in dispersion by labour market, it is unlikely that they will be adequate measures of the absolute degree of dispersion at any given point in time. This being so, their use in the wage adjustment equation, makes it likely that while the statistical significance of these dispersion variables may be unaffected, the actual size of the coefficients on these variables may be considerably distorted. This, in turn, can result in a distorted value for the parameter h.

In so far as any conclusion can be drawn from the empirical results regarding the strength of the transfer mechanism, it is that h tends to be rather high, i.e. that employees in the non-leading sector are able to eliminate a large proportion, if not all, of the difference between wage changes in their sector and those in the leading sector.

For Model IIA, since $\hat{s}^2$ is small compared with s^2 (see above), if $h = 1$ the wage adjustment equation reduces to equation (4.12). Accordingly this equation was estimated using the three functional forms for $f(u)$.

$$\dot{W} = 3{\cdot}88 + 0{\cdot}455\dot{P} - 2{\cdot}39 \log \hat{u}$$
$$\phantom{\dot{W} = 3{\cdot}88}\ (0{\cdot}25)\ \ (0{\cdot}052)\ \ \ \ (0{\cdot}45) \tag{5.1}$$
$$\bar{R}^2 = 0{\cdot}931 \qquad d = 2{\cdot}00$$

$$\dot{W} = 1{\cdot}20 + 0{\cdot}451\dot{P} + 2{\cdot}63\,1/\hat{u}$$
$$\phantom{\dot{W} = 1{\cdot}20}\ (0{\cdot}38)\ \ (0{\cdot}050)\ \ \ \ (0{\cdot}46) \tag{5.2}$$
$$\bar{R}^2 = 0{\cdot}937 \qquad d = 1{\cdot}89$$

$$\dot{W} = 8{\cdot}62 + 0{\cdot}462\dot{P} - 4{\cdot}39\,\sqrt{\hat{u}}$$
$$\phantom{\dot{W} = 8{\cdot}62}\ (1{\cdot}05)\ \ (0{\cdot}054)\ \ \ \ (0{\cdot}88) \tag{5.3}$$
$$\bar{R}^2 = 0{\cdot}925 \qquad s = 2{\cdot}05$$

When aggregate unemployment is replaced in the wage equation by unemployment in the leading sector there is a marked rise in $\bar{R}^2$. From the first section of Table 1 the relevant $\bar{R}^2$'s when aggregate unemployment is included are 0·895, 0·901 and 0·892. This confirms the view that in any attempt to explain aggregate rates of wage change, the existence of some form of transfer mechanism must be allowed for.

Summarizing the post-war results, we may say that Model IIA fits the regional data much better than Model I. In so far as any conclusions can be drawn from purely regional data, it would therefore seem that a transfer mechanism which implies a process of wage-change determination which is 'stable' over time is the more appropriate for the post-war period.

The composite unemployment variables S_i^* generally perform better than normal unemployment variables, suggesting that non-linearity in the market wage equations is an important factor in the determination of aggregate wage change.

Of the three functional forms for $f(u)$ the reciprocal formulation gives marginally the better fit. However for this case the imposition of the a priori restriction causes a slight fall in $\bar{R}^2$ in contrast to the logarithmic and square root equations. Further doubt is cast on this equation when it is observed that the constant term is invariably positive. Because of the reciprocal form of the unemployment variable this implies that, given zero price change and zero unemployment dispersion, the rate of wage change will always be positive no matter how large is the aggregate unemployment rate. Of the remaining two functional forms, the logarithmic formulation appears slightly superior in terms of overall performance.

The dispersion of unemployment by region has been shown to have a statistically significant effect on changes in aggregate wage rates. However, we have not yet shown whether this effect is important in a quantitative sense—that is whether the existence of unemployment dispersion has given an appreciable upward push to aggregate wage rates and resulted in an aggregate wage adjustment function which is some way above the market adjustment function.

Consider again the final estimated equation in, for example, the logarithmc formulation (see fourth section of Table 1).

$$\dot{W} = 3{\cdot}04 + 0{\cdot}431\dot{P} - 2{\cdot}57\,(\log U - S_1) + 6{\cdot}56A_1 \quad (5.4)$$

The average values of the variables included in this equation were for the years 1950–66:

$$\dot{W} = 5{\cdot}46 \quad \dot{P} = 3{\cdot}90 \quad \log U = 0{\cdot}54 \quad S_1 = 0{\cdot}22 \quad A_1 = 0{\cdot}24$$

Using these figures we may now make some estimate of the typical upward shift given to the wage adjustment function by the existence of unemployment dispersion. Equation (5.4) implies a market adjustment function of the form

$$\dot{w} = 3{\cdot}04 + 0{\cdot}431\dot{P} - 2{\cdot}57\log u \qquad (5.5)$$

It follows that, given zero unemployment dispersion and average values of $\dot{P}$ and $\log U$ as above, the average annual wage change would have been 3·33%. The actual average annual wage change was in fact 5·46% suggesting that the existence of dispersion in unemployment levels has shifted the aggregate wage adjustment upwards by just over two percentage points. It can therefore be maintained that the dispersion variables are not only statistically significant but quantitatively important in their effect on the aggregate rate of wage change.

We now turn to brief examination of the years 1967–9, previously omitted from the analysis because of the possible distorting effects of attempted government control over wages and prices. A recent study of post-war wage and price inflation in the United Kingdom by Lipsey and Parkin [7] arrived at the conclusion that wage and price restraints 'have sometimes actually had the effect of raising the rate of inflation above what it would otherwise have been', and that this effect 'is very noticeable in the most recent periods of restraint since 1966'. It was decided to investigate the possibility that a dispersion-type wage-price model might be able to predict this acceleration in the rate of inflation. Accordingly a price equation was added to the wage equation and the reduced form of the resulting two-equation model used to predict inflation rates in 1967, 1968 and 1969.

$$\dot{P} = \alpha + \beta(\dot{W} - \dot{X}) + \gamma\dot{M} \qquad (5.6)$$

The price equation used was a variant of the mark up equation usually employed for estimating purposes. $\dot{X}$ and $\dot{M}$ are the percentage changes in productivity and import prices respectively. Price changes are therefore related to wage costs and import costs. We also placed the restriction $\beta + \gamma = 1$ on the equation, ensuring that if there is a difference of 1% in the rate of change of each cost category between one year and the next, then there will also be a difference of 1% between the respective rates of price change.

The price equation was combined with the logarithmic version of the wage equation and two stage least squares estimates of the two equation model obtained for the years 1950–66. The estimated equations were as follows:

$$\dot{W} = 3 \cdot 02 + 0 \cdot 443 \dot{P} - 2 \cdot 51 S_1^* + 6 \cdot 38 A_1$$
$$\qquad (0 \cdot 45) \quad (0 \cdot 060) \qquad (0 \cdot 44) \qquad (2 \cdot 03) \qquad\qquad (5.7)$$
$$\bar{R}^2 = 0 \cdot 945 \qquad d = 1 \cdot 93$$

$$\dot{P} = 1 \cdot 14 + 0 \cdot 779 (\dot{W} - \dot{X}) + 0 \cdot 221 \dot{M}$$
$$\qquad (0 \cdot 37) \quad (0 \cdot 054) \qquad\qquad\qquad (0 \cdot 016) \qquad\qquad (5.8)$$
$$\bar{R}^2 = 0 \cdot 929 \qquad d = 1 \cdot 42$$

The coefficients in the wage equation are very similar to the ordinary least squares estimates. There is a slight upward movement in the coefficients of the price and composite unemployment variables counterbalanced by a slight fall in the size of the coefficient on the dispersion variable. The coefficients in the price equation are broadly similar to those found in previous studies of the post-war period.

The reduced form of equations (5.7) and (5.8) was now used to predict values for $\dot{W}$ and $\dot{P}$ for the years 1967, 1968 and 1969. Actual and predicted values for these years are shown below.

	actual $\dot{W}$	predicted $\dot{W}$	actual $\dot{P}$	predicted $\dot{P}$
1967	5·37	3·61	3·58	3·15
1968	5·88	3.89	4·96	3·36
1969	6·74	4·10	5·27	3·92

Actual wage changes and to a lesser extent actual price changes are considerably higher than those predicted by the model—contrary to what would be expected in a period of attempted wage and price control. There appears to have been a distinct upward shift in the wage adjustment equation.

Our findings for the years 1967–9 parallel those of Parkin and Lipsey. To determine whether or not there was a similar parallel in the results for 1950–66 the dispersion equation was re-estimated for what Lipsey and Parkin term 'policy-on' and 'policy-off' periods. Since the dispersion data is annual and not quarterly data our 'policy-on' and 'policy-off' periods do not exactly coincide with those of Parkin and Lipsey. We have taken as the policy-on years 1950, 1956 and 1962–6. The results were as follows:

1950–66

$$\dot{W} = 3 \cdot 04 + 0 \cdot 431 \dot{P} - 2 \cdot 57 S_1^* + 6 \cdot 56 A_1$$
$$\qquad (0 \cdot 44) \quad (0 \cdot 048) \qquad (0 \cdot 41) \qquad (1 \cdot 95) \qquad\qquad (5.9)$$
$$\bar{R}^2 = 0 \cdot 946 \qquad d = 1 \cdot 97$$

policy-on

$$\dot{W} = 2·59 + 0·343\dot{P} - 2·32S_1^* + 10·08A_1$$
$$\phantom{\dot{W} = } (0·77) \quad (0·094) \quad (0·49) \quad (4·42) \qquad (5.10)$$
$$\bar{R}^2 = 0·963 \qquad d = 2·50$$

policy-off

$$\dot{W} = 3·05 + 0·416\dot{P} - 3·08S_1^* + 7·10A_1$$
$$\phantom{\dot{W} = } (0·62) \quad (0·067) \quad (0·62) \quad (2·56) \qquad (5.11)$$
$$\bar{R}^2 = 0·942 \qquad d = 2·21$$

The coefficients in the wage equation are well determined in both the policy-on and the policy-off periods. Moreover, although the number of degrees of freedom is small in both equations, so that little confidence can be placed in the point estimates of the coefficients, an F-test performed on the hypothesis that the vector of policy-off coefficients is equal to those for policy on, yielded an F-value of only 0·95. The 0·05 critical value for F with (4,9) degrees of freedom is 3·63.

We find, then, in contrast to Lipsey and Parkin, no difference in the results for policy-on and policy off-years. It must be remembered however that the sample priod (1950–66) used is slightly different to that of Lipsey and Parkin (1948–67) and also that we are using annual rather than quarterly data.

It appears that we cannot, on the evidence of equations (5.10) and (5.11) explain the recent upward shift in the wage equation as being the result of the operation of an incomes policy. It has been suggested that this upward shift is caused by a change in the relationship between the excess demand for labour and the level of unemployment. The N.I.E.S.R. annual report on the economic situation (February 1970), [8], suggested that this has been caused by three major institutional changes since the middle of 1966—the introduction of S.E.T. and the resultant rises in the cost of labour, improved redundancy payments and the introduction of earnings related unemployment benefit. Parkin [9] however, has found that while the relationship between unemployment and excess demand is significantly different between policy-off and policy-on periods, there is no evidence that this is caused by anything other than the existence of incomes policy. Parkin moreover provides evidence to suggest that not only the wage-change unemployment relationship but also the wage-change excess demand relationship is broken after 1966.

We are essentially concerned in this paper with the influence of unemployment dispersion on aggregate wage change and hence have paid little attention to the reasons for the recent upward shift in the wage equation. However, it does appear that the recentness of this apparent shift and hence the limited data available since its occurrence makes any choice between the different explanations of it extremely difficult. Rational choice between the alternative hypothesis about the shift will probably have to wait until the passage of time makes further data available.

6   The pre-war years, 1925–38

In this section we examine the possible effects of unemployment dispersion on aggregate wage change during the pre-war years. The years between the first and second world wars represent a period, vastly different as far as general economic conditions are concerned from the post-war era. The overall level of unemployment varied between 10% and 20% and in many years there was a fall in the aggregate wage level. This presents a marked contrast from the low levels of unemployment and steadily rising wage-levels of more recent years. However, if the dispersion hypothesis, already shown to be successful in explaining rates of wage change during the relatively prosperous post-war period, proved equally successful in explaining wage movements in such radically different conditions as in the 1930's, this would give added confidence in such a hypothesis.

Previous empirical studies of the determination of changes in wages have almost invariably found difficulty in explaining pre-war movements in wage rates. Contrary to *a priori* theoretical expectations demand for labour variables, such as the level of unemployment appear to be statistically unimportant in explaining rates of wage change. Only A. G. Hines [4] has succeeded in providing a statistical explanation of wage changes for this period and his wage equation relies not on demand for labour variables but on 'union aggressiveness' represented by such variables as the rate of change in the percentage of the labour force which is unionized. However, in this section we show that, *provided the aggregate wage adjustment equation is correctly specified, with the appropriate dispersion variable included, variations in pre-war rates of wage change can, after all, be adequately explained by a combination of price-change and unemployment variables.*

We now turn to an examination of available data for the inter-war period. It is here that data problems are most serious. It is possible to obtain data on unemployment dispersion by industry on a basis broadly similar to the post-war classification. However, as for the post-war period, preliminary examination of the industrial data proved unfruitful. Regional data, on a similar basis to the post-war classification, is more difficult to obtain. The Ministry of Labour regional classification is more broadly defined and the regions are correspondingly fewer in number. However, we were able to construct a series broadly consistent with post-war series for the period 1925–38. Figures for regional unemployment dispersion before 1925 would have been largely guesses and those for the years 1925–30 are highly speculative. Details of the series are again given in the Appendix.

Examination of the pre-war data reveals that there is one region— London and South-East—which throughout the period was the minimum unemployment region. It is possible, then, to fit a model of type IA to the pre-war regional data. A model of type IIA, similar to that used for the post-war period, may also be employed since three regions may be identified which throughout the years 1925–38 were those with the three lowest unemployment rates. These regions are London and South-East, Midlands and the South-West, which may therefore be regarded as forming a leading sector.

While unemployment dispersion within these three regions is small (average $\hat{s}^2 = 0.99$) compared with overall unemployment dispersion (average $s^2 = 34.3$), it is still large compared with post-war dispersion levels, so that the possibility arises of there existing a transfer mechanism within the leading sector. However, both the estimated dispersion equation for the post-war period and previous studies of the 'Phillips curve', suggest that at levels of unemployment such as those experienced in the pre-war years, the relationship between rates of wage change and unemployment rates is a relatively insensitive one, i.e., we are on the 'flat' portion of the Phillips curve. This being so, while there may be considerable dispersion in unemployment rates within the leading sector, the disparity in rates of wage change within that sector may be relatively small. It is not, then, unreasonable to assume that no transfer mechanism works within the leading sector.

Models IA and IIA were estimated for the pre-war period and the results are presented in Table 2. For the sake of brevity only the equations for the logarithmic formulation are shown.

Table 2

Dependent variable	const	P	$\log U$	S_1	S_1^*	A_i (Model IA)	A_i (Model IIA)	$\bar{R}^2$	d
$\dot{W}$	0·611 (2·015)	0·572 (0·076)	0·028 (0·762)					0·818	1·07
$\dot{W}$	−3·48 (2·22)	0·437 (0·087)	−0·222 (0·682)	−15·69 (24·15)			17·85 (7·62)	0·902	1·86
$\dot{W}$	−4·10 (1·97)	0·408 (0·073)			0·048 (0·543)		13·71 (4·02)	0·908	1·77
$\dot{W}$	−2·95 (2·71)	0·439 (0·081)	0·678 (0·718)	57·29 (24·93)		5·92 (4·49)		0·862	1·68
$\dot{W}$	−5·85 (3·00)	0·574 (0·082)			0·101 (0·803)	2·00 (3·46)		0·806	1·06

Very similar equations were obtained for the reciprocal and square-root formulations. At first glance these results are not nearly as impressive as those for the post-war period. The only variables to perform consistently well are the price variable $\dot{P}$ and the Model IIA transfer dispersion variable A_i.[3] However, the inclusion of the dispersion variables results in a large increase in $\bar{R}^2$, while if they are omitted there is evidence of considerable serial correlation in the residuals.

The unemployment variable, $\log U$, is invariably insignificant. This, however, is not altogether surprising, since, as mentioned above, we know of no previous empirical study which has found a statistically significant role for the unemployment variable in the pre-war period.

The pre-war results suggest, so far then, that unemployment dispersion is a significant factor in determining variations in pre-war wage change and that Model IIA is likely to be most successful in explaining the available data.

It is, however, possible to rationalize the apparently poor showing of the unemployment and non-linearity dispersion variables. Lipsey [6, p. 16] maintains that at high levels of unemployment, where the market wage equation lies below the horizontal (i.e., unemployment) axis, wage changes no longer react to changes in unemployment in a non-linear fashion. We are at present dealing with a period when aggregate unemployment varied between 10% and 20% of the total

---

[3] Models of type II with $m \neq 3$ and the identity of the leading regions varying over time were also considered. However none performed as well as Model IIA.

labour force. In using data from this period we may in fact be handling observations drawn from a linear section of the wage adjustment function. If this is the case, we should not be surprised at the poor showing of the non-linearity dispersion variable in the aggregate function. However as we have shown in section 3 of this paper, the possible existence of the wage transfer mechanism is not affected by the existence or otherwise of non-linearity in the market functions.

If the market functions are of linear form

$$\dot{w} = a + k\dot{P} + bu \qquad (6.1)$$

then adopting the transfer mechanism of Model IIA, the aggregate wage adjustment function will then be (from section 3)

$$\dot{W} = a + k\dot{P} + bU + bh(\hat{u} - U) \qquad (3.12)$$

This yields an estimating equation

$$\dot{W} = a + k\dot{P} + bU + cA_4 \qquad (6.2)$$

where $A_4 = \hat{u} - U$ and an estimate of the strength of the wage transfer mechanism may be obtained from the ratio of the coefficients b and c.

Estimating equations (6.1) and (6.2) by ordinary least squares yielded for the period 1925–38:

$$\dot{W} = 0{\cdot}790 + 0{\cdot}569\dot{P} - 0{\cdot}0073U$$
$$(0{\cdot}758) \quad (0{\cdot}077) \quad\quad (0{\cdot}0511) \qquad (6.3)$$
$$\bar{R}^2 = 0{\cdot}818 \qquad d = 1{\cdot}06$$

$$\dot{W} = -0{\cdot}079 + 0{\cdot}437\dot{P} - 0{\cdot}268U + 0{\cdot}946A_4$$
$$(0{\cdot}685) \quad (0{\cdot}079) \quad (0{\cdot}104) \quad\ (0{\cdot}350) \qquad (6.4)$$
$$\bar{R}^2 = 0{\cdot}889 \qquad d = 1{\cdot}54$$

When the transfer dispersion variable is included in the equation, the unemployment variable becomes significant with the correct sign and there is a marked rise in both $\bar{R}^2$ and d. Equation (6.4) represents the best result in terms of *a priori* expectations obtained for the pre-war period. It is also *the only estimated wage equation we know of, for the pre-war period, which gives a statistically significant role to the unemployment variable*. The result, then, gives strong support to the view that dispersion variables should be included in the wage equation.

16

Summarizing the pre-war results, it appears that a linear form of the market wage equation, combined with the transfer mechanism of Model IIA is most appropriate.

We may obtain some idea of the quantitive importance of the dispersion effect for this period by re-examining equation (6.4). The mean values for the variables in the equation during the period 1925–38 were:

$$\dot{W} = 0{\cdot}24 \qquad \dot{P} = -0{\cdot}78 \qquad U = 14{\cdot}7 \qquad A_4 = 4{\cdot}84$$

Equation (6.4) implies a wage equation at the market level of the form

$$\dot{w} = -0{\cdot}079 + 0{\cdot}437\dot{P} - 0{\cdot}268u \tag{6.5}$$

It follows that in the absence of any unemployment dispersion in the pre-war period, the average rate of wage change would have been $-4{\cdot}34\%$. The actual average rate was $+0{\cdot}24\%$. Unemployment dispersion then, on average, gave an upward shift to aggregate wage rates of over four percentage points.

Superficially there appears to be considerable difference between the results obtained for the pre- and post-war periods. The implied wage equations for the individual labour markets are for these periods:

$$1925\text{–}38 \qquad \dot{w} = -0{\cdot}079 + 0{\cdot}437\dot{P} - 0{\cdot}268u \tag{6.5}$$

$$1950\text{–}66 \qquad \dot{w} = 3{\cdot}04 + 0{\cdot}431\dot{P} - 2{\cdot}57 \log u \tag{5.5}$$

At first sight these equations bear little similarity to one another. However, the coefficients on the price variable are practically identical and moreover, given $\dot{P}$, for unemployment rates similar to those experienced in the pre-war period both equations imply similar rates of wage change. In Table 3 the implied rates of change are given for varying unemployment rates, given a zero price change.

It can therefore be seen that for pre-war employment rates, *the two estimated market wage equations are in fact almost identical.*

Table 3

Level of unemployment u	8·0	10·0	12·0	14·0	16·0	18·0	20·0
implied $\dot{w}$ using equation (6.5)	−2·2	−2·8	−3·3	−3·8	−4·4	−4·9	−5·4
implied $\dot{w}$ using equation (5.5)	−2·3	−2·9	−3·3	−3·7	−4·1	−4·4	−4·7

We are now able to reconcile the apparently conflicting pre-war and post-war results. This is possible if we accept that the relationship between wage change and unemployment at the market level is a non-linear one similar to equation (5.5). This is perfectly consistent with post-war data. In the pre-war period, however, we are dealing with observations from a section of the 'Phillips curve' where non-linearity is either small or non-existent. The non-linearity is not pronounced enough to be picked up by statistical techniques and for this reason the pre-war market wage equation appears to be of linear form and the non-linearity dispersion variable performs badly in the aggregate wage equation. That this apparently linear pre-war equation is not inconsistent with an overall non-linear wage equation similar to (5.5) is demonstrated by the similarity of equations (6.5) and (5.5) for pre-war unemployment rates.

On the basis of regional data only, the following conclusions may be reached from a comparison of post-war and pre-war results.

(1) The implied wage equation for the individual labour market appears to be very similar for both periods, post-war results suggesting it has a non-linear form.

(2) A dispersion model of type IIA appears to fit both post-war and pre-war data best. This suggests that the process of wage change determination was, in both periods 'stable' in the sense described in section 3.

(3) Examination of the estimated coefficients of equation (6.5) yields a value for the parameter h of 3·5 in the pre-war period. This compares with values of around 2·5 for post-war data. This suggests that a strong wage transfer mechanism was operative in both periods.

Conclusions

We have presented in this paper an explanation of variations in the rate of change of wages, which lays great stress on the dispersion of unemployment rates over different sectors of the economy. The importance of such dispersion is the result, firstly of non-linearity in the market wage adjustment functions and secondly of the existence of a transfer mechanism whereby wage increases in low unemployment markets are passed on to areas of higher unemployment.

A rigorous testing of the dispersion hypothesis is not possible using currently available data. There is a need for complete and comprehensive data on unemployment classified by labour market. We have not in this paper, questioned the existence of a relationship between the level of unemployment and the rate of change of wages at the market level, but have instead concentrated attention on the aggregate function which must hold if such a relationship exists. The empirical work of, for example, Hines (*Economic Journal*, 1969) using dis-aggregated industry data and Cowling and Metcalf (*Bull. Ox. Inst.*, 1967) using regional data failed to uncover such a relationship at either industry or regional level. However, adequate testing of the hypotheses at a dis-aggregated level cannot be carried out until unemployment data by labour market is generally available.

Data problems also hinder progress at the aggregate level. Although unemployment dispersion measured over regions appears to be a good proxy for dispersion over labour markets, the two measures apparently moving in similar directions over time, the findings of this paper suggest that the measures are not of sufficiently similar absolute size to enable adequate measures of the strength of the transfer mechanism to be obtained. Despite these problems, however, it does appear that, at the aggregate level, variations in the rate of wage change can be adequately explained, for both pre-war and post-war periods, by the inclusion of the appropriate dispersion variables in the normal Phillips curve. This is a particularly important finding for the pre-war years since previous empirical studies for this period have generally found difficulty in establishing any link between labour market variables and the rate of wage change.

Finally, the results suggest that not only are dispersion variables a statistically significant factor in the determination of rates of wage change, but that they are also of quantitative importance. The preliminary estimates in this paper suggest that unemployment dispersion exerted an upward pressure on aggregate rates of wage change of more than two percentage points in the post-war period and of more than four percentage points in the pre-war period.

Appendix   Definitions of Variables

$$\dot{W} = \left(\frac{W_{t+1} - W_{t-1}}{2W_t}\right)100$$ Where W_t is an index of hourly wage rates centred at end June of year t.

$$\dot{P} = \left(\frac{P_{t+1} - P_{t-1}}{2P_t}\right)100$$ Where P_t is an index of retail prices centred at end of June of year t.

U = percentage of the total labour force unemployed—centred at end of June of each year.

$$\dot{M} = \left(\frac{M_{t+1} - M_{t-1}}{2M_t}\right)100$$

Where M_t is an index of import prices centred at June t.

$$X = \left(\frac{X_{t+1} - X_{t-1}}{2X_t}\right)100$$

Where X_t is an index of output per head centered at June t.

The dispersion variables are as defined in the main text. All the basic data series are annual averages of monthly data, unless otherwise stated.

Sources

Regional unemployment data
For the post-war period 1950–66, monthly data on both unemployment and total employees can be obtained on a regional basis from the Ministry of Labour Gazette. This monthly data was averaged to obtain annual series. There is, however, an important change of classification in 1962, when three regions—Midland, North Midland, and the East and West Ridings were replaced by two regions covering the same area—Midlands, and Yorkshire and Lincolnshire. Consistent series were obtained by applying the 1962 pro-portions of employees and unemployed in the post-1962 regions to the totals

Table 4 Regional unemployed weights

	L–S–E	SW	M	Y–L	NW	N	Scot.	Wales	N.I.
1925	24·7	6·7	14·9	10·4	18·0	6·6	11·2	5·3	2·3
1926	24·8	6·8	14·9	10·3	18·0	6·6	11·1	5·3	2·3
1927	25·2	6·9	14·8	10·3	17·9	6·6	10·9	5·2	2·2
1928	25·7	7·0	14·9	10·2	17·8	6·5	10·7	5·0	2·1
1929	26·0	7·0	15·0	10·2	17·7	6·5	10·6	4·9	2·2
1930	26·0	7·0	15·1	10·0	17·8	6·4	10·7	4·8	2·2
1931	26·3	7·1	15·0	10·0	17·6	6·4	10·7	4·8	2·1
1932	26·6	7·2	14·9	10·1	17·3	6·4	10·6	4·9	2·1
1933	26·7	7·1	15·0	10·0	17·2	6·4	10·6	4·9	2·1
1934	27·1	7·2	15·1	9·9	16·9	6·3	10·5	4·8	2·1
1935	27·4	7·2	15·1	9·8	16·7	6·3	10·5	4·8	2·2
1936	28·0	7·3	15·2	9·7	16·3	6·2	10·5	4·6	2·2
1937	28·3	7·3	15·3	9·6	16·1	6·2	10·4	4·5	2·2
1938	28·6	7·3	15·3	9·6	15·9	6·1	10·3	4·5	2·2
1950	33·8	5·1	15·3	9·4	13·8	5·9	10·2	4·4	2·2
1951	34·1	5·0	15·3	9·4	13·7	5·9	10·0	4·4	2·2
1952	34·1	5·0	15·3	9·4	13·9	5·9	9·9	4·3	2·2
1953	34·2	5·1	15·2	9·3	13·9	5·8	9·9	4·3	2·2
1954	34·0	4·9	15·3	9·8	13·8	5·7	9·9	4·3	2·2
1955	35·0	5·3	15·1	9·7	13·2	5·6	9·7	4·4	2·2
1956	34·3	4·9	15·2	9·7	13·8	5·9	9·8	4·4	2·1
1957	35·0	5·0	15·1	9·7	13·3	5·7	9·8	4·3	2·2
1958	35·3	5·2	14·9	9·5	13·4	5·8	9·5	4·3	2·1
1959	35·7	5·5	14·7	9·4	13·0	5·8	9·6	4·3	2·1
1960	35·8	5·3	14·9	9·5	13·3	5·6	9·3	4·2	2·1
1961	34·8	5·6	15·2	9·7	13·5	5·7	9·4	4·2	2·1
1962	34·1	5·7	15·4	9·3	12·8	5·7	9·5	4·3	2·1
1963	35·3	5·5	15·7	9·3	13·0	5·6	9·4	4·2	2·1
1964	35·3	5·8	15·9	9·3	12·7	5·5	9·2	4·2	2·1
1965	35·3	5·6	15·9	8·8	12·9	5·6	9·3	4·3	2·2
1966	36·5	5·6	16·2	8·7	12·4	5·5	9·0	4·1	2·1

Table 5   Regional unemployed rates

	L–S–E	SW	M	Y–L	NW	N	Scot.	Wales	N.I.
1925	7·3	8·5	9·1	12·0	11·4	19·6	15·2	16·5	23·9
1926	6·5	8·4	11·0	14·0	14·7	22·3	16·4	18·0	23·2
1927	5·6	7·2	8·4	11·5	10·7	17·3	10·6	19·5	13·2
1928	5·5	8·1	9·9	13·8	12·4	17·1	11·7	23·0	17·0
1929	5·6	8·1	9·3	12·7	13·3	15·4	12·1	19·3	14·8
1930	8·1	10·4	14·7	11·2	23·8	22·8	18·5	25·9	23·8
1931	12·1	14·5	20·3	25·1	28·2	31·0	26·6	32·4	27·8
1932	13·7	17·1	20·1	25·0	25·8	33·9	27·7	36·5	27·2
1933	11·7	15·7	17·4	21·6	23·5	33·0	26·1	34·6	26·5
1934	9·0	13·1	12·9	18·3	20·8	29·4	23·1	32·3	23·4
1935	8·4	11·6	11·2	17·1	19·7	27·5	21·3	31·2	24·8
1936	7·2	9·4	9·2	13·5	17·1	22·1	18·7	29·4	22·7
1937	6·3	8·1	7·3	13·1	14·5	17·8	17·4	24·3	24·1
1938	8·0	8·5	10·0	15·0	18·7	18·1	18·1	26·9	31·3
1950	1·15	1·4	0·7	0·7	1·6	2·8	3·0	3·7	5·8
1951	0·90	1·2	0·6	0·6	1·2	2·2	2·5	2·7	6·1
1952	1·30	1·5	1·3	1·3	3·6	2·6	3·3	2·9	10·4
1953	1·25	1·6	1·0	1·0	2·1	2·4	3·1	3·0	8·1
1954	1·05	1·5	0·7	0·7	1·5	2·3	2·8	2·5	7·0
1955	0·75	1·1	0·6	0·6	1·4	1·8	2·4	1·8	6·8
1956	0·85	1·3	0·8	0·8	1·3	1·5	2·4	2·0	6·4
1957	1·10	1·8	1·1	1·1	1·6	1·7	2·6	2·6	7·3
1958	1·40	2·2	1·7	1·7	2·7	2·4	3·8	3·8	9·3
1959	1·30	2·1	1·6	1·6	2·8	3·3	4·4	3·8	7·8
1960	1·00	1·7	1·1	1·1	1·9	2·9	3·7	2·7	6·8
1961	1·05	1·4	1·2	1·2	1·6	2·5	3·2	2·6	7·5
1962	1·35	1·7	1·6	1·7	2·6	3·8	3·8	3·1	7·5
1963	1·60	2·2	1·9	2·1	3·1	5·0	4·8	3·7	8·0
1964	1·05	1·5	0·9	1·3	2·1	3·4	3·7	2·6	6·6
1965	0·90	1·6	0·9	1·1	1·6	2·6	3·0	2·6	6·1
1966	1·00	1·8	1·2	1·2	1·5	2·6	2·9	2·9	6·1

of employees and unemployed for the three pre-1962 regions. In this way it was possible to obtain consistent series for ten regions in the post-war period— London and South Eastern, Southern–Eastern (combined), South Western, Midlands, Yorkshire and Lincolnshire, North-Western, Northern, Scotland, Wales and Northern Ireland.

Data on a comparable basis for the pre-war period is more difficult to obtain. The Abstract of Labour Statistics provides data on totals of insured employees and insured unemployed for nine regions up until 1936. These series were updated to 1938 using Ministry of Labour Gazette data. The nine regions were —London, South Eastern, South Western, Midlands, North Eastern, North Western, Scotland, Wales and Northern Ireland. Of these regions, all except London, South Eastern, South Western and North Western, correspond to the post-war classifications. To obtain a consistent classification for all series, covering both pre-war and post-war data, two major adjustments were made.

(1) A single region London–Southern–Eastern was defined. This covered the two post-war regions—London and South Eastern, and Southern–Eastern and the two pre-war regions London, and South Eastern. In the pre-war period using Ministry of Labour Gazette data for major towns and cities in the relevant regions, appropriate transfers were made between the South Western region

and the London–Southern–Eastern division. The result of these re-classifications is that the London–Southern–Eastern division contains up to one-third of the total labour force and is by far the largest region. However, since the dispersion of employment levels in the different areas of this combined region is small throughout the period concerned, it was felt that any errors introduced into the calculation of the final dispersion series by this aggregation were likely to be small.

(2) The pre-war region—North Eastern, corresponds to the two post-war regions—Northern, and Yorkshire and Lincolnshire. It was decided to estimate separate pre-war series for the Northern, and Yorkshire and Lincolnshire regions. Estimates of total employees in the two regions for the pre-war years were obtained by applying post-war proportions to the totals for the pre-war North-Eastern region. Unemployment totals for the pre-war years were obtained from the Ministry of Labour Gazette data on the major towns and cities of the regions. Since the coverage of this data becomes progressively poorer as it moves into the past, the final estimates for the early years of the period 1925–38 are unreliable and at best guesses. The same criticism applies to the transfers between the South Western and the London–Southern–Eastern regions.

By making these adjustments, reasonably consistent series for nine regions were obtained. The nine regions are—London–Southern–Eastern, South Western, Midlands, Yorkshire and Lincolnshire, North Western, Northern, Scotland, Wales and Northern Ireland. The series are presented below. The various dispersion variables may then be calculated as indicated in the main text.

Index of hourly wage rates
For the pre-war period this index is obtained by deflating an index of weekly wage rates by an index of hours worked. Both indices are obtained from the Ministry of Labour Gazette. The wage index for 1924–34 is an average of December–June–December figures and thereafter is an annual average of monthly figures. The hours worked index is centred in June. The final pre-war series is given a base 1924 = 100.

The post-war series is also obtained by deflating the Ministry of Labour Gazette weekly wage rate index by the index of hours worked. All series for this period are annual averages of monthly data.

Index of retail prices
The pre-war index used is the Ministry of Labour Gazette cost of living index with 1914 = 100. The post-war index is simply the index of retail prices with 1950 = 100. Both series are annual averages of monthly figures.

Level of unemployment
This is the percentage of the total labour force unemployed obtained from the London and Cambridge 'Key Statistics of the British Economy'. It is again an annual average of monthly figures.

References

[1] G. C. Archibald, 'The Phillips Curve and the Distribution of Unemployment', *American Economic Review*—Papers and Proceedings, May, 1969.

[2] K. Cowling and D. Metcalf, 'Wage–Unemployment Relationships. A Regional Analysis for the U.K. 1960–65', *Bulletin of the Oxford Institute of Statistics*, 1967.

[3] L. A. Dicks-Mireaux, 'The inter-relationship between Cost and Price Changes 1946–59. A study of Inflation in Post-War Britain', *Oxford Economic Papers*, 1961.

[4] A. G. Hines, 'Trade Unions and Wage Inflation in the U.K. 1893–1961', *Review of Economic Studies*, 1964.

[5] J. Johnston, *Econometric Methods*, McGraw-Hill, 1963.

[6] R. G. Lipsey, 'The Relation between Unemployment and the Rate of Change of Money Wage Rates in the U.K. 1882–1957. A further study', *Economica*, 1960.

[7] R. G. Lipsey and M. Parkin, 'Incomes Policy: A Re-appraisal', *Economica*, 1970, and Chapter 4 above.

[8] National Institute for Economic Research, February, 1970, *Economic Situation Annual Review*, Chap. 3.

[9] M. Parkin, 'Some Further Results on the Determination of the Rate of Change of Money Wages', *Economica*, November, 1970, and Chapter 5 above.

[10] A. W. Phillips, 'The Relationship between Unemployment and the Rate of Change of Money Wages in the U.K. 1861–1957', *Economica*, 1958.

P. G. Saunders
and A. R. Nobay

Chapter 12 Price expectations, the Phillips curve and incomes policy

Introduction

The Phillips curve represents a major contribution to the theory of economic policy. As is well known, this relationship establishes the proposition that the authorities have a long-run choice or trade-off between inflation and unemployment. This analysis can be shown to depend upon money illusion, adjustment lags and other frictions. Friedman [3], Phelps [12] and others have argued that this trade-off is a short-run phenomenon arising from unanticipated inflation, and that in the long run there exists no trade-off, but a natural rate of unemployment at which any inflation rate is possible.

This controversy is of considerable significance for policy purposes. The empirical validity of the existence of a trade-off suggests a seductive avenue for improving it via incomes policy. On the other hand, the Friedman-Phelps view would preclude such a policy choice. It is the *a priori* coefficient on the price or price expectations variable which divides these two alternative views. Solow [14] and others have examined this issue extensively and, it would be fair to say that the consensus of the results point towards the value for the price term which is significantly less than one. Johnson's [6] summary of the issue is that 'The outcome is a "sophisticated" Phillips curve, based on a dynamic version of "money illusion", which still offers a trade-off to the policy-makers, though its slope is steeper than that implied by the "naive" Phillips curve.'

One such study which has assumed some prominence, and which has prompted a considerable amount of useful work in this field is the Lipsey-Parkin [8] and subsequent Parkin paper [11][1] which attempted to study the effectiveness of post-war incomes policy in the United Kingdom. In this paper we concentrate primarily on the

[1] Chapters 4 and 5 above.

validity and interpretation of their findings on the role of price expectations, in order to focus on the Friedman-Phelps/Solow controversy. This is undertaken within the framework of an alternative specification of price expectations which, whilst yielding the same reduced-form equation, implies quite different structural parameters. The result follows from a not unreasonable restriction on a general model, and offers us the main advantage of being able to reinterpret the published results of Parkin without having to re-estimate the model. Additionally, we undertake a statistical analysis of the results to test the null hypothesis that the coefficient on price expectations is indeed not significantly different from unity, thus validating the Friedman-Phelps hypothesis.

1   An alternative framework for price expectations

In empirical studies, price expectations are typically assumed to be linear combinations of past actual price movements only,[2] and hence involve the use of distributed lag models. This is a particularly difficult area of applied econometric analysis, and as Griliches [5] warns, 'Interpret the coefficients of a distributed lag model with great care, since the same reduced form can arise from very different structures. Moreover different reduced forms may not differ much in the fit they provide to the data, but have widely different implications as to the underlying structure that generated the model.'

A number of studies, including Parkin's, have specified the generation of price expectations via the familiar adaptive expectations framework. It can be shown that the adaptive expectations model leads to minimum mean-square error predictors which are 'optimal' for certain types of non-stationary stochastic processes c.f. Muth [10], Theil and Wage [16]. Muth also notes that under these conditions, 'the best forecast for the time period immediately ahead is the best forecast for any future time period'.

This has important implications for including price expectations in labour market analysis, as the problem of wage bargains being struck at discrete intervals[3] is automatically dealt with in such a framework.

In a recent paper Sargent [13] has forcefully asserted that distributed lag schemes which constrain the weights to sum to one, as does

---

[2] For an alternative more general view of the determinants of expectations see Georgescu-Roegen [4].

[3] For a recent study which explicitly recognizes the discrete nature of wage bargains see Sparks and Wilton [15].

the adaptive expectations model, impose a considerable downward bias on the price coefficient and hence do not provide a valid test of the Friedman-Phelps hypothesis. In particular, the validity of the assumption of non-stationarity of the inflation rate time series is questioned and it is shown that when this is approximated by a covariance-stationary stochastic process the weights must sum to less than one.[4]

An additional important limitation of the adaptive expectations framework is noted by Bierwag and Grove [1]. If we assume that predictions are made by *individual* economic units *via* the adaptive expectations framework, and that the adjustment parameters, the λ_i's vary across the population, the aggregate prediction consists of a distributed lag of past observations whose weights do *not* decline geometrically. The usual adaptive expectations scheme can only be derived in this framework on the assumption that the λ_i's are equal for all economic units.

Symbolically, if

$$(X_t^*)^i = (\lambda_i) \sum_{j=0}^{\infty} (1 - \lambda_i)^j X_{t-j} \qquad (1.1)$$

and

$$(X_t^*) = \sum_{i=1}^{i=m} w_i (X_t^*)^i \qquad (1.2)$$

then

$$(X_t^*) = \sum_{i=1}^{m} w_i \sum_{j=0}^{\infty} (\lambda_i)(1 - \lambda_i)^j X_{t-j}$$

$$= \sum_{j=0}^{\infty} W_j X_{t-j} \qquad (1.3)$$

where

$$W_j = \sum_{i=1}^{m} \lambda_i (1 - \lambda_i)^j w_i \qquad (1.4)$$

Following Jorgensen [7] we can represent the infinite lag distribution in equation (1.3) by the ratio of two finite lag polynomials, to yield a more general lag structure where the weights are not restricted to sum to unity.[5] This procedure however loses the simplicity of the one-

---

[4] An inspection of the inflation rate in the United Kingdom confirms that the series are better approximated by a covariance-stationary stochastic process. We abstract, of course, from the real problem of choosing the appropriate rate of inflation.

[5] The rational distributed lag function has been used earlier in this context by Lucas and Rapping [9] who reject the adaptive expectations model on the grounds that economic units whose behaviour the model describes will never fully 'catch up' to any steady rate of inflation. It is worth noting the importance of this point for the Friedman-Phelps hypothesis of a vertical long run trade off which relies on prices being fully expected in the long run.

parameter adaptive expectations formulation as the number of coefficients in general increases substantially.

Consider the usual Phillips curve relationship

$$\dot{w}_t = \alpha_1 + \beta_1 U_t + \Phi_1 \dot{p}_t^e + v_t. \tag{1.5}$$

It is usual to derive $\dot{p}^e$ from the *aggregate adaptive expectations scheme*, which yields the following reduced form equation:

$$\dot{w}_t = \alpha_1 \lambda + \beta_1 U_t - \beta_1 (1 - \lambda) U_{t-1} + \Phi_1 \lambda \dot{p}_t + (1 - X) \dot{w}_{t-1} + Z_t \tag{1.6}$$

where $Z_t = v_t - (1 - \lambda) v_{t-1}$.

An alternative scheme is to derive price expectations via the rational form

$$p^e = \frac{\mu(L)}{v(L)} p_t,$$

where $\mu(L) = \mu_0 + \mu_1 L + \mu_2 L^2 + \cdots + \mu_{n-1} L^{n-1}$
$v(L) = 1 + v_1 L + v_2 L^2 + \cdots + v_n L^n$

yielding

$$v(L)\dot{w}_t = \alpha_1 v(L) + \beta_1 v(L) U_t + \Phi_1 \mu(L) \dot{p}_t + v(L) v_t. \tag{1.7}$$

As is well known (c.f. Jorgensen's work on investment) the estimation of such a model involves a considerable search procedure for the appropriate order of polynomial and it also introduces severe problems of multicollinearity.

However, as a special case of the above, consider the following assumption:

$$\mu_i = v_i = \gamma(1 - \gamma)^i \qquad i \geq 1, \ \mu_0 = \gamma \tag{1.8}$$

This assumption implies the following finite approximation to the price expectations formulation

$$\dot{p}^e = \sum_{j=1}^{n} c_j \dot{p}_{t-(j-1)} \qquad (m > n) \tag{1.9}$$

where $c_j = \gamma(1 - \gamma)^{2(j-1)}$.

It is easily seen that the weights sum to $\gamma/[\gamma(2 - \gamma)]$ which is in general less than one except for $\gamma = 0$ or $\gamma = 1$. The first case represents the case where $\dot{p}^e$ does not enter the analysis and the second case the naive forecasting model $\dot{p}^e = \dot{p}$. Then equation (1.7) becomes:

$$
\begin{aligned}
\dot{w}_t &+ \gamma(1 - \gamma)\dot{w}_{t-1} + \gamma(1 - \gamma)^2 \dot{w}_{t-2} + \cdots + \gamma(1 - \gamma)^n \dot{w}_{t-n} = \alpha_1 v(L) \\
&+ \beta_1(U_t + \gamma(1 - \gamma)U_{t-1} + \gamma(1 - \gamma)^2 U_{t-2} + \cdots \\
&\quad + \gamma(1 - \gamma)^n U_{t-n}) \\
&+ \Phi_1(\gamma p_t + \gamma(1 - \gamma)p_{t-1} + \gamma(1 - \gamma)^2 p_{t-2} + \cdots \\
&\quad + \gamma(1 - \gamma)^{n-1}p_{t-n+1}) \\
&+ (v_t + \gamma(1 - \gamma)v_{t-1} + \gamma(1 - \gamma)^2 v_{t-2} + \cdots + \gamma(1 - \gamma)^n v_{t-n})
\end{aligned} \tag{1.10}
$$

lagging equation (1.10) multiplying by $(1 - \gamma)$ and subtracting we obtain:

$$
\begin{aligned}
\dot{w}_t &+ \dot{w}_{t-1}(\gamma(1 - \gamma) - (1 - \gamma)) - \gamma(1 - \gamma)^{n+1}\dot{w}_{t-n-1} \\
&= \alpha_1 v(L)(1 - (1 - \gamma)) \\
&\quad + \beta_1(U_t + (1 - \gamma)(\gamma - 1)U_{t-1} - \gamma(1 - \gamma)^{n+1}U_{t-n-1}) \\
&\quad + \Phi_1(\gamma p_t - \gamma(1 - \gamma)^n p_{t-n}) \\
&\quad + (v_t + (1 - \gamma)(\gamma - 1)v_{t-1} - \gamma(1 - \gamma)^{n+1}v_{t-n-1})
\end{aligned}
$$

If $\gamma < 1$ this becomes

$$
\begin{aligned}
\dot{w}_t &- (1 - \gamma)^2 \dot{w}_{t-1} \\
&= \alpha_1 \gamma(2 - \gamma) + \beta_1 U_t - \beta_1(1 - \gamma)^2 U_{t-1} + \Phi_1 \gamma p_t + Z_t' \quad (1.11)
\end{aligned}
$$

where $Z_t' = v_t - (1 - \gamma)^2 v_{t-1}$.

The reduced form may be written as

$$
\dot{w}_t = \theta_0 + \theta_1 U_t + \theta_2 U_{t-1} + \theta_3 p_t + \theta_4 w_{t-1} + Z_t'
$$

where
$$
\begin{aligned}
\theta_0 &= \alpha_1 \gamma(2 - \gamma) \\
\theta_1 &= \beta_1 \\
\theta_2 &= -\beta_1(1 - \gamma)^2 \\
\theta_3 &= \phi_1 \gamma \\
\theta_4 &= (1 - \gamma)^2 \\
Z_t' &= v_t - (1 - \gamma)^2 v_{t-1}
\end{aligned} \tag{1.12}
$$

It will be noted that this reduced form is identical to that derived for the adaptive expectations formulation of price expectations by Parkin. His structural parameters are as follows:

$$
\begin{aligned}
\theta_0 &= \alpha_1 \lambda \\
\theta_1 &= \beta_1 \\
\theta_2 &= -\beta_1(1 - \lambda) \\
\theta_3 &= \phi_1 \lambda \\
\theta_4 &= (1 - \lambda) \\
Z_t' &= v_t - (1 - \lambda)v_{t-1}
\end{aligned} \tag{1.13}
$$

The *a priori* restrictions imposed,

$$\theta_4\theta_1 + \theta_2 = 0 \qquad (1.14)$$

are the same for both reduced forms. A significant point to note is that the empirical validity of the Friedman-Phelps expectations hypothesis is that $\Phi_1 = 1$. A comparison can be made of the Φ_1 in both the adaptive expectations [Parkin] and the alternative formulation proposed

$$(\Phi_1)_{ae} = \frac{\hat{\theta}_3}{\hat{\lambda}} = \frac{\hat{\theta}_3}{1 - \hat{\theta}_4} \qquad \text{adaptive expectations}$$

$$(\Phi_1) = \frac{\hat{\theta}_3}{\hat{\gamma}} = \frac{\hat{\theta}_3}{1 - \sqrt{\hat{\theta}_4}} \qquad \text{alternative specification} \qquad (1.15)$$

Now, on the assumption that $0 < \lambda < 1$, then $0 < \theta_4 < 1$. Hence $\sqrt{\hat{\theta}_4} > \hat{\theta}_4$ and $\hat{\phi}_1 > (\hat{\phi}_1)_{ae}$. Thus we can see that Parkin's structural parameter on price expectations will assume a value which is lower than that derived from our own formulation. The Parkin structural parameter for price expectation, $(\hat{\phi}_1)_{ae}$ is compared with the imputed value of the alternative formulation in Table 1 below.

Table 1   Comparison of structural parameters of alternative specifications: $\rho = 0$

	α_1	β_1	Φ_1	
Policy-on				
Parkin	−0·098	1·701	0·347	0·240 (λ)
Revised model	−0·098	1·701	0·650	0·128 (γ)
Policy-off				
Parkin	6·967	−2·542	0·472	0·554 (λ)
Revised model	6·967	−2·542	0·787	0·332 (γ)
Entire period				
Parkin	2·097	0·069	0·650	0·282 (λ)
Revised model	2·097	0·069	1·200	0·153 (γ)

The other difference between the two models, and it is a crucial one, is in the interpretation that can be given to the lag parameters, λ and γ. Within the adaptive expectations framework, the λ indicates the speed of adjustment of the economic units. However, as we have stated earlier, it is difficult to give *any* meaningful interpretation to an aggregate λ (unless all the individual λ_i's happen to coincide). The estimated γ only represents the form of the lag polynomials in equation (1.7).

Parkin further approximates the moving average error process in equation (1.13),

$$Z_t' = v_t - (1 - \lambda)v_{t-1}$$

by a first order Markov process,[6]

$$v_t = \rho v_{t-1} + Z_t''.$$

Applying the usual Koyck transformation he obtains

$$\dot{w}_t = b_0' + b_1'U_t + b_2'U_{t-1} + b_3'U_{t-2} + b_4'p_t + b_5'p_{t-1} \\ + b_6'\dot{w}_{t-1} + b_7'\dot{w}_{t-2} + Z_t''$$

where
$$\begin{aligned}
b_0' &= \alpha_1\lambda(1 - \rho) \\
b_1' &= \beta_1 \\
b_2' &= -\beta_1(1 - \lambda + \rho) \\
b_3' &= \rho\beta_1(1 - \lambda) \\
b_4' &= \Phi_1\lambda \\
b_5' &= -\rho\Phi_1\lambda \\
b_6' &= (1 - \lambda + \rho) \\
b_7' &= -\rho(1 - \lambda).
\end{aligned} \qquad (1.16)$$

The comparable assumption in the revised model again gives the same reduced form, but now the coefficients are related to the structural coefficients by the following:

$$\begin{aligned}
b_0' &= \alpha_1\gamma(2 - \gamma)(1 - \rho) \\
b_1' &= \beta_1 \\
b_2' &= -\beta_1((1 - \gamma)^2 + \rho) \\
b_3' &= \rho\beta_1(1 - \gamma)^2 \\
b_4' &= \Phi_1\gamma \\
b_5' &= -\rho\Phi_1\gamma \\
b_6' &= (1 - \gamma)^2 + \rho \\
b_7' &= -\rho(1 - \gamma)^2.
\end{aligned} \qquad (1.17)$$

[6] Whilst approximating a first order moving average error scheme *via* a first order Markov is better than doing nothing, it does not necessarily follow that such a transformation yields unbiased estimates. One needs to test for higher order Markov processes. We are indebted to Pravin Trivedi for this point.

Again the restrictions imposed for estimation are the same in both cases:

$$b_1'b_6' + b_2' = 0$$
$$b_1'b_7' + b_3' = 0. \tag{1.18}$$

Hence Parkin's restricted estimates of the reduced-form can again be used to calculate the revised structural parameters.

As in equation (1.15) above, a comparison can be made between the alternative interpretation of Parkin's results, in the case when $\rho \neq 0$.

$$(\Phi_1)_{ae} = \frac{b_4'}{1 - [b_7'b_4'/b_5']}$$

and for the alternative specification

$$(\Phi_1) = \frac{b_4'}{1 - [b_7'b_4'/b_5']^{1/2}}. \tag{1.19}$$

On the assumption that $0 < \lambda < 1$ and $|\rho| < 1$, it follows that $\Phi_1 > (\Phi_1)_{ae}$, and so once again, our structural parameters for price expectations will have a value greater than those derived by Parkin.

Table 2 Comparison of structural parameters of alternative specifications: $\rho \neq 0$

	α_1	β_1	Φ_1	ρ	
Policy-on					
Parkin	1·223	1·390	0·166	0·516	0·475 (λ)
Revised model	1·223	1·390	0·286	0·516	0·276 (γ)
Policy-off					
Parkin	7·283	−2·629	0·421	0·277	0·609 (λ)
Revised model	7·283	−2·629	0·685	0·277	0·375 (γ)
Entire period					
Parkin	3·007	0·005	0·440	0·483	0·439 (λ)
Revised model	3·007	0·005	0·770	0·483	0·251 (γ)

2 Some further analysis of the Friedman-Phelps hypothesis

We have seen that a re-interpretation of Parkin's results yields parameter estimates for price expectations which are higher than those implied by the adaptive expectations model, thereby questioning the validity of his results as a test of the Friedman-Phelps-Solow controversy.

Statistically, of course, the issue reduces to a test of the null hypothesis H_0; $\Phi = 1$, the appropriate test statistic, $t(\Phi)$, being

$$t(\Phi) = \frac{\hat{\Phi} - 1}{SE(\hat{\Phi})} \tag{2.1}$$

where $SE(\hat{\Phi})$ is the asymptotic standard error of $\hat{\Phi}$.

In order to calculate the test statistic for the revised model we require knowledge of the reduced-form 't values' $t(\theta_i)$. These we derive via the method outlined below.

Using a method suggested by Deming [2],[7] it can be shown that the relationship between $t(\Phi)$ and the $t(\theta_i)$, given Parkin's structural model is as follows:

$$t(\Phi) = \frac{t(\theta_3)t(\theta_4) - [(1 - \theta_4)t(\theta_3)t(\theta_4)/\theta_3]}{\sqrt{t^2(\theta_4) + z^2 t^2(\theta_3) + 2rt(\theta_3)t(\theta_4)z}} \tag{2.2}$$

where $z = \theta_4/(1 - \theta_4)$, and r is the correlation between θ_3 and θ_4.

Similarly, for the revised model we obtain:

$$t^*(\Phi) = \frac{t(\theta_3)t(\theta_4) - [(1 - \sqrt{\theta_4})t(\theta_3)t(\theta_4)/\theta_3]}{\sqrt{t^2(\theta_4) + \frac{1}{4}t^2(\theta_3)\tilde{z}^2 + rt(\theta_3)t(\theta_4)\tilde{z}}} \tag{2.3}$$

where $\tilde{z} = \sqrt{\theta_4}/(1 - \sqrt{\theta_4})$.

We derive $t^*(\Phi)$ using equations (2.1), (2.2) and (2.3) via the following steps:

(a) From equation (2.1), we calculate $t(\Phi)$
(b) Using $t(\Phi)$ in equation (2.2) we derive paired values of $t(\theta_3)$ and r [8]
(c) Substitute $t(\theta_3)$ and r, obtained above, in equation (2.3) to yield $t^*(\Phi)$, since all the other values are known.

---

[7] If v is the structural parameter and θ_i and θ_j are the reduced form parameters from which it is derived, then in general

$$v = v(\theta_i, \theta_j)$$

Taking a first order Taylor series approximation we obtain;

$$dv \simeq \frac{\partial v}{\partial \theta_i} d\theta_i + \frac{\partial v}{\partial \theta_j} d\theta_j.$$

Squaring and taking expected values we obtain a relationship between the variance of v and the variances of θ_i's.

[8] Note that $t(\theta_3)$ and r are the only unknowns in equation (2.2) since in the Parkin model $t(\lambda) = t(\theta_4)$ as $\theta_4 = 1 - \lambda$, and $t(\lambda)$ is known.

17

Whilst this method is in principle applicable generally we have confined ourselves to computing $t^*(\Phi)$ only for the case $r = -1$,[9] as being indicative of the results using the revised model. No calculations have been undertaken for the case where ρ (the auto-regressive parameter) $\neq 0$ as this involves extensive computation, although the method is adequate for this case. Table 3 indicates the test statistics obtained from the Parkin and the revised models.

Table 3   Alternative asymptotic 't-values'

	Parkin model		Revised model
	$\rho = 0$	$\rho \neq 0$	$\rho = 0; r = -1$
(a) $H_0: \Phi = 1$			
Policy-on	1·39*	1·67*	0·42*
Policy-off	5·28	4·56	1·83*
Entire period	2·08	2·77	0·81*
(b) $H_0: \Phi = 0$			
Policy-on	0·74*	0·33*	0·74*
Policy-off	4·72	3·31	6·80
Entire period	3·87	2·18	4·13

* Indicates that there is no statistical grounds for rejecting H_0 at the 5% significance level.

The implications of these results are fairly obvious. Parkin's coefficient on price expectations is not significantly different from unity in the policy-on period. However, not much confidence can be attached to this result as the large variance attached to the estimates makes any meaningful conclusion difficult. His results imply a rejection of the Friedman-Phelps hypothesis for the policy-off sub-period and for the entire period, and a structural change on the effect of price expectations on wage settlements during periods of incomes policy. The revised model, however, consistently over the periods yields a statistical validation of the Friedman-Phelps hypothesis. Note however that as in the Parkin case the coefficient on price expectations during policy-on is badly determined. This confirms the structural change in the role of price expectations which the Parkin results suggest.

[9] One would expect a reasonable high negative correlation between θ_3 and θ_4 [see equation (1.13)].

It is worth spelling out the possible implications of this result. The acceptance that the presence of price expectations steepens the Phillip's curve leads to the conclusion that the policy-off/policy-on break in the role of price expectations would imply a steeper curve in 'off' than in 'on' periods, thus achieving the Lipsey-Parkin result that incomes policy pivots the trade-off. This, however, is derived in our case via the change in the role of price expectations. This can be demonstrated as follows, consider the general case

$$\dot{p} = f(u) + \Phi\dot{p}^e. \tag{2.4}$$

Using the relationship

$$\frac{d\dot{p}^e}{du} = \frac{d\dot{p}^e}{d\dot{p}} \cdot \frac{d\dot{p}}{du},$$

and differentiating the above, we obtain:

$$\frac{d\dot{p}}{du} = \frac{f'(u)}{1 - \Phi(d\dot{p}^e/d\dot{p})} \tag{2.5}$$

The results reported earlier suggest values of zero and one for Φ in policy-on and policy-off respectively. Using equation (2.5) it follows that

$$\text{policy-on} \quad \frac{d\dot{p}}{du} = f'(u)$$

and

$$\text{policy-off} \quad \frac{d\dot{p}}{du} = \frac{f'(u)}{1 - (d\dot{p}^e/d\dot{p})}$$

Assuming $0 < d\dot{p}^e/d\dot{p} \leq 1$, then it follows that the policy-off curve is geometrically steeper.

Note that this result holds for all values of Φ between zero and unity. Hence even on the basis of their own results, the pivoting effect of incomes policy established by Lipsey and Parkin can be derived from the changing role of price expectations.

The above results assume that the structural break is in the role of price expectations, rather than in the underlying generating scheme used to derive the price expectations. If, however, the latter is the case, i.e., it is the arguments in the generating function and not the parameter estimates attached to the variable that change, the above results do not necessarily hold as the model is now mis-specified. Such a situation could arise during 'policy on' periods when the expected inflation rate was exogenously given, by government statements perhaps.

The finding of a unitary coefficient on price expectations is not in itself a sufficient condition for rejecting the existence of a trade-off between inflation and unemployment in the short run. However, *on the assumption that prices are fully anticipated eventually*, the result confirms that no such long run trade-off exists: the choice more appropriately is one of inter-temporal unemployment.

Therefore incomes policy operated in the conventional sense is of limited effectiveness in improving the trade-off between inflation and unemployment.

Summary and conclusions

The empirical verification of the existence of a trade-off between inflation and unemployment rests strongly on the appropriateness or otherwise of the price expectations generating scheme. The adaptive expectations formulation in an *aggregate* model requires that all the individual adjustment parameters, the λ_i's, be equal for all economic units. In general, of course, such a condition cannot be expected to hold, in which case it can be shown that the aggregate prediction is not approximated by a distributed lag of past observations whose weights decline geometrically. However, it is difficult to give any meaningful economic interpretation to the λ in an aggregate adaptive expectations model. Further, it can be shown that the adaptive expectations scheme yields a parameter for price expectations which is biased downwards, thus 'falsely implying' the existence of a Phillips trade-off, albeit a steeper one, between inflation and unemployment. We have demonstrated that an alternative expectations scheme yields the same reduced form as an adaptive expectations model but implies a structural parameter for price-expectations which is substantially higher and nearer in the region of unity. Since we have shown that empirical conclusions drawn depend crucially upon the precise specification of the price expectations generating scheme we conclude that more care is required before any definitive conclusions can be drawn as to the existence or otherwise of the trade-off between inflation and unemployment.

References
[1] G. O. Bierwag and M. A. Grove, 'Aggregate Koyck Functions', *Econometrica* 1966.
[2] W. E. Deming, *Some Theory of Sampling* (Wiley, 1950).
[3] M. Friedman, 'Monetary Theory and Policy', *American Economic Review*, 1968.

[4] N. Georgescu-Roegen, 'Choice, Expectations and Measurability', *Quarterly Journal of Economics*, 1954.
[5] Z. Griliches, 'Distributed Lags: A Survey', *Econometrica*, 1967.
[6] H. G. Johnson, 'Recent Developments in Monetary Theory; A Commentary', in *Money in Britain 1959–1969*. D. R. Croome and H. G. Johnson, Eds. (Oxford University Press).
[7] D. Jorgensen, 'Rational Distributed Lag Functions', *Econometrica, 1960*.
[8] R. G. Lipsey and J. M. Parkin, 'Incomes Policy: A Re-appraisal', *Economica*, 1970, and Chapter 4, above.
[9] R. E. Lucas and L. A. Rapping, 'Price Expectations and the Phillips Curve', *American Economic Review*, 1969.
[10] J. F. Muth, 'Optimal Properties of Exponentially Weighted Forecasts', *Journal of the American Statistical Association*, 1960.
[11] J. M. Parkin, 'Incomes Policy: Some Further Results on the Determination of the Rate of Change of Money Wages', *Economica*, 1970, and Chapter 5, above.
[12] E. S. Phelps, 'Phillips Curves, Expectations of Inflation and Optimal Unemployment over Time', *Economica*, 1967.
[13] J. J. Sargent, 'A Note on the "Accelerationist" Controversy', *Journal of Money, Credit and Banking*, 1971.
[14] R. M. Solow, *Price Expectations and the Behaviour of the Price Level* (Manchester University Press, 1969).
[15] G. R. Sparks and D. A. Wilton, 'Determinants of Negotiated Wage Increases; An Empirical Analysis', *Econometrica*, 1971.
[16] H. Theil and S. Wage, 'Some observations on Adaptive Forecasting', *Management Science*, 1964.

J. A. Bispham [1]

Chapter 13 The current inflation and short-term forecasting

Introduction

A year ago M. J. Artis [2] summed up the forecasting experience of the National Institute in the context of the recent inflation in the form of three propositions: (a) . . . '(it) is clear that there are now no usable econometric relationships for forecasting wages', (b) '. . . the position with respect to prices, on the other hand, is quite different' and (c) '. . . the errors in wage forecasting are of a second order of importance when it comes to generating predictions for "real" magnitudes, e.g., the volume of consumers' expenditure.'

Experience over the intervening year has not led to any significant revision of these views, though the second may be subject to some minor qualification concerning cost-price lags (see below). It will be clear therefore that the current paper has no new econometric results to present so far as wages are concerned—indeed, we argue that formal approaches based on historical data may not be of help to the forecaster, at least over the next year or two. A fairly sharp change of structure cannot be accurately measured with so few observations, while a 'hiccup' can be seen to be just that only after some time has elapsed. In these circumstances one is thrown back on *a priori* reasoning and judgement in the light of the most recent and relevant data, including those on claims and settlements in addition to the usual indices.

Because of these problems we set ourselves a fairly limited task in this paper. Firstly, we bring up to date the historical record. It

[1] National Institute of Economic and Social Research. I am grateful to M. J. Artis, F. T. Blackaby, P. Phillips and G. D. N. Worswick, all of the National Institute, for helpful discussion during the preparation of this paper.
[2] 'Some aspects of the present inflation and the National Institute model', in H. G. Johnson and A. R. Nobay (eds.), *The Current Inflation*. This paper was, in large part, based on chapter III of *N.I.E.R.*, no. 55, February 1971.

should be a useful way of beginning the present conference for someone working with the latest data to present it and draw out the important developments. Secondly, we try to assess in a non-formal way some current theories of wage inflation in the light of the figures and thirdly we look briefly at some of the consequences of the present inflation. Next we discuss some aspects of short-term macroeconomic forecasting in the inflation context and finally[3] present some tentative suggestions for forecasting from now on and some thoughts on the direction which research should take.

The record, 1968–71

Table 1 reproduces the information given a year ago together with observations for the third quarter of 1971. The run-up to the wages explosion which began towards the end of 1969 is by now well known: a sharp rise in import prices following devaluation together with large increases in indirect taxes in both 1968 and 1969 were accompanied in those years by a moderate increase in wage inflation compared with the trend between 1959 and 1966 despite the maintenance of a high level of unemployment by post-war standards. However, with productivity rising at twice its previous trend rate in 1968, unit wage and salary costs did not accelerate until 1969. The figures

Table 1   Movements in costs and prices

Annual % rates of change

	1959–66 Trend	1966–7	1967–8	1968–9	1969–70	1971(III)– 1970(III)
Retail prices	3·2	2·5	4·7	5·4	6·9	10·1
Consumer prices[1]	3·1	2·5	4·5	5·3	5·4	8·0
G.D.P. deflator (factor cost)	2·9	3·7	2·7	3·5	7·8	11·6
Hourly wage rates	5·0	4·1	6·8	5·4	10·3	13·2
Wages and salaries per head[2]	5·4	5·4	7·7	7·8	12·5	12·6[6]
Output per head[3]	2·3	2·3	4·6	2·4	2·5	3·7[6]
Wages and salaries per unit of output	3·1	3·1	3·0	5·2	10·0	9·0
Import prices[4]	1·3	1·3	11·5	2·6	6·7	4·5[6]
Indirect taxes[5]	5·3	−0·1	11·0	14·7	3·3	−7·7

Source: *Economic Trends.*
[1] Implicit deflator of consumers' expenditure (1963 prices).
[2] Wages and salaries per employee in employment.
[3] G.D.P. (compromise estimate) per employee in employment.
[4] Implicit deflator of imports of goods and services (1963 prices).
[5] Implicit deflator of the adjustment to factor cost series (1963 prices).
[6] Estimate.

[3] This section of the paper is largely due to F. T. Blackaby of the National Institute.

suggest that the wage acceleration began at the firm or plant level rather than around the national bargaining tables. In 1967 and 1968 the gap between the rates of increase of wage rates and earnings (wages and salaries per head) widened as compared with the previous trend, though in 1968 some of this can be ascribed to increased overtime working. In 1969, however, when average weekly hours began to fall, the gap widened to 2·4%, compared with a long-run 0·4%, and this gap continued into 1970. Hourly wage rate increases appear to have followed earnings with a lag, and the gap began to close again in 1971 partly because average hours worked fell sharply, but perhaps also because of the steep rise in unemployment.

The end result of the explosion has been to take the rate of increase of the G.D.P. deflator (the most comprehensive index of domestic prices) in 1970 to over twice the previous trend, and in 1971 to three times this rate, 11 to 12%.

Another way of looking at the figures is in the form of a literal 'cost-accounting' framework (Table 2). This procedure does not explain the inflation in any causal sense—it merely shows the relative sizes of the various cost contributions to the rise in prices *given* the movements in wages, import prices, etc. The method of calculating the figures uses the primary input coefficients of consumers' expenditure given in the 1963 input-output tables and applies these weights to the percentage changes in the various cost indicators which go to make up final prices. The results of the exercise seem plausible to the

Table 2   Contributions to the rise in prices

% rates of change

	1968(III)–1967(III)	1969(III)–1968(III)	1970(III)–1969(III)	1971(III)–1970(III)
Consumers' price index	5·3	5·0	5·7	8·0
of which, accounted for by:				
Import prices	1·6	0·4	1·2	0·8[2]
Indirect taxes[1]	1·7	2·6	−0·1	−1·1
Unit labour costs[3]	0·9	1·5	4·7	3·6
Unit non-labour factors costs	1·0	0·1	0·3	4·3
Total identified	5·2	4·6	6·1	7·6

[1] Includes S.E.T.
[2] Unit value index, otherwise, import prices are implicit deflator of constant price imports of goods and services.
[3] Wages and salaries, forces' pay and employers' contributions to national insurance and other pension etc. funds.

extent that the total identified contribution is reasonably close to the measured rise in the C.P.I. Complete agreement is not to be expected as fixed weights are being applied which in any case refer to an earlier period, while the data itself will be subject to some random error.

The table indicates, as would be expected, that import prices and indirect taxes each accounted for about one third of the rise in consumer prices in 1967–8, and that indirect taxes alone accounted for more than half the increase in 1968–9. In 1970, however, unit labour costs (including a large rise in employers' national insurance contributions) moved up very sharply to account for well over 80% of the recorded rise, while at the same time the contribution of import prices moved up again reflecting in part the general inflation in other industrial countries as well as the successful attempt by the oil-producing countries to secure higher crude oil prices. The addition of a further year's data is particularly interesting and appears to bring the circle full close. Between the third quarters of 1970 and 1971 the largest single contribution (over 50%) to the recorded rise in consumer prices of 8% was unit non-labour factor costs—in particular profits. The figure is biased upwards somewhat by the cut in S.E.T., while rebates were still being repaid at the previous rate; nevertheless the qualitative conclusion remains. The unit labour cost contribution declined in absolute terms, though this was due almost entirely to the acceleration in output and productivity (see Table 1) and to a slower rise in employers' contributions, rather than to any deceleration in the rate of rise of average earnings. The negative contribution of indirect taxes is made up of the cuts in purchase tax and S.E.T., the latter including the effect of the delayed timing of rebates already mentioned.

Perhaps one of the most significant points to emerge from the 1971 figures is that even in the face of declining demand pressures entrepreneurs can (and will) recoup profit margins if the latter are squeezed hard enough. This experience contrasts with that during previous cyclical downturns when profits bore the brunt of the squeeze. Part of the explanation for this change in behaviour may lie in a secular increase in the fixed cost proportion, and it also seems likely that the prolonged period of low growth (in other words the absence of the old cycle in its full form) and the severity of the recent recession would have made for an unprecedented (post-war) squeeze anyway. But there is evidence to suggest that the wages explosion itself was to blame for much of the profits squeeze—in contrast to past experience when wage inflation tended to moderate during recessions.[4] At all events the latest figures suggest that labour does not make itself unemployed by pushing for higher wages—at least through the mechanism of causing bankruptcies. (There may, of course, be longer-run effects, for example on international competitiveness, which do work in this direction, see below.) We touch on the topic of the recovery of profits again in our later discussion of the behaviour of price equations through 1970 and 1971.

The record since July 1971

Several important developments in the recent past make it of interest to bring the record as far up to date as possible. The most significant developments probably concern changes in government policy—the cuts in purchase tax and S.E.T., the lowering of the standard rate of income tax (in April) and the raising of child allowances (effective from the third quarter). In addition, the Government has committed the nationalized industries to the 5% limit on price increases contained in the C.B.I. initiative, and has continued its policy of trying to force down the level of wage settlements in the public sector.

Table 3 shows the annual rates of increase of various wage and price measures between the second and fourth quarters of 1971 (or between July and the latest month for which data are available) and between the latest month or quarter and the same period a year ago. Two basic conclusions can be drawn at once—first that the rate of consumer price inflation has moderated significantly and secondly, that wage inflation has also abated somewhat, the deceleration being more pronounced in earnings than in wage rates. From earlier annual rates of increase of around 13%, basic hourly rates have decelerated to around 10%, and average earnings from the 14–15% range to 9–10% per annum. It is important to stress, however, that these figures pre-date the miners' settlement.

Table 3 also shows the N.I.E.S.R. estimate of the effect of recent policy changes affecting prices—purchase tax, S.E.T., the restraint of nationalized industry prices (assumed to allow 5% increases where 10% would otherwise have occurred) and a small reverse effect from

---

[4] See M. J. Artis in Johnson and Nobay, op. cit., pages 27–8, where it is reported that the 1970 fall in the share of profits in total domestic incomes was about three times that expected on previous relationships with output.

Table 3 Recent price and wage developments

% changes, annual rates

	1971(II)–1971(IV) or July–latest month[1]	Change on same period a year ago[1]
Basic hourly wage rates	10·0 (J)	9·4 (J)
Average earnings[2]	8·9 (D)	9·4 (D)
Retail price index[3]	5·2 (J)	8·2 (J)
Consumer price index[4]	5·3 (Q)	7·7 (Q)
Real average earnings[6]		0·3 (D)
Real disposable average earnings[7]		1·6 (Q)[8]
Wholesale price index of manufactures—home sales (excl. food, drink and tobacco)	3·0 (D)	7·4 (D)
Import prices, basic materials	−2·0 (D)	2·5 (D)
Import prices, fuels	−9·6 (D)	16·3 (D)

	1971		1972	
	(III)	(IV)	(I)	(II)
Policy (per cent of C.P.I.)[5]	−0·3	−0·7	−0·9	−1·1

Source: *Economic Trends, Department of Employment Gazette*, and N.I.E.S.R. estimates.

[1] Key: Q: fourth quarter 1971; D: December 1971; J: January 1972.
[2] Great Britain: all employees (monthly inquiry).
[3] Excluding seasonal food.
[4] Estimate from R.P.I.
[5] Includes (negative) purchase tax cut, July 1971; cut in S.E.T., 3rd quarter 1971, restraint on nationalized industry prices and (positive) raising of employers' national insurance contributions.
[6] Monthly inquiry index divided by R.P.I.
[7] Estimate of wages and salaries, forces' pay and net contributions, less tax, deflated by C.P.I. Per employee in employment.
[8] Estimate.

the raising of employers' national insurance contributions. The estimates do *not* allow for the pressure on public sector wages, however. In terms of the consumer price index the estimates suggest that by the fourth quarter of 1971 the level of the index was about $\frac{3}{4}\%$ below what it would otherwise have been—giving a rise over the preceding twelve months of about $8\frac{1}{2}\%$—much the same as in the preceding two quarters. In other words, because of the lags in the wage–cost–price relationship no lowering of the rate of price inflation would have been apparent by the end of 1971 in the absence of the policy changes mentioned.

It is worth noting in passing the fallacy in recent press comment which suggests that the C.B.I. price initiative in the private sector is having some independent impact. The assertion is made on the basis of the sharp slowing in the rate of rise of wholesale prices of manufactures, see Table 3. It can be seen that this deceleration can be almost wholly ascribed to falls in import prices of basic materials, and particularly of fuels since July, rather than to any paring of profit margins.

Tables 3 and 4 also present some estimates of the movement of average earning in real terms and in real disposable terms, i.e., after allowing for inflation and for all effects of policy including income tax and national insurance contribution changes. Although there have been rather sharp quarter-to-quarter fluctuations, the figures show that by the end of 1971, earnings were beginning to be squeezed again in real terms, showing little change over the same period a year ago. Even in disposable terms, which allows for the cuts in income tax, the increase is less than 2%. To the extent that real increases are the target of bargainers this development is clearly significant, though it follows fairly sharp increases earlier (see Table 4) as prices lagged behind costs. The deceleration of earnings growth, combined with the price lags involved, is the main explanation for this development and follows the pattern forecast by the Institute in February 1971,[5] though the full rigour of the squeeze has been mitigated by the changes in both direct and indirect taxes, and by the pricing policies of nationalized industries.

The impact of the downward pressure on wages in the public sector is (perhaps surprisingly) very difficult to measure because of problems concerning the comparability of data between the two sectors—in particular because of the likelihood of much less earnings

[5] *N.I.E.R.*, no. 55, pages 49–51.

Table 4 Real disposable personal incomes[1]

£ million, 1963 prices or %

	1967(III)	1968(III)	1969(III)	1970(III)	1971(III)
Wages and salaries[2]	4,196	4,131	4,222	4,411	4,533
	(68·5)	(67·3)	(68·1)	(68·9)	(69·5)
Other personal income	1,237	1,234	1,192	1,184	1,155
	(20·2)	(20·1)	(19·2)	(18·5)	(17·8)
Current grants[3]	692	771	787	808	830
	(11·3)	(12·6)	(12·7)	(12·6)	(12·7)

	1967(III)	1968(III)	1969(III)	1970				1971			
				(I)	(II)	(III)	(IV)	(I)	(II)	(III)	(IV)[5]
Real disposable wages and salaries per employee in employment (1967(III)=100)	100	99·3	101·9	103·6	105·5	107·5	109·3	110·4	109·2	112·5	111·1
C.P.I.[4](1967(III) = 100)	100	105·1	110·6	113·2	115·1	116·9	118·6	121·1	124·5	126·3	127·8

Source: *Economic Trends*, Inland Revenue and N.I.E.S.R. estimates. Figures in parentheses are percentages of total and disposable income.

[1] I.e., after allowing for taxes, national insurance contributions and transfers abroad, and deflated by consumer price index.
[2] Including employers' contributions and forces' pay, but net of employers' contributions to national insurance.
[3] Assuming no tax is payable on these incomes.
[4] Consumer price index.
[5] Estimate.

drift in the public sector. For what it is worth, the data on increases in *basic rates* suggest a far bigger deceleration (pre-miners' strike) in the public sector.[6] However, when compared with *earnings* in the private sector the relative deceleration (in public *rates*) is nowhere near so marked. Even if we could accurately measure the relative deceleration, of course, we are still left with the question of whether the Government's policy has had any demonstration effect on private sector settlements. The rise in unemployment and slowdown of price inflation could plausibly account for all the relatively small slowdown in basic hourly rates so far accomplished.

Causes

The movement of prices between 1966 and 1969 is relatively easy to explain in terms of devaluation and the associated changes in policy, and, although wages were rising somewhat faster than pre-1966 Phillips-type relationships would have suggested, the discrepancy was not large, especially as a weakening of the relationship had already been detected.[7] By fairly common consent it is the sharp change in wage behaviour (at a time of high unemployment) beginning towards the end of 1969 that requires explanation. Although several theories have been propounded, they are difficult to 'prove' in the accepted sense either because proof requires observations on variables such as 'militancy', expectations, etc. which we do not measure directly, or else because we do not yet have sufficient observations of the phenomenon (particularly post-explosion data). At the present time one is therefore largely thrown back on *a priori* theorizing and attempts to eliminate at least the other unlikely candidates, i.e., other than demand pressure in the labour market, whether measured by unemployment or vacancies.

Among the latter it is fairly safe to place the *direct* effect, i.e., through import prices, of general inflation in the industrial countries (see Table 2)—the orders of magnitude are simply not large enough. It is true, however, that the general world inflation began with demand inflation in the United States following failure to prevent excess demand associated with the war in Vietnam. Nevertheless, when eventually deflationary policies were adopted (in 1968) they

---

[6] These comments are based on an examination of recent data in some detail, carried out by P. Phillips of the National Institute.

[7] See National Board for Prices and Incomes, *Third General Report, August 1967–July 1968*, H.M.S.O., *Cmnd* 3517, Appendix A, July 1968.

did not have the expected effect,[8] and, although the United States experience has not been as dramatic as that of the United Kingdom, economists there are left with exactly the same type of behaviour-change to be explained. We return to other aspects of the international environment below.

The lapse of incomes policy at the end of 1968 is also cited as a reason for the wages explosion and it certainly 'fits' well with respect to timing. It has two drawbacks, however: firstly, that it cannot explain, at least directly, the similar experiences of other countries and secondly, that it requires one to assume (given there were no sharp changes in other variables such as unemployment and prices) that the policy was having a large effect, when most people assumed that it was not.

We come therefore to explanations based on changes in behaviour on both sides of the wage-bargaining table—increased 'militancy' on the part of labour and/or increased 'permissiveness' on the part of management. On the part of the unions the possible 'triggers' for an increase in militancy are fairly easy to see, in particular, the squeeze on real disposable earnings following devaluation and the high marginal rates of taxation effective at the lower end of the income scale. Table 4 shows that between the third quarters of 1967 and 1969, real disposable average earnings rose by less than 1% per annum. In addition, there were probably induced expectations of continued inflation which the unions wished to anticipate, as well as political considerations connected with the Industrial Relations legislation, which was revived by the Conservative Government. The feeling of militancy probably also fed on an international demonstration effect as workers began to see the success achieved elsewhere.

[8] See *Fortune*, March 1972, 'The emerging debate about inflation'. A passage from this article is worth quoting for the summary it gives of the United States experience:

The latest report of the Council of Economic Advisers includes an arresting table that suggests why the wage record this time seemed so baffling. In the first post-war recession, compensation per man-hour in the private economy rose by 8% in the twelve months before the economy peaked out in the fourth quarter of 1948; from then until the economy hit bottom, in the fourth quarter of 1949, the rate of increase was only 0.4%. In the 1953–54 recession, the rate of increase fell from 6% to 3.3%. In the 1957–58 recession, the decline was from 5.4 to 3.3%. In the 1960–61 recession, it went from 4.3 to 1.7%.

But in this last recession the rate of compensation increases *rose*. It was moving up at a 6.5% rate in the year before the economy peaked out (in the fourth quarter of 1969). It rose at a 7% rate in the following year. In manufacturing alone, the rate went from 6.1% in the year before the peak to 6.9% in the following year.

A *feeling* of militancy does not of itself make for increased inflation, however; this requires that the employers do not resist with like
force. The high cost of strikes relative to the cost of concessions has
been put forward by many businessmen as a reason here, though this
cannot have emerged suddenly. What *could* have happened quite
quickly, however, is an increased degree of awareness of this fact on
both sides of the table, but particularly on the union side. For the
employers, two aspects of the international scene were favourable to
permissiveness, first, that devaluation had enabled them to restore
profit margins on exports while improving competitiveness, hence
giving them more leeway with export prices, and secondly, and re-
inforcing this, that prices were accelerating internationally in any
case. It is plausible too that employers became increasingly aware of
the possibilities for passing on wage increases in domestic prices,
though the evidence from the recent behaviour of price equations
(see below) suggests that they delayed for some time before doing
this fully.

Explanations couched in terms of militancy, permissiveness,
oligopoly and the realization of bargaining power, thus seem at the
moment the strongest candidates. Recent events have merely
strengthened this conclusion, it being difficult to envisage any
account of the miners' settlement which does not pay appreciable
regard to some, if not all, of these factors.

Some consequences

In one sense the consequences of the current inflation have not so
far been severe, given that the pensioners have now been 'reim-
bursed', certainly not as severe as the extent of the public debate
suggests. There is one important caveat to this, however, concerning
the possible 'endogeneity' of the Government in addition to its role
of protecting the real standard of living of the pensioners. If the
'propensity to reflate' is related to the rate of inflation, then at least
some of the recent rise in unemployment can be ascribed to inflation.
In other words, the fear of perpetuating or even worsening the inflation may have led in 1970 and 1971 to more cautious demand
management policies than might otherwise have been the case given
the amount of slack existing. But this is certainly not what Ministers
have meant in their assertions that wage inflation leads to unemployment. The implication is that the increasing cost of labour has
led to economy in its use either by cutting back 'unnecessary'

employees or by substituting capital for labour. It follows that we should have noticed a further change in the relationship of unemployment to output in addition to the shift which occurred in 1966–7 and which was partly associated with the introduction of S.E.T. Such a further shift has not been observed, however, in the sense that the assumption of a trend rate of increase of productivity of 3–3¼% between 1967 and the end of 1971 gives a satisfactory explanation of the present level of employment when allowance is made for time lags in the adjustment of actual to 'desired' or 'equilibrium' employment.

In the short-run at least, the converse of the ministerial statements seems to have been true, given the lags in the adjustment of prices to costs, which we have already noted. Table 4 shows that real disposable average earnings grew by 5½% between the third quarters of 1969 and 1970, so that with little change in employment, the effect on aggregate real demand was positive. Not only was total real income increased, but, as Tables 4 and 5 show, there was a strong shift in the distribution of incomes towards wages and away from profits and dividends, i.e., in the direction of sections of the community with higher marginal propensities to consume. As the lags began to work themselves out and as the acceleration of earnings came to an end,

Table 5 Factor income shares[1]

%

	Peak: 1960–6	Trough: 1960–6	1967	1968	1969	1970	1971[2] (I) + (II)	(III)
Income from self-employment	8·6	7·8	8·1	8·0	7·9	7·5 ⎫		
Public sector gross trading surpluses	3·5	3·0	3·6	4·0	4·0	3·4 ⎬ 17·9	17·8
Rent	6·3	5·5	6·5	6·6	6·9	7·1 ⎭	
Gross trading profits of companies[3]	16·0	12·8	13·0	12·2	11·0	10·1	9·6	11·8
Income from employment	69·5	66·7	68·9	69·1	70·2	72·0	72·5	70·4

Source: *Economic Trends*.
[1] Shares in total domestic income after providing for stock appreciation.
[2] Estimates. Seasonally adjusted.
[3] Including S.E.T. on a cash basis. The third quarter 1971 figure is somewhat inflated because of the cut in S.E.T. while rebates were still being paid on earlier tax payments.

18

this process began to reverse itself, being only partially offset by fiscal policy in the third quarter of 1971.

In the longer run, however, the effects of the inflation may do more than merely work themselves out. Not only has fiscal drag been raised to more than negligible proportions[9] but, perhaps more importantly, there has now been a sizeable deterioration in international competitiveness. Export prices have recently been rising at around 10% per annum, and given further inflation since the third quarter of last year and a settlement of exchange rates which was marginally unfavourable to the United Kingdom, it is likely that the whole of the relative price advantage secured by devaluation has now gone, but because of long lags, the effect has not shown up in export demand. Assuming a more flexible exchange rate policy in the future, the consequences for domestic employment would be offset, though there are doubts about this assumption in the context of E.E.C. entry.

Table 6   Ratio of United Kingdom prices of exports of manufactures to world prices[1] in United States dollars, 1963 = 100

1965	1966	1967	1968	1969	1970	1971(III)
101	102	103	97	97	97	102

[1] Including United Kingdom.

The recent changes in the distribution of income are fairly clear from Tables 4 and 5 and require little comment beyond noting again the sharp increase in labour's share, at least temporarily, a much greater increase than would have been accounted for by reference to previous cyclical experience. The fairly stable share of current grant incomes in total personal income is somewhat misleading in that the number of benefit recipients has been increasing. The married couple's pension, for example, showed little absolute change in real terms between 1968 and 1970, though the recent increase works out at about $8\frac{3}{4}\%$ initially, this real gain will of course be partly eroded before the next uprating in October. One must assume that fixed incomes not subject to government control have continued to decline in real terms.

[9] See *N.I.E.R.*, no. 59, February 1972, pages 35–7 where the National Institute estimated that, at constant employment and current rates of inflation, the figure is of the order of £400 million per annum.

Forecasting

(a) *Prices.* As was reported in the Introduction, the forecasting of prices does not present a serious problem *given wages.* Basically we use a cost mark-up hypothesis, the costs being unit labour costs and import prices. The behaviour of this type of equation over the last two years is of interest, though it only mirrors developments we have already noted, in particular, the exceptional squeeze on profits and the more recent sharp catching up. In other words, in the context of a high degree of slack and an unprecedented wages explosion the adjustment of prices to costs did not follow the previous lag pattern, and [see Table 7, equation (1)] on the pure cost mark-up equation prices have still not fully caught up. It is possible that slack demand could be holding back the full cost adjustment and indeed [Table 7, equation (2)] a crude pressure of demand term does improve the statistical results up to the end of 1969, though there is still slight over-prediction between 1970(I)–1970(IV). However, with this equation, given the amount of slack still existing, the degree of catching up has been too great, though, again, longer delayed than the estimated lags would suggest. Once the adjustment has occurred, however, it is worth noting that the errors do not show any noticeable trend, at least, so far.

The comparatively satisfactory performance of pricing relationships recently is another way of saying that inflation does not much matter from the point of view of the short-term macro-economic forecaster interested mainly in 'real' magnitudes, given that the effects on the foreign balance are relatively long-delayed. Prices merely adjust to costs with a lag, and there are only minor uncertainties connected now with the precise length of this lag.

(b) *Wages.* Our present method of forecasting wages is wholly informal and is discussed below. The only point to note here is the rather startling success of the method: our forecast a year ago of the increase in average earnings in 1971 (on unchanged policies) was a rise of 14%. The out-turn (after changes in policy, including pressure on public sector wages) looks like being about 12–13%.

The prospects for prediction: direction of thought

At the Institute, we never in fact relied wholly on any equations for the forecasting of wage rates and earnings. In the 1958–68 period, one or other of the various relationships was used, depending on the preference of the person who was forecasting at the time; however, it

Table 7   The recent behaviour of two aggregate price equations. (Estimated by Almon least squares.)

Equation (1) $C.P.I.F.C. = f\left(\dfrac{W.S.^*}{G.D.P.}, M.P., Constant\right)^1$

Estimation period: 1960(I)–1969(I). S.E. = 0·60. D.W. = 1·0.

Lag coefficients

Variable	t	$t-1$	$t-2$	$t-3$	$t-4$	Sum	T-value
W.S.*/G.D.P.	50·1	19·8	12·3	14·9	15·1	112·1	25·7
M.P.	−0·02	0·10	0·09	0·02	−0·03	0·159	3·8

Actual-calculated (points)

1970				1971			
(I)	(II)	(III)	(IV)	(I)	(II)	(III)	(IV)²
−2·1	−2·0	−2·7	−3·2	−3·1	−1·6	−1·6	−1·3

Equation (2) $C.P.I.F.C. = f\left(\dfrac{W.S.^*}{G.D.P.}, M.P., G.D.P.^*/T, Constant\right)$

Estimation period: 1960(I)–1969(I). S.E. = 0·41. D.W. = 1·8.

Lag coefficients

Variable	t	$t-1$	$t-2$	$t-3$	$t-4$	Sum	T-value
W.S.*/G.D.P.	28·1	7·4	14·4	28·8	30·9	109·5	28·3
M.P.	0·10	0·05	0·02	0·02	0·01	0·20	5·8
G.D.P.*/T.	0·06	0·08	0·11	0·13	0·10	0·47	4·8

Actual-calculated

1970				1971			
(I)	(II)	(III)	(IV)	(I)	(II)	(III)	(IV)²
−0·9	−0·3	−0·2	−0·5	−0·2	+1·3	+1·1	+1·2

[1] Definitions of the variables:

C.P.I.F.C. = consumer price index net of indirect taxes and subsidies;
  W.S.* = wages and salaries plus employers' contributions;
  G.D.P. = gross domestic product (1963 prices), compromise estimate;
G.D.P.*/T = rates of G.D.P. to trend; trend measured over 1960(I)–1967(IV) equivalent to 3% per annum;
  M.P. = import unit value index.
[2] Partly estimated.

was always subject to adjustment in the light of information about recent claims and awards. For three successive years now—1970, 1971 and without doubt 1972—every one of the equations used for explaining wage rates or earnings in 1950–69 has given answers which are wrong by a significant margin.

The wage rates and earnings forecasts, therefore, are made on the basis of an examination of claims and settlements. The judgement of these includes using our limited knowledge of comparabilities; it requires a view of how far the Government incomes policy will be effective in the public sector, and how far that might spread to the private sector; and it requires some judgement about militancy—what Christopher Dow used to call 'trade union pushfulness'.

It is true, of course, that the requirements of a forecaster are rather special; a good general relationship will not do if there is year-to-year variability above a certain size. So inspection processes may be better for short-term forecasting even if there are some variable long-term relationships in play.

We do not see any early prospect of returning to a forecast based on indicators of pressure of demand, past prices, or previous rises in real income. No doubt in time new relationships will be presented, which will be more successful in explaining 1970–2 by some combination of these, perhaps by cutting in prices heavily at some point. From our point of view, new constructions of this kind would have to predict well for a number of years before they were acceptable. Further, the forecaster must accept that some kind of incomes policy is likely to continue for the indefinite future. At a minimum, the Government is virtually certain to try to influence the size of wage settlements in the public sector; and the public sector accounts for one quarter of total employment.

The model implied by the current method of forecasting is a 'bargaining model'. The rate of inflation is set by the wage bargains struck in negotiations. Further, the model accepts the concept of 'key negotiations' (which no doubt change from time to time), and the concept of wage negotiating contours, so that large numbers of negotiators can as it were coast along in the wake of certain crucial bargains.

Essentially, therefore, one is attempting to quantify the pressures on the negotiators on either side. It has always been a defect of the 'pressure of demand' model that it mainly quantifies just one pressure on just one side—on the employers' side. Certainly unions in the past have adjusted their claims to the cycle, putting in big claims in prosperous years, and smaller claims in less prosperous years; now they appear no longer to be doing this. When they did do it, there is some reason to think that they were adjusting to the economic pressure on the employer, rather than thinking of the employment consequences of their wage claims. That is, they did not, and do not, really believe that they would benefit the unemployed by putting in low claims.

One can envisage a number of other economic pressures on negotiators. A shift in price expectations will increase the pressure on the union side and reduce it on the employers' side. A period of stagnant real wages, after tax, will increase the pressure on the union side. But in particular bargains there are likely to be a number of other factors which are not directly economic. There is almost certainly an element of militancy which is independent of the economic pressures bearing on the trade union negotiators. If this element is important in key bargains, then it is not difficult to see that it may be impossible to forecast the rise in wage rates in any particular year from economic variables alone.

The year 1972 is a case in point. It is reasonably clear that the coal miners' settlement will shift up the level of wage bargains reached in the rest of the year substantially. The railwaymen are already being offered an 11% increase, 3% above the previous public sector ceiling. So the success of the coal miners will be a fairly strong determinant of the rise in wage rates in 1972. No set of economic variables could have predicted that success.

The case for giving an independent weight to some kind of militancy is strengthened by international experience. It is not easy to think of a set of economic terms which could explain the simultaneous deviations from 'pressure of demand' wage rate predictions in a number of countries.

To some extent, the improvement of the present Institute method of wage rate prediction will depend on increased knowledge of the bargaining process. We shall be interested in any studies of wage rounds, of wage contours and comparabilities used, and in attempts to identify key bargains. We shall also be interested in any detailed studies of arguments presented on either side, not only in negotiations, but also in presentations before arbitration tribunals. Granted that the arguments may differ from the 'true' pressures, nevertheless there may be some correspondence between them.

We have been wondering whether there is any possibility of getting direct information on expectations, particularly expectations of negotiators. One of the problems here of course is that any series would have to be built up over a number of years before it became useful. Still, some series of actual expectations as opposed to presumed expectations has to be started by some one at some time. There is little reason to trust any of the standard economists' 'expectation-generating' schemes, and true *ex ante* series are needed.

We would obviously be interested if any group, more sociologically inclined than the Institute, produced any material from which some kind of quantification of 'militancy' might be made. In any case, there is unlikely to be a convenient lag: so one would be confronted with the problem of forecasting militancy.

Harry G. Johnson

Chapter 14 Notes on incomes policy and the
balance of payments

Incomes policy is usually recommended in the context of the domestic
economy, as a means of circumventing the fact that the rate of unemployment deemed politically tolerable has proven inconsistent
with the degree of price stability also deemed politically tolerable.
In these circumstances, economic theory would suggest that either
the definition of 'full employment' is mis-conceived—since in other
markets economists typically identify equilibrium with stability of
the price and disequilibrium with price increases reflecting excess
demand or price decreases reflecting excess supply—or that inflation
ought to be considered as a means of preserving a socially desired disequilibrium in the labour market. In the latter case, which raises the
theory of the so-called 'Phillips curve', economic theory raises two
sorts of questions: the first is whether the costs of inflation as the
price of maintaining a level of unemployment below that which
would prevail with price stability are really as high as is commonly
made out, since most of the commonly recognized effects are income
redistributions rather than resource wastes and therefore in principle
compensable and not a source of real social loss; the second and
more fundamental is whether a situation of permanent disequilibrium
in the labour and product markets can be maintained by inflation,
given that the expectations that influence money wage and price
adjustments will, assuming rational behaviour on the part of those
concerned, adjust to the fact of on-going inflation. On this second
question there is a well-known controversy between the 'mone-
tarists' and the 'Keynesians', the former asserting that the employ-
ment-creating effects of monetary expansion must be transitory,
lasting only until the resulting inflation becomes fully expected, the
latter asserting that these effects can be permanent, either because
of 'dynamic money illusion', according to which inflationary ex-

pectations do not become fully incorporated in the wage-determination process, or because 'transactions costs' prevent the wage-determination process from ever catching up on (though it may keep pace with) inflation, with the result that real wages suffer a once-over reduction which makes a lower unemployment rate more profitable to employers. The empirical evidence on these points is by no means conclusive; and in fact the whole Phillips curve approach has suffered a severe set-back in recent years as a result of the prevalence of a combination of abnormally high unemployment and abnormally rapid inflation in the United States and the United Kingdom. These phenomena are in my view easily explicable in terms of the more sophisticated quantity theory that has emerged in recent years and which makes use of complex models of expectation-formation and lagged responses of price and wage determination to changes in macroeconomic policies; nevertheless, they have been widely interpreted by those whom I shall refer to as 'political economists' as evidence that the Phillips curve has broken down (or even never existed), that inflation is a matter of sociology or 'trade union militancy' or the abuse of monopoly power by giant corporations, and that the appropriate remedy for it is some form of social control over the determination of money wages and prices, described generically as 'incomes policy'.

Political economy, then, in contrast to economic theory, instead of recognizing and insisting on the existence of a politically-determined dilemma that government would like to pretend does not exist, regards the problem as being created by the irresponsible failure of important groups of citizens, notably trade unions and corporations, to do their political duty, by responding to the market signals coming to them and indicating inflationary wage and price responses, instead of maintaining price stability by 'appropriate' and 'responsible' self-denying refusals to take as much in money terms as the market forces offer them, and thereby to relieve government of the dilemma it has created for itself by its irresponsible promises to give the electorate more employment and less inflation than the facts of economic nature will permit. 'Incomes policy', it should be clearly recognized, constitutes an attempt to solve a politically-created economic policy problem by political means; and that raises the two main problems about incomes policy, whether a political solution is possible in principle, in the political context, and whether a political solution can be effective in beating an economic problem.

19

The evidence of past experiments along these lines is overwhelmingly negative; but it is characteristic of political animals that they have the infinite self-confidence that is born of solipsism and the disregard of past and others' experience as irrelevant, which is expressed in the view that past failures are attributable to the lack of determination or the lack of astuteness of others than oneself.

From the point of view of economic theory, still within the context of a closed economy, the recommendation of an incomes policy contains several fatal errors of logic or economic understanding. One elementary one is that there is such a thing as a price or a wage for a clearly defined quality and amount of product or labour delivered to the purchaser under clearly defined transaction conditions and contingent obligations. Transactions have an infinite number of dimensions, and agreement or insistence on fixing the ratio of money to commodity quantity exchanged in a single transaction leaves all the other dimensions of the bargain free to vary in response to economic circumstances. A second one is that, while the prime purpose of an incomes policy as usually recommended is to provide a more comfortable substitute for a restrictive fiscal or monetary policy—in other words, an alternative to macroeconomic control of the economy—it inevitably becomes concerned with the micro-economic issues of relative wages and prices. This involves the two quite conflicting social aims of improving the efficiency of operation of the microeconomy by eliminating or at least reducing monopoly power, and of counteracting the allocation and pricing of resources resulting from market competition in order to implement minority views of social justice in the distribution of income. The macro-economic purpose then becomes cluttered with quite irrelevant microeconomic objectives. Third, and most important, the policy attempts to stabilize the value of money essentially by decree, regardless of its quantity—a fallacy disregarding the laws of demand and supply which is only too common in other aspects of govern-mental policies, and which in those contexts is well known to produce problems of deficiencies or surpluses that require further interventions in production and consumption.

The argument for incomes policy here is deceptively simple—why should people bother or be allowed to attempt to increase their real income shares by pushing up money wages and prices, when the end result in real terms will either be market-determined or amenable to social agreement on the desirable distribution of income? In theoretical terms, the fallacy of this argument is its neglect of the fact that, in addition to determining the relative prices of goods and services in terms of one another, a general equilibrium system which contains money has to determine a money price level such that the quantity of real balances is equal to the amount that people want to hold. The equilibrium relative prices consistent with monetary equilibrium could be determined in principle without reference to money; but their expression in terms of money could not be, and expression of them arbitrarily in terms of money of an assumed constant purchasing power would in general make them disequilibrium prices not merely in absolute but also in relative terms.

I have heard it argued that in feudal times men had their wages fixed by royal decree, guild bargaining, etc., and should be happy enough to return to that system in return for the presumed feudal benefits of full employment. But in those days money was not under the direct and immediate control of the state (and in any case did not matter so much in the organization of economic activity, the degree of division of labour being smaller by several orders of magnitude than at present) so that money bargains were for the most part real bargains as well; and there are to be found in economic history since the year A.D. 1 many cases, such as the commutation of real into money rents in the later stages of feudalism, of monetary disturbances disrupting the equivalence of real and money bargains. Incomes policy, therefore, in my judgement, makes no sense in the context of a closed economy; it is an attempt to solve a political dilemma by a political solution pseudo-justified by spurious economic analysis in defiance of basic economic principles.

Almost all of the advocacy of incomes policy proceeds in the context of a closed economy assumed in the argument above; but this is another fundamental analytical mistake. All relevant national economies are engaged significantly in international trade and other kinds of current and capital account transactions, and therefore are open and not closed economies. Arguments about wages and prices based on the assumption of a closed economy can only extend to an open economy if that economy adheres to a floating exchange rate without official intervention aimed at influencing the level of that rate, because only in that case do the national monetary authorities enjoy autonomy with respect to controlling the trend of national wage and price levels. Under a system of fixed rates of international exchange among currencies, the 'ideal type' of the present international monetary system (the qualification being the ability of countries to change their pegged exchange rates by international agreement in cases of 'fundamental disequilibrium'), the national economy becomes only one component part of an integrated world economy, and the national wage and price level must be adjusted to keep in line with the world price level, according to the standard law of markets or more formally the principle of purchasing power parity.

The implications of this long-run proposition will be discussed below. In the short run, however, national wage and price levels can get out of line with world levels, leading respectively to balance-of-payments surpluses or deficits; and this fact, in conjunction with the fact of a general upward trend of world prices in the period since World War II, has produced an additional and in many respects a politically more cogent argument for incomes policy in deficit countries—chronically in the United Kingdom, and recently in the United States—namely an argument for restraint on the rise of money wages and prices in the deficit country as a means of restoring its international price competitiveness, by reducing its money prices for traded goods not absolutely but relatively to the inflating prices of its international competitors, and so avoiding the need for a devaluation of its currency. Three points about this argument should be noted, apart from the questions raised earlier about the feasibility of an incomes policy operation in the first place. First, rectification of the deficit requires not only the rectification of the relative prices of internationally traded goods, but also the diversion from home-market to export and import-competing production of the resources required to produce the extra quantities that will be demanded from exporters and producers of import substitutes as comparative cost advantage is tilted in their favour by the incomes policy. In other words, the incomes policy will require to be backed up (in normal circumstances of relatively full employment of resources) by policies of deflation of domestic demand; action on wages and prices only is theoretically insufficient. Second, once the deficit has been remedied by the appropriate adjustment of relative prices, the character of the incomes policy will have to be changed, if the emergence of an obverse balance-of-payments surplus problem is to be avoided: wages and prices will have to be allowed to rise in line with world prices. This is obviously a more difficult problem to manage than that of persuading everyone to accept the objective of price stability and to govern wage and price decisions accordingly. Third, the starting point of the problem was an increase in domestic wages and prices above the levels consistent with international equilibrium, presumably the result of excessive laxity of demand management prompted by the desire to reduce domestic unemployment. To maintain the newly-restored equilibrium in the balance of payments, the authorities will have to resist the political pressures to commit the same mistake again.

To summarize, the use of incomes policy to correct a balance-of-payments deficit is a far more complicated matter than the simple appeal to everyone to accept the desirability of domestic price stability and act accordingly would imply, because it involves a species of short-run 'voluntary' relative wage and price deflation in the context of a long-run acceptance of inflation at an externally-determined rate.

In the longer run, as previously mentioned, the national members of an international fixed exchange rate system will be obliged to accept the common rate of world inflation, unless *either* for domestic purposes they prefer a higher rate of inflation, and are willing therefore to accept an alternation of periods of deficit and periods of surplus on their balance of payments associated with periods of currency over-valuation and periods of currency under-valuation respectively preceding and following devaluations of their currency from a higher to a lower pegged international value, *or* for domestic purposes they prefer a lower rate of inflation and are willing therefore to accept an alternation of periods of surplus and periods of deficit on their balance of payments associated with periods of currency under-valuation and periods of currency over-valuation respectively preceding and following revaluations of their currency from a lower to a higher pegged international value. It should be noted that in the former case the country concerned must go through an initial period of unwanted imported deflationary pressure, and in the latter case an initial period of unwanted imported inflationary pressure.

In the long-run context of a fixed exchange rate system and an inflating world economy, an incomes policy as conventionally conceived for a national economy—i.e., a policy of restraining wage increases to rates proportional to the growth of productivity and therefore resulting in stable prices—must engender a policy dilemma and ultimately fail. Assume first that it is temporarily successful in holding down national prices in the face of rising foreign prices. The result must be an increased foreign demand for exports and a switch of demand from imports to domestic substitutes; on the monetary side this implies a balance-of-payments surplus and a reserve inflow that must be sterilized by the central bank; on the real side it implies a growing demand for domestic productive resources that must be offset by matching deflationary domestic monetary and fiscal policies. The capacity of the central bank to sterilize monetary inflows is obviously limited, and the reduction of domestic resource utilization for the benefit of foreigners via the balance-of-payments surplus raises obvious political problems. The attempt to reduce domestic absorption by monetary as distinct from fiscal policy also is likely to raise domestic interest rates and so increase the inflow of foreign money and aggravate the monetary sterilization problem. The conclusion is that the very assumed success of the incomes policy will generate consequences for the money supply and for effective demand that will make that success necessarily temporary, in both economic and political terms. I advance political as well as economic considerations, because the implied process of restraining domestic consumption, public and private, and investment in order to lend to foreigners at low or zero (or even negative, given the assumption of background world inflation) rates of return will eventually generate political opposition from those who question why their apparent prosperity has to be secured at the price of denying them the public goods—schools, hospitals and cheap housing—and the private consumption that prosperity ought to imply. A futher important point is that, given the high degree of substitutability among the manufactured goods produced by the leading industrial countries in each others' markets, there will be strong economic pressures working against the effective continuance of the incomes policy. On the one hand, employers will sooner or later recognize the irrationality of continuing to sell their goods in the home and export markets at prices below the prevailing world price for comparable products, and specifically the irrationality of trying to hold wages down, and incurring the costs of doing so, in order to continue subsidizing their sales. On the other hand, the workers will sooner or later recognize that their conformance with the incomes policy is putting them in the position of subsidizing domestic and foreign consumers by accepting money wages below the potential money value of their real marginal product. The pressures for adjustment of domestic money wages and prices in the internationally competitive sectors will sooner or later break the incomes policy as it applies to those sectors. And while the government can probably continue to enforce the policy for the non-internationally-competitive sectors, the costs of doing so in terms of labour emigration, labour shortage, and deterioration of the quality of production in those sectors will eventually force the abandonment of the policy for those sectors as well.

A national incomes policy for a country maintaining a fixed exchange rate therefore makes no sense, if the policy is defined on the conventional lines of seeking to maintain price stability by confining wage increases to the growth rate of productivity. The only rational, and also feasible, policy in the long run would be a policy that sought to raise wages and prices in line with the general world inflationary trend, so as to keep the balance of payments balanced and avoid either unwanted resource transfers to other countries through balance-of-payments surpluses or politically embarrassing dependence on resource transfers from other countries through balance-of-payments deficits. For some countries, abnormally inflation-prone, this would involve wage and price restraint, but not restraint of a kind expressible in a simple formula such as equating wage increases with productivity increases. For other countries, abnormally devoted to maintaining price stability, it would involve deliberate inflation of wages and prices, but again inflation that could not be expressed in any simple and easily comprehensible formula.

The foregoing analysis assumes a given world rate of inflation, to which the individual country must adjust, if it insists on adhering to a fixed exchange rate. In the world as it is, however, and also in general equilibrium monetary theory, the world rate of inflation is an average of the rates of inflation chosen or permitted by the member countries of the international monetary system—and specifically and concretely, given the relative size of the United States in the world system, of the rate of inflation chosen or permitted by the United States. If one accepts this fact as immutable, effective national incomes policies in other countries would have to be policies of making national wage and price levels in terms of domestic currency rise in line with whatever rate of inflation was going on in the United States. (The phrase 'in line with' is used here and previously to allow for the possibility that various kinds of economic change in the world economy, together with differential rates of productivity increase in different countries which have the effect of altering the relationship between the prices of internationally-traded goods and of non-traded private and governmental services, will alter the equilibrium relationship between measured price or cost-of-living indexes among countries.)

An emerging but still inchoate recognition on the part of the staff of the Organization for Economic Cooperation and Development of the impossibility of implementing national incomes policies of the simple traditional price-stabilization kind within the framework of a fixed exchange rate system subject to an inflationary trend has led that body to the elementarily obvious next stage of advocating a coordinated set of incomes policies among the advanced countries as a means of controlling world inflation. This proposal embodies the same sort of pious hope of solving a politically-created dilemma by political means as does the recommendation of a national incomes policy on the closed-economy assumption discussed earlier. But it raises an extra and extremely problematical political question. Summoning up the political will within a nation required to induce the conflicting claimants to shares in the real national product to resolve their claims in monetary terms that will ensure stability of prices is in principle much easier than summoning up the international political will to agree on the division of the world real product both among nations and among the claimants within each nation in terms consistent with stable world prices. The mind boggles at the possibility of convincing American trade unions to hold down their wage claims so that the rentiers in Germany will have the advantage of stable money prices for the goods they consume. This is entirely apart from the economic proposition that, in the world economy as in the domestic, inflation is a problem created by excessively expansionary fiscal and, especially, monetary policy, and that incomes policy is an attempt to relieve governments of the economic consequences of their own irresponsibility to their electorates.

In summary, incomes policy is no easy answer to the three problems discussed above, domestic inflation, balance-of-payments adjustment, and world inflation. Proper economic analysis requires the recognition that in the closed-economy, or world, economic context the control of inflation requires adequate macroeconomic management policies, not the persuasion or coercion of the citizen into making good by individual self-denying behaviour the irresponsible failures of his government collectively to exercise appropriate macroeconomic management policies. In the open-economy world-system-member context it requires recognition that exchange-rate adjustment, whether by free floating of the rate or by frequent adjustments of the pegged rate on other currencies, is the appropriate method of securing domestic autonomy with respect to the trend rate of change of domestic prices and wages, whereas the use of incomes policy raises problems of determining the appropriate relative and absolute domestic price level that cannot be subsumed in the simple idea of aiming for domestic price stability.

Author index

Subject index